Shining in Shadows

Movie Stars of the

2000s

★★★★★★★★★★★★

EDITED BY

MURRAY POMERANCE

RUTGERS UNIVERSITY PRESS

NEW BRUNSWICK, NEW JERSEY, AND LONDON

LIBRARY OF CONGRESS CATALOGING-IN-PUBLICATION DATA

Shining in shadows : movie stars of the 2000s / edited by Murray Pomerance.
    p. cm. — (Star decades : American culture / American cinema)
  Includes bibliographical references and index.
  ISBN 978–0–8135–5147–0 (hardcover : alk. paper)
  ISBN 978–0–8135–5148–7 (pbk. : alk. paper)
  1. Motion picture actors and actresses—United States—Biography. I. Pomerance,
Murray, 1946– .
  PN1998.2.S493 2011
  791.4302'80922—dc22
  [B]

                                    2011001086

A British Cataloging-in-Publication record for this book is available from the British
Library.

Visit our Web site: http://rutgerspress.rutgers.edu

Manufactured in the United States of America

"They never see the ventriloquist for the doll."

—F. Scott Fitzgerald, *The Last Tycoon*

CONTENTS

★★★★★★★★★★★

ACKNOWLEDGMENTS
☆☆☆☆☆☆☆☆★★

I must express profound gratitude to Mary Beltrán, Madison; Emmanuel Burdeau, Paris; Andrea Eis, Oakland University, Rochester, Michigan; Ned Comstock, Film-Television Library, University of Southern California; Dominic Lennard, Lindisfarne, Tasmania; Adrienne L. McLean, Dallas; Ron Mandelbaum and his loyal staff at Photofest, New York; Adam Miller, Toronto; Jenny Romero, Margaret Herrick Library, Beverly Hills; and Sean Springer, Brooklyn. Matt Thompson has been an incomparably deft research assistant and a joy to work with. My colleagues at Rutgers University Press, Marilyn Campbell, Bryce Schimanski, Leslie Mitchner, and Eric Schramm, have made it a delight once again to labor in their charming company. The Office of the Dean of Arts at Ryerson University has provided assistance, as have many of my friends, often unwittingly. To Nellie Perret and Ariel Pomerance, my hopes that this book will bring inspiration.

Shining in Shadows

INTRODUCTION

☆☆☆☆☆☆☆☆☆★

Stardom in the 2000s

MURRAY POMERANCE

These pages contain discussions of twenty-five stars of Holly-wood cinema who flourished, all to a distinctive degree in the international eye, in the decade between 1 January 2000 and 31 December 2009. Although these stars were as bright as stars have ever been in Hollywood, producing a kind of illumination that had staying power and global effect, the book itself is called *Shining in Shadows* because all of them shone within an intensively American darkness brought on by the surprise attacks of 11 September 2001. In our economy, our philosophy, our social thought, our poetic hopes, and the screen dreams that energized and mirrored us, 9/11 lasted throughout the decade in one way or another: as a memory, as a wound, as a pretext for the withdrawal of civil liberty, as an incitement to ongoing fear. Whether or not it affected any particular cinematic endeavor or begrimed any actual performative work (beyond the relatively small number of films actually depicting it, such as the omnibus *11'09"01* [2002], Oliver Stone's *World Trade Center* [2006], or Paul Greengrass's *United 93* [2006]), 9/11 can generally be said to have shocked, slowed, rigidified, and made self-conscious the entire cultural apparatus of the United States and the West; to have tinted the decade and leeched out some of the light that might otherwise have illuminated our world. Perhaps it can be suggested that if after the Great Depression of 1929 American cinema turned to a "feel good" aesthetic, with morally uplifting drama, ebullient social comedy, and gay musicals working to take people's minds off the bleakness of their real conditions, the cinema of the 2000s largely worked through spectaculariza-tion, intensified distribution, and oddball dramatic setups to perform the same escapist function, to give people reasons for believing the "War on Terror" declared by the Bush administration and its apparently incessant side effects were not all there was to life.

The 2000s were born in a storm of global panic and alarm, something of a foundation for the numerous American and global crises that would follow. Y2K, a "millennium bug," had already been bruited around the world, a virus that would strike all computer systems at the stroke of midnight on

1 January 2000, ready and eager to produce manifold forms of infrastructural damage (on New Year's morning, vast populations awoke in a worldwide wave to discover that nothing had happened at all, thus instantly rendering parodic the "need" for the so-called "preparations" that had been put in place as much as eighteen months before). Hardly had nervous systems settled when the dot.com bubble, in which the stock market, which had promised an unending upward spiral of growth and munificence, burst unceremoniously. Wall Street's richest suddenly found themselves indicted (shades of Oliver Stone's *Wall Street* [1987], a film that would be sequelized as soon as the decade was over). The George W. Bush presidency came into effect, and with it a climate of irresponsible aggressiveness and tarnished dignity. If Bush couldn't antagonize America's partners and neighbors, he could at least—and routinely—turn himself into a public fool through malapropisms that not only made the news but were catalogued in Mark Crispin Miller's *The Bush Dyslexicon*. Inauspiciously at first—but by the end of the decade causing major international upheavals in monetary value—the euro entered the marketplace (on 1 January 2002). By 2003, conflict had erupted in Darfur, a site that would ground a humanitarian crisis of major proportions. The U.S. Army entered Iraq, and by the summer of 2003 a severe acute respiratory syndrome (SARS) epidemic was threatening on several continents (during the summer, a major rock concert in Toronto brought megastars including the Rolling Stones to beg for help). Ronald Reagan, once a screen star and labor leader, then a governor, finally president of the United States, and the man responsible for trickle-down economics—the somewhat unlikely proposition that the wealthy and successful would naturally invest in such a way as to benefit the poor and unemployed—died, his funeral attended by luminaries from the worlds of politics and entertainment equally. North Korea began nuclear testing, Pluto lost its status as a planet, a tsunami ravaged Southeast Asia, and a fictional teenaged wizard named Harry Potter took over the imaginations of legion adolescents and adults worldwide, his final adventures, released in the summer of 2007, selling to eleven million book buyers within twenty-four hours and thus constituting the fastest-selling book of all time. Apple released a new product called the iPhone. In 2008, the economies of the world joined one another harmoniously in a resounding crash, with major banks requiring government bailouts and automobile manufacturing teetering on the brink of bankruptcy. And with a flu virus spreading around the world, the first black person was elected to the American presidency, after an Internet campaign intensively aimed at young voters.

Superseding all this in the viral speed of their popularity and density of their usage came two technological innovations, both computer-based:

A magical boy who could wave his wand and fix the world. Daniel Radcliffe as a maturing wizard in *Harry Potter and the Prisoner of Azkaban* (Alfonso Cuarón, Warner Bros., 2004). By decade's end, the young star had a personal fortune of some forty million pounds. Digital frame enlargement.

YouTube would make possible the virtually instantaneous broadcasting, from any point on Earth, of moving images created by anybody, thus annihilating the hegemony of professional image-makers and forcing screen performers into a condition where the image bite could replace the integrated performance. Facebook led the way toward digital interaction, again platforming cinematic downloads and providing a new context in which movie stars could peddle their "monopoly personalities" (to paraphrase Janet Staiger). By Armistice Day 2010, even the queen of England had a Facebook page and David Fincher's ode to Facebook, *The Social Network*, was bringing Jesse Eisenberg and Andrew Garfield an immense new audience for their young stardoms.

Cinematically speaking, the 2000s was a decade of high-concept extravaganzas and quirky, small-scale independent dramas, all of which captured serious public and critical attention and brought to the fore screen performers who had not been particularly recognizable earlier, while consolidating the careers of some who had. With the decade's television—now heavily infused with independent production and far from its glory days as a three-network operation—offering its addicts seductive and morally challenging dramatizations of crime and forensic investigation— "C. S. I.," "C. S. I.: Miami," "C. S. I.: NY," "Law & Order," "Law & Order: Special Victims Unit," "Law & Order: Criminal Intent," "Criminal Minds," "Bones," "NCIS," "NCIS Los Angeles," "Without a Trace"—as well as ironic and bizarre quasi-comedies such as "House," "The Office," and "30 Rock," not to mention the new teen musical sensation "Glee" or the tidal wave of "reality programming," Hollywood had to stretch in order to keep its bank accounts full. Moviegoers could marvel at the stunning wire effects of *Crouching Tiger, Hidden Dragon* (2000), the CGI effects of *The Lord of the Rings* (2001, 2002, 2003), the historical reenactments of *Master and Commander* (2003) or *The Aviator* (2004) or *Letters from Iwo Jima* (2006), the artful manipulations of *Sin City* (2005), the pulsing action of *The Bourne Ultimatum* (2007) or *The Dark Knight* (2008), and the eccentric characterizations of *The Curious Case of Benjamin Button* (2008) and *Avatar* (2009), or for a completely different kind of experience they could migrate to the small-scale delights of Juliette Binoche as a chocolatière in *Chocolat* (2000), Julia Roberts as an advocate for toxic waste victims in *Erin Brockovich* (2000), Jake Gyllenhaal as a weird but brilliant high-school depressive in *Donnie Darko* (2001), Nicole Kidman with a putty nose as Virginia Woolf in *The Hours* (2002), Bill Murray as an alienated movie star trapped in Tokyo while making a commercial in *Lost in Translation* (2003), Hilary Swank as a fated female boxer in *Million Dollar Baby* (2004), Johnny Depp as Sir James M. Barrie in *Finding Neverland* (2004), Gyllenhaal and Heath Ledger as homoerotically bonded cowboys in *Brokeback Mountain* (2005)—pundits mused: was homosexuality being forefronted in mainstream cinema, or was it not?—David Strathairn as Edward R. Murrow in *Good Night, and Good Luck* (2005), Brad Pitt and Cate Blanchett as suffering tourists in Morocco in *Babel* (2006), the charmingly "natural" Anne Hathaway in *The Devil Wears Prada* (2006), Abigail Breslin as a teeny-weeny beauty queen in *Little Miss Sunshine* (2006), Helen Mirren seeming more credibly queenly than Elizabeth II in *The Queen* (2006), Tommy Lee Jones as an aging sheriff facing a hideous danger in *No Country for Old Men* (2007), Kate Winslet as an illiterate former SS guard in *The Reader* (2008), or Carey Mulligan as a British teen who decides that school isn't for her in *An Education* (2009)—not to mention the work of Frank Langella (an old hand on Broadway and with film character roles) putting on Richard M. Nixon in *Frost/Nixon* (2008) to raving critical acclaim. The movie canvas in the 2000s thus essentially presented a sweeping panorama of action, color, effects, and often metaphysical wonders; or else a stunning character portrait in the context of a deeply involving, typically starkly limned drama on themes of contemporary relevance.

Some stars had successes piled upon one another. In *Gladiator* (2000), *A Beautiful Mind* (2001), and *Master and Commander* (2003), the Australian-born Russell Crowe was established as a many-dimensional talent for both intensive character development and bravado action entertainment. Some younger faces became iconic only because of the vehicles that were providing notable continuing character opportunities: Daniel Radcliffe with Emma Watson and Rupert Grint in the apparently unceasing Harry Potter series

Anne Hathaway's principal accomplishment in *The Devil Wears Prada* (David Frankel, Fox 2000, 2006) is withstanding the critical glare of fashionistas, wannabees, designers, and a rather conventional boyfriend. No matter how horrible things are, she helps us believe, feeling good about the way one looks is a major source of strength. Digital frame enlargement.

(2001, 2002, 2004, 2005, 2007, 2009), Elijah Wood and Orlando Bloom in the three *Lord of the Rings* features, Keira Knightley working with the already well established Johnny Depp in the *Pirates of the Caribbean* franchise (2003, 2006, 2007).

A number of films offered coverage for a scintillating group of noteworthy character performances (as in 1932 and 1933, *Grand Hotel* and *Dinner at Eight* had originally done). These films constituted something of a new style, with multiple stories interlaced (as opposed to chained, as had happened with Robert Altman's *Short Cuts* [1993]) and a narrative eye jumping hither and thither among them, the viewer finding himself saddled with the task of either weaving all the plotlines into a coherent picture or else waiting for the director and editor to sum up in the last few moments. Steven Soderbergh's *Traffic* (2000) embroiled Michael Douglas, Benicio Del Toro, Catherine Zeta-Jones, Topher Grace, Albert Finney, James Brolin, Dennis Quaid, Amy Irving, Benjamin Bratt, and hundreds of others in a complex socio-realistic narrative about a disintegrating American family in the shadow of the international drug trade. Paul Haggis's *Crash* (2004) had Sandra Bullock, Don Cheadle, Keith David, Terrence Howard, Thandie Newton, Brendan Fraser, Matt Dillon, and many others tied up in a complex L.A. police corruption saga. Robert Altman's *Gosford Park* (2001) involved Alan Bates, Michael Gambon, Helen Mirren, Ryan Phillippe, Clive Owen, Jeremy Northam, and many others in a complex British country-house mystery that revolved upon upstairs-downstairs relationships. "And many others" was an experiential hallmark, as though cinema overflowed with limitless fascinating characterization, stardom beyond what any story could hold.

Some major stars (most from earlier decades) faded permanently from screen life—among them Anne Bancroft, Alan Bates, Marlon Brando, James Coburn, Yvonne De Carlo, Vittorio Gassman, Katharine Hepburn, Charlton Heston, Bob Hope, Betty Hutton, Janet Leigh, Jack Lemmon, Walter Matthau, Paul Newman, Donald O'Connor, Anthony Quinn, Jason Robards, Robert Stack, Fay Wray, Loretta Young, and Heath Ledger—this last drawing a sharp image for fans and admirers of the arbitrary nature of star construction and the essentially "everyday," mortal nature of the life experience that undergirds fame. The accidental-overdose death of Ledger elicited considerable press attention and speculation, since many observers stressed that he had led a healthy and normal life and that he had been in good spirits. That so young and promising a vitality should have been cut off so abruptly seemed stunning in the world of movie stars, who, regardless of their essential humanity, are productively and routinely touted as superhuman talents who transcend normal limits. Perhaps stars may die, and their intensive illumination vanish, but surely not so suddenly, not by way of a simple accident.

Stars who still thrived tended often to build new personae in this decade. Having produced a definitive presence in sensitive and quirky roles during the 1990s, Leonardo DiCaprio put on a little weight physically and gained immense weight economically with a series of much-heralded and intensive dramatic performances: as a revolutionary youth in *Gangs of New York* and a con man in *Catch Me If You Can* (both 2002), as Howard Hughes in *The Aviator* (2004), as a cop caught up in a corruption intrigue in *The Departed* (2006), in *Blood Diamond* (2006), where he sported an Afrikaans accent, and in *Revolutionary Road* (2008), where he became an angry and repressed 1950s commuter. By decade's end he was to have appeared in Martin Scorsese's *Shutter Island*, but Paramount's jittery financial situation forced the studio to hold off its major advertising push and to recut trailers that had already been screening nationwide, in order that the film could open in the first quarter of 2010—which, in fifty-five countries including Estonia, Malaysia, Syria, Canada, Israel, and Kazakhstan, it somewhat sputteringly did. DiCaprio had graduated in this decade from playing offbeat and hypersensitive youth roles under competent directors to work that caused the critical establishment to speculate he had perhaps become the "new" Robert De Niro. Other notable performers re-formed themselves. Julia Roberts settled into being Danny Ocean's stolid ex. Kate Winslet turned sour and ugly, to vast acclaim. Depp got lost in myriad disguises. Nicole Kidman turned quiet and chilling, then quietly and chillingly seemed to disappear. Ian McKellen left Shakespeare behind, found action

Michael Cera as the bumbling, brilliant Paulie Bleeker in *Juno* (Jason Reitman, Fox Searchlight, 2007). His performances show again and again that life might seem disconnected, the world a forest of monsters, but innocence, sensitivity, and exceptional wit at least provide us a chance to talk back, and talk back with unlimited charm. Digital frame enlargement.

film. Jake Gyllenhaal got buff. Daniel Day-Lewis and Meryl Streep continued to give eccentric, forceful, dynamic, memorable, and even gaudy performances in the style of Great Theater. Matt Damon continued to show his vast range and continued to elude notice. Clint Eastwood directed, and directed, and directed, and directed . . .

No one would choose to claim that the stars focused upon here were the very most important of movie stars (if movie stars are ever important in the overall balance of things). But as the pages of a volume such as this are necessarily limited, and the tastes and opinions of the contributors necessarily biased and constrained by their observations and positions of vantage, some arbitrariness must attach to our selection, some pointed motive to our selections, and so it came about that a huge number of fascinating performers who did strong and popular work in this decade—Tom Cruise, Christian Bale, Reese Witherspoon, Tobey Maguire, Jennifer Garner, Ben Affleck, Shia LaBeouf, Tilda Swinton, Anne Hathaway, Streep, and Gyllenhaal, to name only some—aren't to be found here. Absent, too, are performers who gained considerable attention from a widely ranging public, but this only for character performances or mass-mediated activity, none of which quite accomplished the "magic" of turning them into stars. A signal example is the young Canadian Michael Cera. The star, after all, is more than a celebrity, more than a well-known face, more, even, than a personage who spends time on red carpets: the star is someone for whom it is widely felt that red carpets *should* be rolled out. While the celebrity culture that intensified after the 1990s—through numerous television entertainment tabloid shows, the late night talk show circuit, the plethora of film and culture festivals, advertising, and the virtually countless award ceremonies made available to global audiences as entertainment fodder—produced and touted plenty of personalities as recognizable, enviable, marketable, red-carpetable, or at least discussable, thus increasing the population of that virtual world we know as "Hollywood," still only a small number of personalities swelled to such a proportion that, more than looking good in Dolce & Gabbana or Karl Lagerfelt or Armani, they might have seemed to actually inhabit a modern-day Olympus. Such folk typically did not give interviews or speak to crowds, beyond making a winking comment that betrayed their own knowledge of the specialness with which we had conferred them.

The stars in these pages represented figureheads of the new New Hollywood, an industry controlled by independent production, global marketing, and multimedia platforming and pervaded by young crossover talent glittering in a publicity atmosphere that has been dominated by computer and video imagery as much as by cinema itself: online movie trailers, downloads, televised interviews, and increasingly, for their films, screenings easily to be found on YouTube or Facebook. With the emphasis on youth, the "old-time" stars in this decade were frequently holdovers from only the 1990s, with eminent faces from previous decades now more and more relegated to quirky character walk-ons or touching but esoteric small-scale dramatic offerings—Lauren Bacall, for example, in *Birth* (2004), or Christopher Walken in *Hairspray* (2007).

The contributors to this volume have offered a range of intriguing propositions about the stars in their focus. Dominic Lennard opens our considerations with an astute reading of Matt Damon, Johnny Depp, and Robert Downey Jr. as "boyish" types, all three somehow resisting the call of adulthood and lingering in a zone in which childhood and its oneiric wonders dominate consciousness and personality. Damon is "both tough guy and little kid, calculating and vulnerable" in roles that center on "instabilities in contemporary heteronormative masculinity, the struggle to manage or surmount inherited understandings of manhood as self-reliant fortress, and . . . to recognize the fallibility of patriarchy." Depp "starred primarily in offbeat character roles, as stylized black sheep, psychos, grotesques," but was also sprung on an international audience with his serio-comic portrayal of a colossal failure at adulthood, Jack Sparrow. And Downey again and again seemed to incarnate "someone who, despite his sins, wound up in Hollywood through unlikely talent, dumb luck, and adolescent adorability."

Moving to the other end of the age spectrum, Robert Eberwein studies two elder statesmen of the screen. Clint Eastwood, he notes, was a star "of such a magnitude that his political positions, real or assumed, are themselves the material for critical discourse," yet also one whose "aging is often foregrounded against his earlier career and personae." Also visibly aging, and in a way that contributed to his star status, Morgan Freeman supported an image that foregrounded his race, "especially in relation to the problematic category of what some designate 'Magical Negroes,'" a category, it is worth noting, of which Freeman had come to be "*the* prime example."

Victoria Johnson studies the presence of, and relation between, two women whose careers moved from stellar positions in television to stardom on the big screen. For Johnson, Jennifer Aniston's and Tina Fey's multi-mediated stardom shows how film and television personalities equally command public attention. With Aniston, we see a career mythology that "symbolically positions" her as "ugly duckling" risen to beautiful "swan," while Fey is "a literal girl with glasses whose career mythology charts revenge of the 'nerd.'" The stardom of Fey and Aniston works to "unify an otherwise disparate media environment."

Brenda Weber has chosen to concentrate on the Frat Pack, a loose but salient affiliation of Jack Black, Will Ferrell, Adam Sandler, and Ben Stiller. These performers have repeatedly worked to create a narrow but deeply evocative narrative identity, one that has worked to mold their off-camera personae as both topical and marketable. "The Frat Pack," writes Weber, "trades in a sort of cheerful and benign masculine moralism in which the male characters build new values, suture their ties to one another through a form of homosocial bonding endearingly termed bromance, learn lessons about themselves, life, and relationships, and become 'better' men, often (and incredibly) getting the pretty girl in the end." While with a succession of characters Black has specialized as the guy who gets "the kick to the groin," and Ferrell as a kind of paragon of "normalcy," Sandler has set himself up as "in constant need of learning a lesson" and Stiller has apotheosized a "put-upon everyman."

Mary Beltrán's two points of focus, the stardoms of Javier Bardem and Benicio Del Toro, signify "a broadening horizon of imagined possibilities for Latino and Spanish actors, particularly regarding notions of Latino masculinity and machismo." Del Toro's star image "was closely fused with awe for his skill as an actor"; thus, that his politics, biography, and cultural background did not easily rise to the surface was credited to his extraordinary capacity at performative disguise. Bardem displayed an "eloquent and ebullient dedication to his family and to the actors and country of Spain" that "furthered his star image as both intelligent but sexy idol and family man."

Examining the work of Philip Seymour Hoffman, Jerry Mosher shows how stardom can emerge from a chain of character performances, "painful, disturbing, funny, enlightening, or sublime, but . . . always electrifying." If Hoffman "would be the first to deny that he is a movie star," he "runs circles" around numerous better-known actors, and does this with remarkable consistency and power. Yet it was true at the end of the decade that "the full extent of Hoffman's range and capability, regrettably, remained untested."

For Corinn Columpar, an examination of the stardom of Maggie Gyllenhaal, Hilary Swank, and Renée Zellweger raises social and political considerations of the status of women in our culture, given the characterizations offered these actresses in their films. While even Swank's relatively unsuccessful performances have "political potential insofar as they undercut the 'idealized, essentialized femininity' that postfeminist culture promotes"; and Gyllenhaal suggests that "women have not necessarily come a long way, baby—at least not in the film industry," Zellweger's definitive Bridget Jones is a character "spurred on by an impetus that is germane to normative definitions of femininity: the need for love, be it from a single partner or a mass audience; the need to complete, and be completed by, someone else."

In the stardom of Heath Ledger, Claire Perkins finds an " 'authentic' historical persona" that "throws his contemporary performances into relief. He never seems quite at home in the modern world"—a quality intrinsic to his role in the groundbreaking *Brokeback Mountain* as well as his earlier work. With Ledger, we are able to evaluate an abbreviated career as having constructed "an image of a character always in the process of becoming something else, indeed, stunningly, always marching toward death."

Michael Hammond reveals that the star personas of Leonardo DiCaprio and Sean Penn in this decade were both constructed upon an open demonstration of the performer's "ability to act." Penn's social involvement, central rather than ancillary to his star career, positioned him in the public consciousness in an unconventional way: he "exists as a celebrity in ways that endorse politicians, react to historical events, and solicit causes rather than sell products." DiCaprio exited the decade as a "new type of old Hollywood star," also showing his public a range of political commitments while playing out his social engagement through a commitment to independent production.

Charlie Keil reveals how "the examples of Cate Blanchett and Kate Winslet proved that actresses who staked out a claim to stardom predicated explicitly on acting talent over celebrity could persevere, generating industry respect and a stream of challenging roles in the process." For both of these actors, there were numerous occasions during the decade when the choice was made to go with a difficult, absorbing, and dramatically important performance rather than a romantic lead that could have garnered a broader fandom. Winslet had to "negotiate the demands that stardom placed on an actress with serious dramatic aspirations," while Blanchett had to "establish that her estimable gifts as an actress would translate into the creation of roles that could draw audiences to her films."

Linda Ruth Williams sees the 2000s careers of Angelina Jolie and her partner Brad Pitt as interwoven, indeed hybridized, through the "Brangelina" construct that motivated the bulk of either actor's publicity. If Jolie "moved from self-harming, bisexual, incestuous wild child to maternal saint" as her image was stabilized in a nuclear family and Pitt changed his physique and acting technique to address varied role demands, including a beefcake physicality, a relentless brutality, and a hyperactive feebleness, it was in their curious match that the stardom of each was magnified and burnished. "Pitt excels in roles where he can capitalize on aspects of his stardom, Jolie in roles where she buries it," offers Williams.

David Sterritt concludes the volume with a chapter on George Clooney, whose "career since 2000 reflects an expanding interest in public affairs that has placed him in the front ranks of Hollywood progressivism." For Sterritt, "Clooney's career rests on a cluster of dialectical relationships: between celebrity status as a profession and as a source of influence, between work in front of the camera and behind it, between taking direction and giving it, between managing a public persona and safeguarding a private self, between performing in fiction films and performing in real-life arenas, between acting as entertainment and acting as intervention—between acting and *acting*."

If these appraisals can provoke some reflection about contemporary Hollywood, if they can make us wonder anew what these icons are that so brightly and intensively attract our attention and concern at a time when things are bad, perhaps we may even find a grounding for optimism—at least optimism about what the motion picture star is, and what she or he can be. The 2000s found us wallowing in an unclear time, but in the shadows of that decade, the stars were still shining.

☆☆☆☆☆☆☆☆☆☆

Wonder Boys
Matt Damon, Johnny Depp, and Robert Downey Jr.

DOMINIC LENNARD

  In the decade from 2000 to 2010, cinemagoers witnessed the ascension to superstardom of Matt Damon, Johnny Depp, and Robert Downey Jr. All three are intense, to varying degrees; disarmingly handsome, to differing effects; and talented, in various modes and rhythms. Additionally, in many of their best and most memorable roles all three pulse with an energy scarcely held in check—poised for action (or violence)—at

Matt Damon, Johnny Depp, and Robert Downey Jr.

the same time as they are tethered by a tremulous, childlike vulnerability. In films like *The Bourne Identity* (2002), *Pirates of the Caribbean* (2003), *Finding Neverland* (2004), *Kiss Kiss Bang Bang* (2005), *The Departed* (2006), *Iron Man* (2008), *Invictus* (2009), *The Informant!* (2009), and beyond, we see riptides of contradiction, men who have learned everything and nothing, grown up quickly and not at all. The characters brought to life by these actors are often both superheroes and lost boys, thrill-seeking loners, self-hating egotists struggling, comically, torturously, and poignantly (and in the often unlikely context of sports films, crime thrillers, blockbusters, swashbucklers, and offbeat comedies) with the people they may or may not be. Throughout the decade, all three played men surveying their foundations, sometimes shifting monoliths of self, and, charmingly (as with Downey Jr.'s loudmouth billionaire Tony Stark in *Iron Man*), finding more solid ground than they expected. Or, alternatively (as with Damon's cockily corrupt Boston cop Colin Sullivan in *The Departed*), finding much, much less.

☆☆☆☆☆ Matt Damon

Matt Damon radiates a familiar, easygoing kind of charm, a brand of stardom both warm and comfortably recognizable. Todd McCarthy of *Variety* supposes him "the most inescapably American-looking of all contempo actors" ("The Bourne Identity," 7 June 2002). He keeps one eyebrow frequently hoisted in a characteristic that, in his film roles, variously conveys suspicion, unembarrassed skepticism, or good-humored self-effacement: an asymmetrical indication of nothing to hide—something imperfectly, endearingly human. "He has fashioned that oxymoronic quality, the normal superstar, to a fine art," writes Ian Nathan of *Empire* (www. empireonline. com). Damon's seductively unaffected appearance and manner are regularly played upon in his film roles: celebrated in jokey crime comedies like *Ocean's Eleven* (2001), *Ocean's Twelve* (2004), and *Ocean's Thirteen* (2007), or portrayed as dangerously misleading, as in crime thrillers like *The Talented Mr. Ripley* (1999) and *The Departed*. The *Sunday Times*'s David Denby points out that Damon "is unique among Hollywood A-list stars for the quality and consistency of his lies. His greatest roles are treacherous façades. His outstanding performances in *The Talented Mr. Ripley* and Martin Scorsese's Oscar-winning *The Departed* are obsessed with identity" ("The Bourne Ultimatum," 16 August 2007). Whether personable, duplicitous, or both, Damon's roles are also frequently underpinned by the vulnerability of the little boy; his characters are usually socially or physically powerful at the same time as they are emotionally precious, in need of some quasi-parental guidance.

At the start of Doug Liman's 2002 film *The Bourne Identity*, the first in a series of three break-neck spy thrillers based on the novels by Robert Ludlum, an unconscious man floats on the ocean surface, seemingly encapsulated in a galactic blue gloom, both stormy and amniotically still. This is Jason Bourne (although he doesn't know it yet): CIA lone-wolf assassin, and Matt Damon's most familiar role to filmgoers in this decade. The target of an assassination attempt that left him with amnesia severe enough to erode even knowledge of his own identity, Bourne's character is ironically forged through the Agency's attempt to erase him. In his earlier major film roles Damon had typically been an awkward physical presence: a wan tortured genius in *Good Will Hunting* (1997) concealing physical signs of childhood abuse, and a master impersonator struggling to manage his homosexual desire in *The Talented Mr. Ripley*. The *Bourne* franchise signaled the transformation of Damon into the tough guy. In relation to Damon's first outing as Bourne, Stephen Hunter of the *Washington Post* wrote, "You wouldn't think of Damon as a tough guy, but he's worked really hard on the physical stuff here and it shows" (103). However, in her review of 2010's *Green Zone*, Kate Muir of the *Sunday Times* referred to Damon giving "his usual hard-as-nails physical performance" (12 March 2010).

It would be easy to overlook Jason Bourne as a (literally) mindless action part. The narrative of *The Bourne Identity*, for instance, is both implausible and mundane—propelled by energetic crosscutting, a sound track of steely techno beats, and a hair-raising car chase that sees Damon pinball through the streets of Paris in a trashed Mini. As opposed to *Good Will Hunting* or *The Talented Mr. Ripley*, which provided several dramatic, monological outlets for Damon's expressive breadth as an actor, Bourne is a creature of overt functionality: perpetually in flight (or fight), or getting ready for it. But that isn't all he does, nor all he is: the role is grounded, elusively humanized, by the implication that as inscrutable as Bourne is to us, he is (forlornly) to himself as well. For *Urban Cinefile*'s Louise Keller, Damon's depiction of Jason Bourne "combin[es] an appealing vulnerability with an [*sic*] chilling automated response action"; Andrew L. Urban of the same web site writes that as Bourne "Matt Damon is gruff and tough and yet vulnerably likeable" ("The Bourne Identity," www.urbancinefile.com.au).

Jason Bourne—the killing machine—is also, paradoxically, tenderly childlike, seemingly too youthful for his fierce physical abilities: *USA Today*'s Mike Clark writes that "we're struck [here] by how young Damon looks" ("'Bourne' Plays Old-School Spy Game," 14 June 2002, www.usatoday.com). In one scene, Bourne's traveling companion Marie (Franka Potente) awakens in the middle of the night to find him staring at the children of the man in whose house they are temporarily staying: "Everything I've found out about myself I've hated," he confesses, mournfully transfixed. This scene, in its muted poignancy, suggests Bourne's desire to return to a blissful childhood Eden, some prelapsarian state of fullness—fullness in nothingness, in the absence of the adult identity and ability he has discovered.

The Damon we see in Martin Scorsese's crime thriller *The Departed* plays out the anxious, childlike undercurrents of his previous films at length and with shocking force. In his review of the film, Ben Walters of *Time Out* noted that there was "something boyish" about Damon's role as crooked cop Colin Sullivan (263). Five minutes or so into the action, a young boy (thirteen or fourteen) gazes into the camera, captured in close-up: he is clean-cut, impressionable, but not foolish. The smoky, vulpine drawl of charismatic crime boss Frank Costello (Jack Nicholson) has already indicated to us that this is Colin, "Johnny Sullivan's kid": it is upon Frank that the boy's gaze is adoringly fixed as the crime patriarch hands down his dubious pearls of wisdom. Colin's father, we assume, is dead or in prison. A match cut exchanges the boy's face for a close-up of Damon, as a much older Colin: the boy's resemblance to the star is a minor coup—same freckles, same broad forehead, same eyebrow. The film does not flash back to the young Colin, whom we've only just learned about, so the biography sticks, framing Damon's character through his childhood of uncertainty and paternal disconnection, peculiarly disposed to an enchantment with male power. Nicholson's throaty affirmation, "That's my boy," lingers on the other side of the transition, indicating his enduring spell over the man.

The Departed returns more noticeably to the troubled-youth overtones of Damon's 1990s work. His performance as Sullivan is complex and shifting, the character variously charismatic, intolerably two-faced, and, again, disarmingly vulnerable. The adult Colin has all the down-to-earth, boyish charm one associates with Damon. In a typically working-class way he is also sexist, homophobic, and intensely careerist—swiftly endearing himself to the corporatized, aggressively patriarchal hierarchy of the State Police even as he feeds information back to crime boss Costello. He woos police psychiatrist girlfriend Madolyn (Vera Farmiga) with practiced yet indifferent charm, and remains terrified of his dependence on a woman, privately ridiculing those police officers who violate masculine prohibitions by seeking out her guidance. As Costello's mole in the State Police, Colin's path in the film is the management of competing father figures, his superiors and his criminal mentor. It is also the energetic avoidance of introspection that implies profound childhood insecurity, and as well as implying the total absence of Colin's father, the film contains three separate references to

Matt Damon (l.) as Colin Sullivan in *The Departed* (Martin Scorsese, Warner Bros., 2006), transformed into the sniveling, abandoned child as he is arrested by undercover officer Billy Costigan (Leonardo DiCaprio). Digital frame enlargement.

pedophilia in the Catholic priesthood after having shown Colin's stint as an altar boy in an early scene.

Additionally, at one point Colin removes his girlfriend's childhood photographs with the evasively jokey excuse that "you don't see any pictures of where I came from." Sullivan is reduced to the exasperated child at several points in the film: "I can fucking investigate anyone I fucking well like!" he screams at a fellow detective, as his boss, like a peacekeeping parent, intervenes between the two men. Eventually, the film culminates in an Oedipal drama in which Colin is forced to murder surrogate father-figure Costello. "Grow up!" the crime patriarch tells him in an insidious blood-clogged gargle as he dies and as his fatherly role emerges as little but wanton manipulation.

As the corrupt cop is arrested toward the film's conclusion, we see the devastating collapse of Colin's cocky façade. Initially boastful of his untouchability, he suddenly realizes the jig is up and stops squirming: "Just . . . kill me. Just fucking kill me," he sobs abruptly as blood streams from his nose. Suddenly he has been reduced to the snotty, helpless little boy he most inwardly is, desolated by the prospect of the total, irredeemable withdrawal of paternal love in its institutional form.

In Steven Soderbergh's 2009 independent comedy-thriller *The Informant!*, Damon again played a thoroughgoing liar—although hardly the virtuoso prevaricator of *The Talented Mr. Ripley* or *The Departed*. Jordan Hiller of Bangitout. com recognized this symmetry to Damon's career, pointing out that the role "eerily evokes a controversial character he portrayed ten years ago" in *Ripley* ("2009: Year End Movie Recap," 1 June 2010, www.bangitout .com). As Mark Whitacre, real-life VP and whistleblower at a large agricultural corporation in the early 1990s, the glammed-down Damon is pudgy and bespectacled, his head topped with a whorl of fallow hair pushed into an unfashionable side-part. Mark's company processes corn into Lysine, and at home he talks to his young boys about corn the way a young boy talks to his parents about dinosaurs or toy trains: passionately, incongruously, exhaustingly. A compulsive but utterly unmalicious fibber, Mark concocts a story about extortion to cover a product contamination for which he has received the blame: a juvenile tale that (with juvenile naiveté) he assumes will evaporate as soon as it has done its job. Damon's Whitacre is the eternal innocent in a culture of greed and misogyny. His voiceover doesn't so much narrate the film's plot as demonstrate his blissful disconnection from it: some of it is muddled corporate-motivational rhetoric (metaphors about the predatory animal kingdom for which the point appears to be lost on him even as he speaks); most, however, is random opinion and observation that we repeatedly try and fail to connect to the (frequently very serious) situation at hand. All throughout the film we are treated to Mark's chipper ruminations on how mysterious the steam from a pool is in the winter; how his hands are his favorite part of his body; the feel of wool garments on skin (he doesn't like it); whether he could buy his ties in bulk; his feeling that "liter" is a nicer word than "quart," and so on.

While *The Informant!* extended Damon's history of playing both boyish and two-faced characters, it also refreshingly counterbalanced the tormented intensity of his roles in *Good Will Hunting*, *The Talented Mr. Ripley*, and *The Departed*, ensuring that he would never threaten to become "too serious. " His role in the 2003 Farrelly brothers comedy *Stuck On You* had a similar effect. Further, upon titling Damon "Sexiest Man Alive" in 2007, *People* magazine praised the star's "irresistible sense of humor" (26 November 2007, www.people.com). *The Informant!*'s relatively small-scale production and oblique sense of humor also ensured that Damon would easily evade the charge of Oscar-baiting austerity that often accompanies an actor's concealment of his good looks for a role. Damon also helped stabilize the emotional exhaustion of many of his most successful roles through his playful humor in interviews: doing impressions of fellow Hollywood stars, as well as participating in an immensely popular comedy skit for "Jimmy Kimmel Live!" (see Edward Wyatt, "Late Night TV Satires Become Online Hits," *New York Times*, 27 February 2008, www.nytimes.com).

More prominent and celebrated than Damon's performance in *The Informant!* in 2009 was his role in Clint Eastwood's *Invictus*, which tells the story of the 1995 South African Rugby World Cup following the abolishment of apartheid. Navigating the hairpin accents of South African English as deftly as Bourne mastered the streets of Paris in his unlikely Mini, Damon played white Springbok captain François Pienaar, whom Nelson Mandela (Morgan Freeman) takes under his wing. Critics consistently praised Damon's depiction of Pienaar. The role was "played with crisp, disciplined understatement" according to A. O. Scott of the *New York Times* ("Invictus," 11 December 2009, movies.nytimes.com). *Empire* praised Damon as "the film's heart," observing that "he doesn't intrude rather than quietly embody his character. Even so, there are De Niro–like levels of immersion going on here" (Nathan). The role was also a softer, more harmless retread of themes from earlier in the actor's career, from *Hunting* to *The Departed*. Again, Damon was the precociously powerful but philosophically undernourished young man, in need of introspection and guidance. Pienaar is a man of few words, benignly reserved almost to the point of melancholia. As with Damon's character in *The Departed* (Colin Sullivan, we note, was also a member of a rugby team), Pienaar's is a masculinity that conceals everything, although here this is less aggressively phrased—not metaphorized through the conventions of the gangster film, which specializes in double identities. The Damon of *Invictus* doesn't have half of the baggage that the Damon of *The Departed* must carry, and that simplicity is also his blessing. Rather, Pienaar is a man tapped on the shoulder by a force bigger than him, and bigger than the game he knows, yet one that does not threaten to denigrate or obscure either. He is the most vigorous participant in the Springboks' World Cup victory, and also a curious, hopeful observer of its larger cultural and political significance.

Damon is thus both tough guy and little kid, calculating and vulnerable. Rather than seamlessly alloying these elements, however, as reviewers imply, one might easily see Damon's most celebrated roles of the decade (including those of the *Bourne* series, *The Departed*, and *Invictus*) as centering on instabilities in contemporary heteronormative masculinity, the struggle to manage or surmount inherited understandings of manhood as self-reliant fortress, and (especially in *The Departed* and *The Informant!*) to recognize the fallibility of patriarchy. The fetishization of machine-gun punches and acrobatic counterattacks in the *Bourne* films indicates the pleasure wrapped up in Jason Bourne the rigorously disciplined, hypermasculine fighting machine; however, he is also prisoner to his training, possessed by it. Early in the film, he speaks a foreign language he does not (at the very same moment he utters the words) seem to understand. He is alarmed at the sounds coming from his mouth—does not own or control something as intimate as his own voice. The initially apolitical François of *Invictus* must suddenly look beyond the simple pride and bunched muscle of the "hooligan's game"; whereas the boyishly arrogant Colin Sullivan of *The Departed* (a film utterly preoccupied with masculinity) is doomed by his destructive, patriarchal attachments as the conspiracy begins to unstoppably unravel, and he must seek solace in the girlfriend whom he has already pushed irretrievably out of reach.

★★★★★ Johnny Depp

Moviegoers of the decade could hardly get enough of Johnny Depp. Hardly get enough because, despite appearing in eighteen films from 2000 to the end of 2009—including blockbusters like *Pirates of the Caribbean* (2003) and its sequels—Depp cultivated a persona that was both celebrated and elusive, cult and commonplace, earnest and ironic, sexy and strange. Whether timorously ensconced within Victor, the soulful animated bachelor of Tim Burton's *The Corpse Bride* (2005), or in full, flamboyant, and gyroscopic lurch as the outrageous Captain Jack Sparrow of the *Pirates of the Caribbean* series, the Depp of the 2000s was as fleeting, unknowable, and auroric as he was in the 1990s—although on a much larger scale.

From 2000 to 2010, Depp was unquestionably one of cinema's most celebrated and yet mysterious presences. He had enjoyed mainstream success before the new millennium with films like *Edward Scissorhands* (1990) and *Donnie Brasco* (1997). However transient a presence he might have been, the average filmgoer certainly knew who Johnny Depp was. *New York Magazine*'s Adam Sternbergh describes him as having "[taken] his inheritance of celebrity and bolted the kingdom, heading first for the art house and, eventually, to France" ("Boy, Interrupted," 21 May 2005, www.nymag .com). Indeed, for an actor so distinctive—and so attractive (for Peter Bradshaw "an almost absurdly attractive man" ["Public Enemies," 3 July 2009, www. guardian.co.uk])—he had been absent from big-budget leading man parts. Instead, he starred primarily in offbeat character roles, as stylized black sheep, psychos, grotesques—cloaking himself with the chilly Gothicism of films like *Sleepy Hollow* (1999) and *From Hell* (2001). Of his agent, Tracy Jacobs, Depp told *Time* magazine in 2004:

> Tracy's taken a lot of heat over the years. . . . She has bosses and higher-ups, and every time I take on another strange project, they're going, "Jesus Christ! When does he do a movie where he kisses the girl? When does he get to pull a gun out and shoot somebody? When does he get to be a f——— man for a change? When is he finally going to do a blockbuster?"
>
> (qtd. in Josh Tyrangiel, "Doing It Depp's Way," 9 March 2004, www.time.com)

A star for consumption: Johnny Depp on display as the fantastical Captain Jack Sparrow in *Pirates of the Caribbean: The Curse of the Black Pearl* (Gore Verbinski, Walt Disney Pictures, 2003). Digital frame enlargement.

An expected (and not unreasonable) cynicism surely undergirds such comments, although they nevertheless accurately indicate Depp's conspicuous elision of a familiar (and familiarly commodified) heterosexual screen persona for the majority of his career—his curious withdrawal from his seemingly preordained status as a figure of mass consumer desire. This unreadable, elusively erotic Depp is to some degree dramatized onscreen in Lasse Hallström's *Chocolat* (2000). Depp plays ponytailed bohemian Roux, whom chocolaterie owner Vianne (Juliette Binoche) attempts over and over again to seduce by guessing his favorite kind of chocolate (which the film never tires of reminding us is a metaphor for sexuality).

Depp's perceived disconnection from the Hollywood mainstream ended with a broadside blast when he accepted the role of Jack Sparrow in Gore Verbinski's *Pirates of the Caribbean: The Curse of the Black Pearl*, the first of three lavish and lengthy family blockbusters based on the Disneyland ride, and which collectively went on to gross well over two and a half billion dollars worldwide (boxofficemojo.com). On the whole, reviews of *Pirates* fizzled, with a mixture of charmed lyricism and utter bemusement for Depp's portrayal of "the worst pirate anybody's ever seen," the arrival of one of his exotic characters to such a glittering and accessible stage. And what a performance it was (worthy, certainly, of some bemusement): bedecked with gypsy puff and buckle, Depp's Captain Jack is both vagabondian and eccentrically regal, his dark hair falling about his shoulders in wild, near-dreadlocked tendrils. Throughout the film his body idles with the weird, liquid roll of an animated character; he moves as if the unrelenting stability of terra firma is altogether more than he can handle, somehow surfing the dry land.

In addition to the camp swish of his movements, Depp's dusky eyes were underscored with eyeliner in a flourish that was read as sexually ambiguous by several critics: this film, too, abstained from presenting Depp as the subject of an uncomplicated heterosexual gaze. Nor is Depp a participant in the romantic heterosexual coupling at the center of the narrative. With his buckled and browned teeth, one might even reasonably have expected Depp's *Pirates* character to signify the actor shedding, for all to see, the sex-symbol allure implied and expected by his agent's superiors—the Depp we were all waiting for. Yet, in 2003, following the release of *Pirates*, the star was decisively relocated in a cultural narrative of heternormativity—repositioned as a conventional object of desire—when he was voted *People* magazine's "Sexiest Man Alive."

At a glance, one might be tempted to think that Depp was awarded this honor in spite of his performance in *Pirates*. However, it wasn't just that the Depp of *Pirates* was roguishly, boozily (and yet unthreateningly) sexy; it was that he was doing something that mass audiences—like those represented by a magazine like *People*—understood. Unlike the Depp of the foreign-filmed *Chocolat* or the grisly *From Hell*, the Depp of *Pirates*—however offbeat his performance—made Johnny accessible again. In the article that named him "Sexiest Man Alive," *People* also ingenuously pointed out that *Pirates of the Caribbean* had "catapulted [Depp's] art-house career into the bright, shiny mainstream. After spending a lifetime rebelling against the Man, Depp has been tamed, at 40, by the Mouse" (Lisa Russell, "The Sexiest Man Alive: Johnny Depp," *People*, 1 December 2003, www.people.com). Film scholar Murray Pomerance writes that *Pirates of the Caribbean* "can be seen to purport and herald a new era for Johnny Depp, one in which he is, finally, as though long-promised and long-expected, the proud proprietor of a much-accepted career; not only a star but a middle-class hero" (224).

Depp may not have been the leading man, but by virtue of his very appearance in the picture, his previously guarded beauty was offered as something for consumption. *People*'s "Sexiest Alive" story imagined (and celebrated) the actor's new willingness to put himself on display, writing that he was "finally coming to terms with his own charisma" (Russell) and indicating the way in which Depp's renowned "sexiness" was strongly determined by the economic circumstances underlying the films in which he chose to appear. The Depp one sees in interviews throughout the decade seems to contradict this supposition. The star continued to baffle and delight interviewers with his self-effacing modesty, grinding conversations to an affable halt with confessions that he hadn't actually seen the film he was promoting, or was uncomfortable watching himself onscreen. Upon winning "Sexiest Man Alive" again in 2009, a mystified Depp pronounced the award "a joke" (qtd. in Oli Simpson, "Depp 'Confused by Sexiest Man Alive Title,'" *Digital Spy*, 18 January 2010, www.digitalspy.co.uk). In his publicity appearances, at least, Depp was as oblivious to "Depp" as ever.

Public and tabloid excitement around Depp's apparent embrace of the mainstream had intriguing implications for the actor's reputation as a challenging, unpredictable performer—a wonderful secret of the indies and a critical, rather than commercial, darling. In a decade in which Hollywood was derided for a steady stream of uninspired remakes and video game adaptations, reviews of the *Pirates of the Caribbean* films often revealed anxieties over Depp's presence in the overtly commercial context of films that found their source material in an amusement park ride. Implicit (and occasionally explicit) in reviews of *Pirates* was the question of whether Depp was with the commercial tide or (given the quirky nature of his performance) against it, conforming or reacting, packaged by the film or somehow triumphantly "above" it.

Prolific UK critic Mark Kermode tore down the carnival lights with the most style, consistently slamming the entire *Pirates* franchise as the epitome of commercial dreck. The plot of *Dead Man's Chest* (2006), he notes, is "business as usual" and "constantly [reminds] us that this is a film franchise based upon a fairground ride"; its director is "a witless hack [who nevertheless] understands the laws of supply and demand and doesn't skimp on the money shots"; collectively the film's faults amass as "rank consumerist decrepitude." Depp's part in this, for him, is no exception. While hailing the star's résumé, Kermode labeled his role in the films as "some of the actor's very worst work to date. . . . A symphony of eye-rolling, hair-tossing, lip-pouting, finger-fiddling narcissism" ("Pirates of the Caribbean: Dead Man's Chest," *Guardian*, 9 July 2006, www.guardian.co.uk).

If Kermode represented a pessimistic minority that saw in *Pirates*—Depp included—nothing but dollar signs, *The Observer*'s David Smith sought to rescue Johnny from the commercial mire, idealistically painting him as inexorably countercultural: "[J]ust when it had become a commonplace to say the maverick Depp was the only A-lister who would never make a blockbuster, he rebelled against type again." For Smith, Depp does not simply "appear" in *Pirates*, and he certainly does not capitulate to it; instead, the film is "stolen comprehensively" by his "riotous" performance ("Rebel Reborn," 13 November 2005, www. guardian.co.uk). This notion that by appearing in a family blockbuster Depp was somehow "rebelling" (in a more comprehensive, extreme, or baffling way than we could probably grasp) was repeated by a number of reviewers similarly oblivious to the notion of that "rebellion" itself being commercialized—that Depp's quirky portrayal was compelling, not subverting, the film's commercial success. For Kevin Maher, by the third *Pirates* film Depp's character could be seen as emblematic of "corporate entertainment's unfathomable ability to transform creative originality into anodyne excess" (*Times*, 24 May 2007, entertainment.timesonline.co.uk). Indeed, upon picking Johnny as "Sexiest" again in 2009, *People* implies the comfortably commercialized form of rebellion he offered by affectionately referring to the star, in the context of the *Pirates* films, as "Hollywood's most irresistible iconoclast" (qtd. in Michelle Nichols, "Johnny Depp Named People's 'Sexiest Man Alive,'" *Reuters*, 18 November 2009, www.reuters.com).

Part of Depp's charm has always been his inscrutability: "What makes Depp so peculiar and so vitally interesting," writes Pomerance, "is exactly that he is ungraspable" (10). After Johnny's performance in *Pirates* formed a successful, successfully disguised (and, for most reviewers and filmgoers, really quite pleasant) commodification of quirkiness, he was able to carry a kind of inscrutability, a dusky occult charm into further mainstream roles like Sweeney Todd, the electric-haired throat-slashing protagonist of the musical *Sweeney Todd: The Demon Barber of Fleet Street* (2007). Here he flashed another glimmer of mystery and unpredictability—added to the Depp mythos—by surprising audiences and critics with his singing prowess. Successful as Depp was, viewers could never quite say what or who he was.

Mainstream commercial success aside, Depp continued to avoid familiar leading-man parts well into the mid-2000s, often playing characters rooted (either delightfully or uncertainly) in an archaic childhood realm. For *New York Magazine*'s Adam Sternbergh, "Depp has always seemed too special an actor to become a true leading man. His tenderfoot good looks and bad-boy lifestyle embodied a fantasy: he, too, is the boy who never grew up." Sternbergh's immediate referent here is Depp's performance as eternal child and *Peter Pan* creator J. M. Barrie in Marc Forster's *Finding Neverland*. Depp's Barrie is a reluctant escapee from the world, inhabiting his own twinkling, liminal plane of existence that he struggles to reconcile with the socially conscious coterie around him. And, as a person out of place around adults, he is utterly sexless. The film also forcefully rejects any inference of pedophilia that viewers (or Barrie's peers within the film) might be inclined to draw from his obsession with the world of children. In one scene, two of the childlike Depps overlap when Barrie pretends to be a gravel-voiced pirate in a high-seas fantasy staged with the Llewellyn-Davies children he has befriended. Captain Jack and this civilized English pirate are clearly distinct characters (one fully developed and recklessly, vertiginously alive, the other temporary and self-knowingly clichéd), but the moment draws attention to Depp's double-dip into roles that blur the line between the world of the child and that of the adult. Depp was still—with intriguing consistency—avoiding "being a man." In 2005 he collaborated with Tim Burton in *Charlie and the Chocolate Factory*, playing a germophobic, ironically child-deploring Willy Wonka, his hair styled into an androgynous mahogany bob, his voice squeezed to a sarcastic twitter, and his face chalkily, prepubescently smooth in a characterization frequently compared to Michael Jackson.

Finally, in 2009 Depp would play the leading man—shoot a few people, kiss the girl—in Michael Mann's John Dillinger biopic *Public Enemies*. Depp played Dillinger surprisingly straight, eschewing the commodified eccentricity of *Pirates*, to the surprise and disappointment of some reviewers, who seemed thoroughly wooed by his larger-than-life portrayals. While the leading man role suggests familiarity, far from finally disambiguating Depp the film sees the star's iconic inscrutability recede into something ineffably transitory and, in this sense, symbolically "cinematic."

As Dillinger, Depp is both murmuringly introverted and flirtatiously brazen. His dialogue is all devil-may-care apothegms, stressing freedom and impulse, yet his manner is curiously guarded, as if he is secretly aware of his own impermanence. The film's breathtaking conclusion gives us Dillinger (and Depp) as someone both otherworldly and powerfully immediate, a wondrous creature of cinema. As Dillinger watches gangster film *Manhattan Melodrama* (1934) in the theater outside of which he will be shot to death, a series of close-ups allows us to register his reactions to the events on the screen before him, to recognize his tender absorption in the figure of Clark Gable being led to his death in a turn we know prefigures the end of our protagonist. (Depp even wears a Gablesque mustache here.) We witness how John Dillinger knows himself through this film, understand his vulnerability—indeed, understand that he is like any of us watching *Public Enemies* at this very moment. We see the screen as he sees it: pristine, ethereal, overwhelming—it becomes, for an urgent moment, our film. The sound swells and becomes everything. We see his acknowledgment and validation of truth in the titanic, shimmering screen, share in the affirmation of what he sees as both unreal and a gorgeously heightened reality.

After the movie, he strolls outside, pleasantly managing his thoughts on what he has seen, visibly immersed in the film—too much, in fact. For, creeping up on him is the burly officer who pummeled his girlfriend in custody, the man's face contorted with hatred, gun thrust balefully before him.

Perhaps in response to some noise behind him, an intrusive scuffle or murmur as the officer approaches, the spell is broken and Dillinger's face becomes gradually, irritably pinched. He turns. The film gives us the point of view of the approaching officer as it is suddenly met, held, and haunted by Depp's orphic gaze, captured in extreme close-up—just as limitlessly close, in fact, as those stunning, dreamlike images we saw in the theater. Gradually, hypnotically even, the man lowers his gun: he reacts as if he has seen a phantom, been confronted by something beyond him, not a man like himself but a force of history. In other words, he is starstruck: not just by Dillinger, but by Depp—for the two are, at this moment, utterly inseparable. Dillinger's status as folk hero in the film complements and at this moment is utterly subsumed by the fact that he is also, and irrepressibly, Johnny Depp.

The fatal shots will not come from this stunned officer, but they will come: the face of suave film-star mystery graphically penetrated by a bullet right before the camera. Dillinger mouths a few words, but their meaning is lost on those who kill him. In Mann's film, the Depp we see is transcendently but fleetingly cinematic, like the images Dillinger has seen onscreen: infinitely alluring but ungraspable, evanescent, much too easily lost (see Pomerance 105–06). Mann gives us the gunshots through Depp's face not as a demystification, a rupture, or a falsification of cinematic truth (or of the gravity of stardom), but as a reminder of cinema's human affective center, its point of reception: Dillinger as the thinking, feeling filmgoer. The character played by Depp in this film is someone both impossible and—with his bloodied face pressed breathlessly to the sidewalk—startlingly, achingly real.

★★★★★ Robert Downey Jr.

By the first years of the 2000s, Robert Downey Jr., the Oscar-nominated star of Richard Attenborough's *Chaplin* (1992), was more familiar to the public from televised news of his arrests than from his appearance in cinematic features. While he appeared in several films across the turn of the century, including *Bowfinger* (1999) and the critically acclaimed *Wonder Boys* (2000), Downey was also repeatedly charged with drug-related offenses and eventually jailed for violating the terms of his parole. In 1999 he told a judge of his struggle to remain clean: "It's like I have a loaded gun in my mouth, and I've got my finger on the trigger, and I like the taste of the gun metal" (qtd. in Jessica Reaves, "Will Robert Downey Jr.'s Case Spark a Change in Drug Sentencing?" *Time*, 7 February 2001, www.time .com). Apparently on the right track again in 2000, Downey provided a significant ratings bump for the legal comedy-drama "Ally McBeal," playing the love interest of star Calista Flockhart. However, the actor was dropped from the show after yet another arrest on 24 April 2001—the media's tendency to phrase commercial as personal success making his fall appear all the more dramatic: "Downey's off-screen addiction left many fans [of the television show] and critics puzzled," wrote CNN (edition.cnn.com).

During his prolonged decline, it was common for the media to draw connections between Downey's personal and legal troubles and his past film roles, especially that of drug addict Julian in *Less Than Zero* (1987), this kind of thinking aided by Downey's own assertion that his role in the film was like "the ghost of Christmas future" (qtd. in "Downey Blames Movie for Addiction," *Contact Music*, 28 April 2008, www.contactmusic.com). And, since getting clean, Downey's cinematic roles, from independent films to blockbusters, have capitalized on his troubled personal life in various guises. The *New York Daily News* points out Downey's "specialty in dissolute guys" (Joel Neumaier, "'Iron Man' Tests Robert Downey Jr.'s Metal," 30 April 2008, www.nydailynews.com). In Richard Linklater's *A Scanner Darkly* (2006), an independent animated feature based on the novel by Philip K. Dick, Downey—his body seemingly perpetually shifting and unrelaxed—played a garrulous expert on and user of the future drug "Substance D." Larger-scale success, however, came with the lead in jokey noir thriller *Kiss Kiss Bang Bang* a year earlier, which played even more noticeably on Downey's high-profile legal and personal troubles. In the midst of a frantic getaway that sees his partner shot, small-time crook Harry Lockhart (Downey) inadvertently finds himself in a late-night audition for a film role. The script, concerning a dead partner, allows his real distress to override his awkwardness, and he gets the role. As Lockhart, Downey is tough yet vulnerable, the troublemaker who never does any real harm: someone who, despite his sins, wound up in Hollywood through unlikely talent, dumb luck, and adolescent adorability. With his skittish energy and seemingly overexposed, near-quivering eyes (conveying a James Dean–like blend of fatigue and alertness), each one capped by a solemn jet-black bushy eyebrow, Downey was especially well suited to playing combinations of vulnerability and destructiveness.

In David Fincher's unnervingly restrained *Zodiac* (2007), Downey's public persona was evoked more uneasily. This film dramatizes the futile search for the eponymous serial killer in the late 1960s and early 1970s. Downey plays Paul Avery, a crime reporter at the paper to which the killer (a flagrant manipulator of the media) sent a series of taunting letters. Downey's Avery is brusque and arrogant, seemingly attentive to only the twitchy rhythms of his own thoughts (a characterization the actor would carry over into his depiction of Tony Stark in *Iron Man* as well as that of Sherlock Holmes in the film of the same name). Avery's stylish green shirts and waistcoats, offset by the dull business attire of his colleagues, mean we pick him as the newsroom maverick immediately. After he arbitrarily describes the Zodiac as "possibly a latent homosexual," in a salacious flourish that reflects his feeling that the case is "good business," he receives a Halloween card from the killer along with a threat: "You're doomed." Seemingly unable to accept the letter as a specious extension of Zodiac's manipulation of the media (Fincher's film frequently reminds us of the serial killer as a mass-media phenomenon), he is consumed by the menace. Profoundly distressed—and instantly famous—he immediately purchases a handgun and begins a rapid descent into alcoholism and drug addiction that uncomfortably reminds us of Downey's own very public decline.

Later in the film—and years later in the narrative—amateur sleuth and protagonist Robert Graysmith (Jake Gyllenhaal) visits the grimy houseboat to which the drug-addled Avery has retreated. As Graysmith tries to reignite Avery's interest in the Zodiac case, the burnt-out journalist cuts him off with a dismissive mumble: "It's not new." The line, like his retreat to the houseboat, like his disposal of his Zodiac files, like the "Pong" videogame (jammed into the shot) whose robotic bops and boops intrusively punctuate their conversation, indicates Avery's insatiable, addictive craving for the new, for acceleration. It bespeaks his desire to escape from the public Avery, the victim-in-waiting, constructed by the Zodiac: to force the obsolescence of a historically specific, public identity that has by now contaminated and totally, debilitatingly reconstituted his private, personal one.

The casting of Downey in the role of Avery amplifies this anxiety by further eroding the boundaries between reality and representation. So complete in its disorder, its jittery, chaotic involution, is Downey's portrayal of Avery's drug addiction that we might reasonably wonder whether the star is not in fact drawing on some lived knowledge of his subject—that is, whether he is doing something that is not quite truly acting. As the dressing-gowned Avery reclines on his couch, speaking only in terse ejaculations, his semiclothed body vulgarly illuminated by the pale sunlight that streams through the window, he is a discomforting vision of wrecked celebrity. Consequently, in *Zodiac*, Downey is both an actor and—disturbingly—not an actor: "performing" and, at the same time, disorientingly too authentic.

Despite impressive and critically admired performances in a number of films from 2005 onward, it was his role in *Iron Man* (2008), as billionaire

Both powerful and puppyish, Robert Downey Jr. as Tony Stark in *Iron Man* (Jon Favreau, Paramount, 2008). Digital frame enlargement.

playboy and inhabitant of a fantastic mechanized metal suit, that Downey hit his commercial stride—giving the media sufficient evidence of his "comeback." The news media's subordination of years of successful independent and lower (yet hardly shoestring) budget work since the actor's commitment to sobriety helped construct Downey as the prodigal son of the mainstream: "Downey's upbringing was loose and anarchic and his private life followed suit but his aspirations were always toward the mainstream," wrote the *Telegraph* in a story on the star subtitled "Return of the Hero" (Murphy Williams, 26 April 2008, www.telegraph.co.uk). "Back from the Brink" ran the title of *Time* magazine's story upon the film's release in 2008, which stressed the length of time that had passed since the high-profile success of *Chaplin* (Rebecca Winters Keegan, 16 April 2008, www.time.com).

Tony Stark again provides a reminder, albeit a more comfortably subdued one, of Downey's public troubles. Stark is a cynical, hard-drinking, womanizing celebrity who develops a conscience to equalize his flamboyant arrogance. In an interview with *Superherohype*, director Jon Favreau indicated the bad boy persona Downey brought to the role: "People are ready for this guy to play this role. . . . He captures that bad boy attitude. . . . That's why we open with 'Back in Black.' That's why it's Robert Downey Jr. This had to have attitude and be rock 'n' roll and in your face" (Edward Douglas, "An In-Depth Iron Man Talk with Director Jon Favreau," 29 April 2008, www.superherohype.com).

"Audiences will be seeing a lot of the real Downey in *Iron Man* when it opens Friday," concurred the *Ottawa Citizen* in their description of a press conference with the star, before quoting Downey as saying about himself and his role in the film that "[he] think[s] the parallels are obvious" ("Hollywood's Iron Man," 30 April 2008, www.canada.com/ottawacitizen).

The *Telegraph* wrote that the story Favreau wanted to tell "is one of a famous, flawed but brilliant, funny, complex character and his redemption. Downey had to be the man" (Williams). The star's vulnerability is also capitalized on in Favreau's film—indeed, Stark is so whimsically arrogant, viewers surely need assurance of a troubled interior.

Downey's comeback and roguish persona were cemented with a high-profile supporting role in Ben Stiller's comedy *Tropic Thunder* (2008). Reviving the extravagant Australian accent he used in *Natural Born Killers* (1994), Downey played white acting virtuoso Kirk Lazarus, whose commitment to his role as a black soldier leads him to undergo a pigmentation procedure that darkens his skin tone—the most alarming and successful element in the film's manifold satirization of Hollywood filmmaking. The actor extended this anti-establishment theme by playing a sinewy, street-fighting reinterpretation of British literature's most famous drug addict, Sherlock Holmes, in Guy Ritchie's 2009 film of that name. While the film clearly capitalizes on Downey's narcotics troubles, its allusions to drug addiction are negligible and lighthearted, easily palatable to mainstream audiences—limited, indeed, to Holmes's fumbling around as the curtains admit a unwanted flood of light into his unkempt room.

Around the release of *Iron Man* and *Tropic Thunder* interviewers lingered on Downey's personal troubles as a matter of convention, playing to this commodified image of dissidence: "He's clutching a Starbucks as though it contained the last drop of caffeine on Earth," observed the reporter from the *Ottawa Citizen*, as if tickled by the prospect of Downey the addict raging forth at any moment. A series of photographs for American *GQ* arranged Downey in a variety of *enfant terrible* poses: his head squashed into a stocking; clutching an aerosol can to a cigarette lighter; letting a woman pull a pistol from his jeans while dragging her tongue across his face (Matthew Klam, "The Man in the Irony Mask," May 2008, www.gq.com).

However, in interviews Downey has communicated some self-consciousness about the media's fascination with his personal troubles: "Downey is keen to stress how conventional he is," noted the *Telegraph*. "I'm not a psychological mess," the actor told the paper, "and I'm actually a very stable and trustworthy and consistent person." Despite this seemingly forceful self-evaluation, the *Telegraph*'s story concludes by interpreting, with perverse optimism, one of the star's many ambiguous metaphors as "hinting, perhaps, that a clean future is no guaranteed bet" (Williams). Similarly, in a story with the abstemious headline "Robert Downey Jr. Can't Imagine Life Without His Wife," online entertainment reporter *ShowbizSpy* nevertheless defaults to Downey the recidivist bad boy, provocatively closing with his appraisal of the actor's co-star Rachel McAdams as "smokin' hot" (27 December 2009, www.showbizspy.com).

Perhaps sensing a clash with his rebellious persona (or an altogether undesirable brand of rebellion), stories on the star tend to note—but not linger on—Downey's expressed Republican leanings. Similarly, the star's 2004 album, *The Futurist*, seems out of tune with Downey the bad boy: swervy mature keyboard-pop swept along by the actor's wistful, smooth, yet smoky vocals, somewhere between those of Joe Cocker and Don Henley (and not an *Iron Man*–esque hard-rock riff around).

While the press delight in seeing Downey the arrogant bad boy, a comfortable commodification of his troubled "real life" image, interviewers have also ensured the accessibility of his persona by stressing his modesty. In interviews, Downey appears to oscillate between untethered rogue and fortunate kid, bewildered by his own dumb luck. In their 2008 profile, the *Telegraph* relayed Downey's description of his meeting with Steven Spielberg: "I couldn't believe it. He's over by the monitors, and I'm like 'Jesus Christ, there he is' and he talks to me about a couple of things, and then he leaves the set and I'm like 'God darn it!' I've only been waiting 25 years to have one of those moments" (Williams).

" 'It's all so new to me,' Downey . . . says with the sparkle of someone half his age," continues the *Telegraph*'s article, its author feeling that "Downey's youthful brightness is his saving grace" (Williams). Without quoting Downey's admission of as much, the *New York Daily News*'s Joel Neumaier wrote that "[The] opening of 'Iron Man' mark[ed the] movie-going season as the summer of Robert Downey Jr. That is something no one, not even Downey, ever expected." When Downey appears to threaten the loser-turned-lucky theme, seeming expectant of his fame for "suggesting that important moments in an actor's life are like astronomy and that the stars need to be in the right configuration," the *Ottawa Citizen* subtly derides him for incongruously "turn[ing] philosopher."

Around 2001, a number of sources reported a supposed obstacle to the revival of Downey's mainstream career: the cost of insuring an actor who couldn't be relied upon to show up on set. The *Ottawa Citizen* raised the question in their report on the star's *Iron Man* press conference in 2008: "Fellow actor Terrence Howard, who plays Tony Stark's military buddy in the movie, says the film's producers balked at the idea of casting Downey because they feared his history made him too much of an insurance risk." In May 2001, *Time* ran a story speculating that "Downey Jr. might have priced himself out of the market" (Jess Cage and Kathleen Adams, "Detention: Would You Buy Insurance from This Man," 21 May 2001, www.time

.com). As a Hollywood star (and an immensely talented one according to critics and peers, one destined for mainstream success), the drug-addicted Downey was not just a personal or media tragedy but, commercially, a broken product: a gigantic, magnetic presence unable to be utilized. What we see in Downey's recent commercial successes, and the dramatization of his rebellious persona (especially in the *Iron Man* franchise and *Sherlock Holmes*), is an intriguing example of high capitalism's ability to take advantage of its glitches—to make an asset from a deficiency, a virtue from a flaw. Even the star's shortcomings, his failures as a product, could be repurposed and sold. Only time will tell whether the true versatility and depth of Downey's ability can also find a mainstream reception given the overpowering presence of, and the insatiable demand for, Bad Boy Downey.

2 ☆☆☆☆☆☆☆☆☆☆☆

Clint Eastwood and Morgan Freeman
Million-Dollar Seniors

ROBERT EBERWEIN

Shortly before Clint Eastwood received an award from the Museum of the Moving Image, the *Hollywood Reporter* dubbed him "The Elder Statesman" (30 November 2009). Soon afterward he was on the cover of *AARP Modern Maturity*, in which he told an interviewer, "You get to a certain age and you go, 'I'm the last man standing.'" Hearing that his friend was about to turn eighty, Morgan Freeman, who is only seven years younger, quipped, "Eighty? Really? Unbelievable! . . . This man absolutely shows no signs of slowing down or losing traction. He's so sharp, so efficient. I hope this won't make him mad, but when I grow up, I want to be like Clint" (David Hochman, "10 Who Inspire," January/February 2010, 24). From one perspective, Eastwood certainly gave no signs of "slowing

Clint Eastwood. Courtesy of Photofest New York. Morgan Freeman.

down" in the 2000s. He directed nine films (two of them featuring Freeman in major roles) and starred in four of them. Freeman himself has obviously already "grow[n] up." Within these ten years, he appeared in at least twenty-eight films with an overall gross of $1.6 billion, as opposed to East-wood's $575 million. Both are stars of the first magnitude, respected by worldwide audiences, a remarkable achievement for two aging actors at a period when youth-oriented fare drives the box office. Of particular inter-est is the way the parts each man plays in films of this decade and the responses to them focus on important issues. Consideration of Eastwood's aging is often foregrounded against his earlier career and personae (the Man with No Name, Dirty Harry Callahan) and the issue of masculinity. Dominant themes for Freeman are his image as an authoritative "voice of God" narrator, and his race, especially in relation to the problematic cate-gory of what some designate "Magical Negroes."[1]

★★★★★ **The Last Man Standing**

A month before being on the cover of *Modern Maturity*, East-wood was on the cover of *GQ*'s last issue of the decade as Man of the Year and the subject of an appreciative tribute by Michael Hainey: "Think about it: His breakthrough role—playing the Man with No Name in those spaghetti Westerns? He's in his mid thirties when he does those. . . . And *Dirty Harry* [1971]? He's 41 when he makes that. . . . The guy doesn't hang it up—he only starts getting stronger. He goes on a stunning run of creativity that a man half his age would kill for. . . . In this youth-obsessed world, the guy is the patron saint of late bloomers. . . . He might be the only guy alive who makes you envy crow's feet" ("Icon: Clint Eastwood," www.gq.com, Decem-ber 2009).[2]

Although he had been considered one of the world's top stars in the 1970s, the 1980s had not been good years for him (see Morrison). But he reached new heights in the 1990s, most particularly in *Unforgiven* (1992), with Oscars for Best Picture and Director, and the popular films *In the Line of Fire* (1993) and *The Bridges of Madison County* (1995). The films of the 2000s registered his trajectory from hardboiled gunman and lawman to mellowed and vulnerable champion of the oppressed, and, in his most recent films, an aging star whose roles chronicle a progressively darkening concern with death. The films in which he acts include a comedy, *Space Cowboys* (2000), that thematizes the maturity of the star and his co-stars while evoking his earlier lighthearted roles such as *Every Which Way But Loose* (1978); a crime film, *Blood Work* (2002), that provides a much darker treatment of the older star, now playing the survivor of a heart transplant, while calling forth memories of his Dirty Harry role; and two melodramas, *Million Dollar Baby* (2004) and *Gran Torino* (2008), that see him playing first a fading manager of a boxing gym who assists a hopelessly paralyzed boxer to die and then an embittered old former automobile worker who finds meaning in his life by sacrificing it for others.

Except for *Invictus* (2009), the third time he has directed Freeman, the theme of death pervades and controls all his other films of this decade: *Mystic River* (2003), which explores the horrific effects of child molestation and murder on a Boston community; *Changeling* (2008), based on a true story about the kidnapping and probable murder of a little boy; and the dyptych *Flags of Our Fathers* (2006) and *Letters from Iwo Jima* (2006), two World War II films that depict the bloody Battle of Iwo Jima from the perspectives of both the American and Japanese combatants (see Eberwein).

★★★★★ Coming to Terms with Death

Space Cowboys concerns a group of aspiring astronauts whose ambitions to go into space as younger men in 1958 were unrealized. Forty years later, Frank Corvin (Eastwood), knowledgeable about the design of earlier spacecrafts, is called on to assist in capturing an errant Russian satellite that is circling the Earth with a deadly payload. He brings his former team back. The other stars are James Garner, as a slightly dotty minister; Tommy Lee Jones, who is dying of cancer; and Donald Sutherland, as an obnoxious skirt chaser. One of the most poignant moments in the film (although played for laughs) occurs when the four have physical exams. We see them naked, from behind, in a manner that uncompromisingly exposes the effects of aging on the male body.

Blood Work examines the condition of aging in a much darker manner. Eastwood plays Terry McCaleb, a police detective who succumbs to a heart attack during a chase early in the film, and then recuperates from a heart transplant. Even though he is on leave from the force, he becomes involved in hunting for a serial killer after discovering that the donor of his heart was one of the victims. Responding to a plea from the victim's sister, Graciella (Wanda de Jesus), he operates outside the purview of the police department, assisted by his apparently supportive neighbor Jasper (Jeff Daniels), who is in fact the serial killer. Terry kills him, assisted by Graciella, with whom he is in love. Throughout the film, Terry constantly puts his hand on his heart. A shot of him shirtless offers an image of the aging male body that's a counterpart to that of the naked old stars in *Space Cowboys*. At one

point he stares at his chest in the mirror. Characters remark on his appearance, noting he looks "bad, like shit." At one point Terry says, "I better go
home to take my pills," and we see him at various times doing just that, or
else being sternly lectured by his cardiologist (Anjelica Huston) for breaking his therapeutic routine.

Reviewers commented on the star's confrontation with his own aging.
Roger Ebert praised Eastwood: "He knows himself, he knows his craft, his
pride as a director is dominant over his ego as an actor, and the results are
films that use a star aura with an uncommon degree of intimacy. Terry
McCaleb is one of Eastwood's best characters because, in a way, he's not a
new character at all but just the same guy farther down the road." Here and
in *Space Cowboys*, for Ebert, "Eastwood has paid attention to his years, and
found stories to exploit them" (rogerebert.suntimes.com, 9 August 2002).
Todd McCarthy made a similar observation about the star's intelligent
choices of parts: "Eastwood, far from ignoring his own advancing years à la
Woody Allen, has incorporated some sort of commentary on getting old
into his characterization. Enjoying the obvious benefit of being in excellent
shape, Eastwood continues to be able to function credibly in genre formats
with only slight modifications to accommodate his characters' encroaching
maturity" (www.variety.com, 4 August 2002). Walter Metz also notes how
Blood Work thematizes aging (207) and discusses how it "engages images of
Eastwood's aging body, as no longer capable of its earlier . . . Dirty Harry
heroics" (210).

Of equal significance, given the way his films display the value of masculinity, is the connection between this sense of mortality and Eastwood's
acknowledgment of the power of the feminine. Drucilla Cornell focuses on
the image of Eastwood observing his scarred torso in the mirror in *Blood
Work*: "When we witness [Eastwood] in front of the mirror, we understand
the integral connection between [his] vulnerability and his metaphysical
and literal embrace of the feminine, which, now that [he] has a woman's
heart is literally a part of him" (Cornell 66). She praises him for "con-
structing a more wholesome masculinity, one that develops out of the inte-
gration, not the rejection, of the feminine other" (67).

Before the opening of *Space Cowboys*, a very different kind of venue was
providing information about Eastwood in a way that continued to support
the media's construction of his masculinity. In "A Star's Star Attraction," Eastwood talks about a huge eucalyptus tree on his Carmel, California, property.
The reporter begins: "What comes to mind when you think of Clint Eastwood? Dirty Harry, probably. Maybe a scene from *Play Misty for Me* [1971] or
The Outlaw Josie Wales [1976]. What about a man who once worked as a

logger and who carries a lifelong knee injury from a load of logs that fell on him at a pulp mill? Someone who is an avid golfer, skier, and helicopter pilot with a passion and loyalty for the Monterey Peninsula and its landscape?" The immediate interest was the giant tree Eastwood was maintaining, having preserved it and the land on which it rests from developers some years before (Dan Smith, *American Forests*, Spring 2000, 14–17). An article the following summer in the same journal concerned another eucalyptus tree that was in fact bigger than Eastwood's, one with a forty-eight-foot circumference as opposed to the thirty-eight feet on his. Asked about his response to a possible challenge by the owners of the other tree as claimants for an entry in the National Registry of Big Trees, Eastwood commented, "Let the best tree win" ("You Have to Ask Yourself a Question: Do You Feel Lucky?" *American Forests*, Summer 2001, 13). (His tree lost.) The article's use of Dirty Harry's line from the original 1971 film and the issue of whose tree is bigger clearly play on issues of phallic power and testify to his continued vitality.

The comments on Eastwood's masculinity, directly or obliquely, continue the ongoing treatment of the subject (see Bingham). The issue surfaces most personally in regard to Eastwood's romantic relationships over the years and the seven children he has fathered with five women. Morgan, his most recent child with wife Dina Ruiz, was born in 1996, when Eastwood was sixty-six. (The child is named after her maternal grandmother, not, as has been incorrectly suggested, after Morgan Freeman.) Fathering a child at that age suggests a potency certainly in keeping with the power that has characterized Eastwood's star image over the decades.

The press commented on Eastwood's late fatherhood and continuing masculine power in connection with the opening of *Blood Work*. In an article titled "Clint Eastwood: For a Few Women More; How Clint Eastwood Has Finally Found Happiness as a Family Man," Anna Day speculates, "This new lease of life can be attributed to many things, but there is no doubt that his young family have played an important part. His constant references to his six-year-old daughter Morgan and his young wife, TV news anchor Dina Ruiz, lead you to believe that the surliest actor in Hollywood has mellowed a little. 'I've waited all my life for a woman like Dina,' says Clint, who has the body of a man half his age, thanks to years of healthy eating and a fierce exercise regime" (*Mirror*, 27 December 2002). The attention paid by the press to his body and health continued. When Dave Carr interviewed Eastwood and his wife, two topics surfaced: their unpretentiousness and their continued sexual relations. The first was affirmed by Eastwood's assertion that his wife wore "a $60 dollar watch to the Oscars, not a $10K loaner," the second by a bit of domestic humor: on her way to the market, Dina asks

Clint what he needs, and he answers in a way that jokes publicly about sexual enhancements: "Levitra, Viagra, Ciallis—deadpanned to shrieks of laughter from the staff. He can make that kind of joke not just because of the children . . . but also because he is not given to anxiety over his image" ("Still Fighting for the Green Light," www.nytimes.com, 13 February 2005).

Million Dollar Baby, his first mega-hit of the decade, is about Maggie Fitzgerald (Hilary Swank), an amateur boxer who wants to break into the sport professionally. She seeks out Frankie Dunn (Eastwood) to help train her. Although initially unwilling, he is convinced to help by his friend Eddie Scrap-Iron Dupris (Freeman), a former fighter who works in the gym and who is blind in one eye as a result of Frankie's error in not attending effectively to his wounds in an earlier fight. After a series of successes, Maggie fights in a championship bout in which her opponent unfairly and cruelly hits her after the bell, causing her to fall in a way that results in complete paralysis. Hopelessly crippled, she wants to die and tries to kill herself by biting her tongue. Even though warned by his priest about the effects that mercy killing will have on him, Frankie injects her with an overdose of adrenaline and ends her misery. The entire film is narrated by Eddie, who, unknown to Frankie, witnessed his administering the fatal dose. The film concludes in a way that suggests the narration we have heard is in fact contained in a letter that Eddie has been writing to Frankie's estranged (and never seen) daughter. Frankie disappears from Eddie's life and the gym in a manner reminiscent of Bill Munny's at the end of *Unforgiven*. But unlike that film's conclusion, with its suggestion of a new and freer life in San Francisco, *Million Dollar Baby*'s gloomy ending suggests a kind of terminal isolation for Frankie.

The film generated debates between supporters and opponents of mercy killing and was seen as another sign that Eastwood, formerly associated with right-wing politics and support of the Republican Party and Libertarian positions, had moved to the left. The issue of whether Eastwood was in fact making a redemptive movie to alter his star image in the film surfaces in commentary by Chris Orr, who offers the most comprehensive treatment of the star's ambivalent position in relation to critics of the left and right. He thinks Eastwood is "sorry or seems so" and that it's "hard to shake the sense that *Million Dollar Baby* is another in a series of efforts by Eastwood to make amends for his early career." Orr cites a comment made by Eastwood, "I'm not haunted by my past," and observes that he "is the rare artist who has gone from being condemned as a fascist propagandist by the left to being condemned as a fascist propagandist by the right. . . . But the two critiques are illustrative of the journey Eastwood has taken over the last 34 years, from conservative icon disparaged by much of the critical establishment to Hollywood statesman (and Academy favorite) widely vilified on the right" ("Dirty Harry or P.C. Wimp?" www.salon.com, 24 February 2005). Significantly, Eastwood's star status is of such a magnitude that his political positions, real or assumed, are themselves the material for critical discourse. As such he joins another icon, John Wayne, whose politics remained securely conservative (and problematic for critics).

What matters most here is the way the film blends the two old men, Eastwood and Frankie. As Mike LaSalle observes in his rave review, "*Million Dollar Baby* ages well in memory because it gradually seems to mean more. Its meaning can't be summed up in a sentence, but it has to do with a view of life as inexpressibly sad and yet always right. . . . This is an old man's view. . . . The trainer is an old man, and so is Eastwood. The weight of years is in *Million Dollar Baby*, technically, artistically and philosophically. It has the gloom and transcendence of an old man's wisdom" (*San Francisco Chronicle*, www.sfgate.com, 25 December 2004).

Eastwood's description of himself as "the last man standing" was given a decidedly negative turn in Akiva Gottlieb's hostile assessment of him and his presumably last acting performance in *Gran Torino*. Many of the reviews used the film's depiction of a biased, aging Korean War veteran as an occasion for talking about the aging actor who had served in the United States during the Korean War, but not in combat. Walt Kowalski, a widower with less-than-warm relations with his children, lives in a modest home in a run-down section of Detroit. His neighbors, Hmong immigrants, elicit initial contempt and impatience from the feisty and racist Walt. Tension increases when a teenaged boy, Thao (Bee Vang), tries to steal Walt's Gran Torino as part of an initiation into the local Hmong gang. Eventually Walt grows closer to Thao and his family, defending them with his rifle from the Hmong gang that harasses them.

Walt is especially protective of Thao's sister Sue (Ahney Her), who has been raped by gang members. His revenge against the gang for that crime comes in the form of preventing Thao from risking his life and by sacrificing himself to a hail of bullets in a way that guarantees the gang will be arrested for having shot an unarmed man. His final speech to Thao before leaving to sacrifice himself concerns the horror he experienced in killing a young Korean soldier and what comes with the sense of having killed at all, a very different kind of sentiment regarding death than we have ever heard from this star in any film.

Gottlieb complains that Eastwood "has been encouraging people to believe that every new film was his last one as long as he has been making

Walt Kowalski (Clint Eastwood) and his Hmong neighbors (Bee Vang, Brooke Chia Thao, Chee Thao, Ahney Her) in an on-set publicity still from *Gran Torino* (Clint Eastwood, Matten Productions, 2008). Courtesy Photofest New York.

movies. [He] repeatedly seeks nostalgic references from his audiences with a kid's petulant sense of entitlement." While acknowledging him as an "icon," a word that appears repeatedly in commentary on Eastwood, Gottlieb finds the film (the biggest box-office success he ever had as the star—$148 million) "a meditation on [his] own obsolescence" ("Last Man Standing," *Nation*, www.thenation.com, 1 June 2009).

Commentary by Mark Harris also positions the film in relation to Eastwood as a venerable star:

> Sometimes the star is actually too big for the movie. I'm not a fan of *Gran Torino*, which seems less like a freestanding, credible story than a flimsy pretext for the estimable Clint Eastwood to continue a dialogue with his own past selves about solitude and martyrdom and toughness and misanthropy. If you've immersed yourself in Eastwood's 40-year record of pondering these themes, this movie is a fascinating if problematic installment in Clint-as-metaphor. But if not, the spectacle of an actor-director who has made himself look like some insane, old sand monster from *The Mummy* rasping, 'Get off my lawn!' seems ludicrous.
>
> ("What Stars Are For," *Entertainment Weekly*, www.ew.com, 2 January 2009)

Although he trashes the film, Mike LaSalle's commentary is relevant. He sees Walt as "the Clint Eastwood of collective memory. Coming back to squint and sneer and look absolutely outraged" ("Clint's *Gran Torino* a Funny Mix," *San Francisco Chronicle*, www.sfgate.com, 19 December 2008). The attack on Walt replays the one in *A Fistful of Dollars* (1964) when the Man with No Name stood seemingly vulnerable against a fusillade of bullets, except that, unlike his forebear, Walt has no plate of steel under a poncho. He falls, armed outstretched in a Christ-like pose, in death. It's a profoundly affecting moment, partly for the reason adduced by LaSalle. When Walt dies, so too does our relationship with the star's persona that has captivated our imaginations for so many years. But there's something else. While Walt's action allows him to redeem himself for his racism and previous acts of violence, Eastwood's role as the sacrificing Walt could be seen as offering his audience a kind of redemptive expiation for its moral investment in and compliance with the violent acts in the cinematic past it shares with Eastwood himself.[3] Even more, the death of Walt is an unsettling precursor of the death of Clint, given his numerous statements that this is in fact the last film in which he will act, even though he continues to direct. As such, it's almost as if the ultimate and inevitable demise of this huge star as performer points to the end of what remains of the Hollywood star system.

★★★★★ The Voice of God

In contrast to Eastwood, Morgan Freeman entered the 1990s with a record of major box-office successes in 1989: *Lean on Me*, *Glory*, and *Driving Miss Daisy* (Oscar nomination as Best Actor). In the 1990s, he was nominated for Best Actor in *The Shawshank Redemption* (1994) and co-starred in Eastwood's *Unforgiven* and the box office successes *Se7en* (1995) and *Deep Impact* (1998). Production of *Million Dollar Baby* reunited Eastwood and Freeman at the ages of seventy-four and sixty-seven. One reporter noted how this film was Eastwood's twenty-fifth as a director and that "Freeman isn't willing to slow down either. 'Obviously I did [the film] because Clint called. And when Clint says to you, "Do you care to go another round with me buddy," you don't say no'" (Phillip McCarthy, "Thudden Impact," *Sidney Morning*, smh.com.au, 4 February 2005). Although this would be the second Eastwood film in which Freeman acted, in one respect he had already gone another round in 2000 when he served as narrator of a documentary about his friend, *Clint Eastwood—Out of the Shadows* (2001; originally made for PBS's "American Masters" series in 2000). Interestingly, while the decade begins with Freeman serving as a *nonfictional* narrator whose commentary in a documentary explores East-wood's cinematic and personal past, *Million Dollar Baby* is perhaps the greatest example of Freeman as a *fictional* narrator, a function he would perform several times in the decade, and the role that got him an Oscar.

The expression "the voice of God" refers to a cinematic narrative technique that uses a speaker, sometimes involved with the principal characters and sometimes not, to offer commentary and explanations about the story we are watching. Obviously the technique parallels the use of the omniscient narrator in fiction. Freeman has served in this capacity, as a non-character narrator, in two films: Steven Spielberg's *War of the Worlds* (2005) and the documentary *The March of the Penguins* (2005). In the first, he describes the initial onslaught by aliens attacking the United States and explains the reasons why they expire. In the second (a commentary replacing that in the original French film by Luc Jacquet), he outlines and responds to the remarkable journey by emperor penguins traveling to their breeding grounds in Antarctica. His voice-of-God narration in the second film elicited positive comments from Stephen Holden, whose review speaks to the way Freeman is perceived as a star, even when describing penguins: "Freeman's warm dignified narration completes the anthropomorphic commentary. He is a human witness, a grandfatherly surrogate who speaks for the loving couples" (*New York Times*, www.nytimes.com, 24 June 2005). The key words here are "warm," "dignified," and "grandfatherly"—all terms that are attached to Freeman the trusted star. He now introduces the "CBS Evening News with Katie Couric," previously presented by the voice of Walter Cronkite, generally regarded as the most trusted man in America when he was alive.

As narrator of fiction films, his manner and decorum are unique. Particularly in *Million Dollar Baby*, his sad and resigned tone as he traces the disturbing progress of events in the lives of Frankie and Maggie adds to our increasing dismay, especially because we sense the irony that this one-eyed man, with his physically impaired vision, has seen it all in a broader sense. One of the most startling moments in the film (besides the shock generated when Maggie is cruelly and unfairly injured by her opponent after the bell sounds) occurs when we realize that Eddie has been able to describe the assisted suicide because of his vantage point.

His other voice-of-God narrations in this decade occur in Robert Benton's *Feast of Love* (2007) and Rob Reiner's *The Bucket List* (2007). Responses to these films indicate some reviewers are tiring of his ongoing role as the all-knowing character. In the first he plays Harry Stevenson, an academic temporarily on leave because he is grieving for his son, who died of a drug overdose. Harry is the force who connects and tries to help a number of

Frankie Dunn (Clint Eastwood) and Eddie Scrap-Iron Dupris (Morgan Freeman) outside the ropes at the Hit Pit in *Million Dollar Baby* (Clint Eastwood, Warner Bros., 2004). Courtesy Photofest New York.

characters with romantic problems. The film establishes his narrative authority by presenting the story as a flashback preceding a conclusion Harry already knows, and his offering of insights that foreshadow the events. Roger Ebert, usually a big fan, gave the film only two stars and was bothered by its use of him "as a wise counselor of the troubled and heartsick. Apart from his great films, of which there are many, this is almost his standard role, although he tends to spend a lot of time playing God" (rogerebert.suntimes.com, 28 September 2007).

The Bucket List was a huge hit (grossing over $93 million) and let Freeman fulfill his longstanding desire to work with Jack Nicholson. They play Carter Chambers and Edward Cole, old men fighting and ultimately succumbing to cancer, but not before they embark on a series of adventures traveling through the world and taking on physical challenges like skydiving. The idea for this comes from Chambers's "bucket list" of things to do before dying. Freeman's narration is somewhat deceptive, since he presents the last events in Cole's life—reunion with his estranged daughter, and death—as if he is still alive. But it turns out Chamber's narration comes from the grave, an unusual but not unheard-of situation in which a film's narrator is already dead, such as occurs in *Sunset Blvd.* (1950), although there we are informed he is dead at the beginning of the film. Despite its popularity at the box office, many critics really hated *The Bucket List*. Their complaints say something about their impatience with the role Freeman is playing. The *Village Voice* reviewer blasts "Freeman's poor but wise man, who narrates in plummy tones . . . as mournful and wry and knowing as ever" (Julia Wallace, www.villagevoice.com, 11 December 2007). Stephanie Zacharek finds the film "shameless" as she criticizes "the fact that Reiner kicks off the movie with one of Freeman's trademark 'This is God speaking' wisdom-clogged voiceovers" (www.salon.com, 25 December 2007).

Significantly, Freeman himself is conscious of the role he has assumed in the minds of his viewing public and wants to avoid it. His biographer quotes an interview: "I think I've been pigeonholed. I have gravitas. I can't play bad guys. . . . I've gotten a little tired of gravitas" (Tracy 107). Michael McKenna described his typical role as "the gentle, wise mentor of usually troubled underlings," to which Freeman responded: "I get all those roles where I'm this very stable and dignified and dependable and gravitas lending character, and after a while I feel as if I'm boring everyone to death. . . . I wanted to break the mould and have a bit of fun" (*TV Guide Sunday Tasmanian*, 6 April 2003, T06). He would do so shortly afterward in *Dreamcatcher* (2003), a film in which he plays a military commander who loses his mind fighting aliens. A similar kind of complaint figures in a later interview he gave to Chrissy Iley, who observed, "He's made his name playing dignified mentors. . . . Generally he has been bored by his own gravitas." This explains his decision to play a crime lord in *Lucky Number Slevin* (2006). "This dignity stuff is getting rather boring and I should really stop. What do they call me? 'The wise man who's always protecting white men?'" ("Million Dollar Morgan," *Daily Mail*, 2 February 2006).

His desire to play against type notwithstanding, Freeman has made such a desire more problematic for himself, not just as the voice-of-God narrator but by actually playing God in two films, *Bruce Almighty* (2003) and *Evan Almighty* (2007). In the first, a tremendously successful comedy with Jim Carrey ($242.6 million gross), Freeman's God lets Bruce see what it's like to be God after he complains about the ways things are; Bruce soon discovers how difficult God's role is. Needless to say, critics saw the appropriateness of the casting. Robert Kroehler wrote, "Freeman appears born in his suit and takes it on with cool gravitas" (www.variety.com, 23 May 2003). Stephen Holden noted, "Freeman playing God is a piece of cake with his quiet, measured drawl, which implies depths of good-humored wisdom" (www.nytimes.com, 23 May 2003). The sequel, with Steve Carell playing a modern-day businessman who's spurred on by God to build an ark in anticipation of a second flood, was much less successful, earning a little more than half its production cost. A. O. Scott pointed to a conceptual problem in the film, caused by casting Freeman: "As I understand it the God of the Old Testament is a pretty tough deity, but it is not in Mr. Freeman's nature to be wrathful or jealous. His God is more a practical joker than a smiter" (www.nytimes.com, 22 June 2007).

The basic point that Freeman is just too nice a guy to play a wrathful God connects to a thesis by Michael Kinsley, who explains his competitive status against James Earl Jones (the voice introducing CNN newscasts):

> Jones' only real competition for the role of God . . . is Morgan Freeman. Jones is the Old Testament God, fierce and forbidding. Freeman is the New Testament version, all wise and all knowing, to be sure, but more approachable. He has done it twice in movies, has been the VOG in commercials for Listerine and Visa cards, among other products, and was the inevitable choice as narrator for that excruciatingly adorable movie about penguins. Freeman told an Associated Press reporter a few months ago that he is "tired of playing God." Who can blame him?
>
> ("Barack Obama and the Voice of God," *Time*, 15 January 2009)

★★★★★ The Magical Negro

Tired as he may be of embodying gravitas and of playing God, Freeman represents perhaps *the* prime example of what has come to be designated "the Magical Negro." For example, Cynthia Fuchs uses the expression twice to describe his characters in her reviews of *Levity* (2003) (www.popmatters.com, 18 April 2003) and *An Unfinished Life* (2005) (www.popmatters.com, 9 September 2005). In the first, Freeman plays Miles Evans, a criminal on the run masquerading as a storefront minister who helps troubled young people. Although he flees at the end of the film, he manages to offer moral guidance to them and to Manuel Jordan (Billy Bob Thornton), an ex-con who murdered someone during a robbery years ago and now seeks atonement from the victim's sister (Holly Hunter). In the second, he plays Mitch Bradley, a partially crippled man being supported by Einar Gilkyson (Robert Redford), who was responsible for his injuries years ago. Freeman is instrumental in helping ease the breach between Redford and his estranged daughter Jean (Jennifer Lopez), who caused the death of his son in an auto accident.

In using the expression "Magical Negro," Fuchs draws on an already established concept. The origins of the expression or similar ones are not clear, one attribution being to Spike Lee. Christopher John Farley refers to the "Magical African-American Friend" ("That Old Black Magic," *Time*, 27 November 2000), as does Rita Kempley ("'Magic Negro' Saves the Day—But at the Cost of His Own Soul," www.blackcommentator.com, July 2003). Krin Gabbard applies the term "magic" "to describe films in which African Americans radically transform the lives of white characters, usually providing them with romance and gravitas" (6). Matthew Hughey begins his assessment of the phenomenon by noting that Freeman was present to offer a preview of *Evan Almighty* at a film festival in Virginia, "Revelations: Finding God at the Movies," in 2007. He argues that the "'magical Negro' (MN) . . . has become a stock character that often appears as a lower class, uneducated black person who possesses supernatural or magical powers . . . used to save and transform disheveled, uncultured, lost, or broken whites . . . within the American myth of redemption and salvation." But Hughey thinks that rather than providing positive images of African Americans, these roles actually confirm the superiority of whites and are supporting racism of a different sort: "The new racism supports the social order while seemingly challenging the racial inequality constitutive of that order . . . and reinforces the meaning of white people as moral and pure characters. . . . These on-screen interactions [with the MN] afford white people centrality, while marginalizing these seemingly progressive black characters" (Hughey 544).

Use of the term and analysis of its significance speak very much to the status of Freeman and other African American actors included in this category, such as Whoopi Goldberg. But by foregrounding the concept, an inevitability given the voiceovers and roles Freeman has played, full consideration of this particular star and his immense talent can be obscured. "I'm good at nasty," Freeman claims (Tracy 107). And so he is. But what we should observe is that when he is "nasty" in films of this decade, his race is irrelevant. In *Nurse Betty* (2000), he plays Charley; he and his son Wesley (Chris Rock) are killers involved in searching for missing drugs. In the process he falls in love with Betty (Renée Zellweger). Nothing connects his criminality to race. In *Dreamcatcher* (as noted), he's a crazy army officer. In the comedy *The Big Bounce* (2004), he is a corrupt judge in Hawaii who succeeds in a complex scam involving murdering his mistress's husband. In *Lucky Number Slevin* he is a crime lord, The Boss, who happens to be black. His rival, The Rabbi (Ben Kingsley), happens to be Jewish. But the enmity between them is not played out in racial or religious terms. They're simply rotten human beings, period. In *The Contract* (2006), he's a paid assassin working for some top-secret organization in Washington. Again, race is irrelevant. In *Gone Baby Gone* (2007), he's head of a police unit in Boston investigating a kidnapping, which he in fact staged. In *Wanted* (2008), he is *really* nasty and at his most demonic as Sloan, the mastermind behind a complex assassination operation that employs the central female character,

Fox (Angelina Jolie). In *Thick as Thieves* (2009), he's a slick con man involved in a jewel theft, and in *The Maiden Heist* (2009) he's a mild-mannered museum guard who with his co-workers successfully creates fake art works to replace the ones they're stealing.

Some of these criminal roles occur in films that went straight to DVD or were not released at all. But the marginality of his blackness applies also to films that fell by the wayside and in which he has positive roles, but not as the stereotypical Magical Negro or wise counselor. In *Under Suspicion* (2000), he's a police inspector trying to solve murders for which Gene Hackman is the prime suspect; in *Guilty by Association* (2003) he's a police lieutenant dealing with delinquents; and in *Edison Force* (2005) he's a straight cop uncorrupted by the slimy higher-ups with whom he has to deal.

All the attention to his Magical Negro roles does more than lock him into a critical box. Worse, it ignores his other roles where his race does not matter. Use of the concept to the extent it has been employed with Freeman diminishes his accomplishments by failing to recognize what a versatile star he is and how his characters interact with other minorities. In a way one of his key roles occurs in the little-seen (but highly regarded) *10 Items or Less* (2006), in which he plays a nameless star scouting out a grocery store as possible location for a future role. He's a kind of surrogate for Freeman himself, signaled when his character finds a videotape (not a real film) on sale, starring himself and Ashley Judd. They had in fact appeared together in *Kiss the Girls* (1997), where he played a criminologist, Dr. Alex Cross, a role he would repeat in *Along Came a Spider* (2001). In *High Crimes* (2002) he's a lawyer trying to help Judd defend her husband against war crime charges. In *10 Items* he befriends the store's cashier Scarlet (Paz Vega), a Spanish woman dealing with various problems, and gives her advice. While he certainly helps her, she's obviously not a weak white male. And the Freeman character is not some powerful angelic force; he's actually forgetful (losing track of an important phone number, uncertain about the way to his home in Brentwood) and not that much in control of his life.

Unleashed (2005) is another film in which Freeman's character is helpful to someone besides a white male. Here he plays Sam, a blind piano tuner who takes on the responsibility of helping an Asian youth named Danny (Jet Li). The nefarious gangster Bart (Bob Hoskins) keeps Danny collared like a dog until he unleashes him to attack his enemies. After Danny escapes he is comforted and supported by Sam and his stepdaughter. In the film's climax, even though blind, Sam manages to knock out Bart and save Danny.

Of special importance are his roles as savvy, trusted, responsible, and connected authorities. In the action thriller *The Sum of All Fears* (2002), he's the director of Central Intelligence, killed when a nuclear bomb explodes in Baltimore but not before having made important discoveries about the villainous forces trying to destroy the United States. And in *Batman Begins* (2005) and *The Dark Knight* (2008) he's Lucius Fox, the brilliant scientist and engineering wizard who creates the Batmobile and other technological marvels used by Bruce Wayne (Christian Bale). *The Dark Knight* ends with Fox turning his back on Wayne because he thinks Batman has abused the powers that the scientist has made available to him.

With the exception of *10 Items or Less*, in which he plays a stand-in for himself, *Invictus* marks the one time in this decade when Freeman actually plays someone whose blackness is thematized as such, the South African savior and hero Nelson Mandela, now president of South Africa but a man who had been imprisoned by white South African leaders for over two decades. Mike LaSalle observes wittily, "Morgan Freeman has become such a notable and noble presence in American film that it would seem almost as appropriate for Nelson Mandela to be playing Freeman . . . instead of the reverse" (www.sfgate.com, 11 December 2009). And Stephanie Zacharek comments, "Admittedly, after you've been the voice of God weighing in on the life-and-death saga of penguins, there probably aren't many heights left to scale. Playing a figure as lauded and beloved as Nelson Mandela is an understandable next step" (www.salon.com, 10 December 2009). Freeman had wanted to make a film about Mandela for many years, a project that wasn't realized until Eastwood made it possible. This inspirational biopic follows Mandela's successful attempt to unite black and white citizens of his country, severely fragmented by apartheid. To do so, he has the brilliant idea of enlisting popular support for the Springboks rugby team (all white with one exception), captained by François Pienaar (Matt Damon). As members of his own personnel team made up of blacks and whites gradually warm to one another, so too does the public become more enthusiastic about the players, who win match after match. Mandela's triumph comes when the team wins the World Cup in 1995, on a tie-breaking goal kicked by Joel Stransky (played by Scott Eastwood, Clint's son). Freeman, who looks like Mandela, plays the leader with a winning and sharply conceived mixture of gravity and canniness. Appropriately, he was nominated for the Best Actor Oscar in 2009.

Given his importance as a major star, Freeman is a subject of interest to the media. Magazines that target black readers regularly provide coverage. For example, he's included as part of a special section on successful achievers ("Top 25 Moneymakers in Hollywood," *Black EnterpriseLexisNexis© Academic*, March 2008, 220), and he appears as the subject of articles in the

Nelson Mandela (Morgan Freeman) exultant as he leads the South African team and nation in *Invictus* (Clint Eastwood, Warner Bros., 2009). Courtesy Photofest New York.

black-centered magazines *Ebony*, *Essence*, and *Jet*. But coverage of him is certainly not race-specific. He's an entrepreneur who operates the Ground Zero Blues Club in Clarksdale, Mississippi, where he lives. Because he couldn't get the kind of meals he wanted in Clarksdale, he opened a restaurant called Madidi (Andrea Sachs, "Morgan Freeman, Down Home," www.washingtonpost.com, 13 November 2005). In a short feature on the restaurant in the upscale cooking magazine *Bon Appétit*, he responds to a reporter's question about three actors from past or present he'd like to host. The first is Humphrey Bogart: "I'd combine him with one of my favorite people, and that's Clint Eastwood. And I'd invite Meryl Streep because she's a terrific conversationalist" ("Morgan Freeman," September 2001, 202). An article in *Sports Illustrated* treats his interest in automobile racing and in NASCAR: "I'm not a car buff but I love driving" (Richard Deitsch, "Q and A: Morgan Freeman," 3 April 2006, 26). Josie Garthwaite interviews him on environmental issues ("The Green Life," *Sierra*, September–October 2008, 8–12). *Vogue*'s coverage of his trip to Africa to make *Invictus* included fashion shots of the star, wearing his own clothes (John Powers, "Takin' It to the Streets," June 2009, 114–21.) His auto accident in 2008 was widely covered in newspapers and popular venues like *People* (Steven Silverman and Michele Diamente, "Morgan Freeman 'Doing Well after Surgery,' " 5 August 2008).

I suggested earlier that the death of Walt in *Gran Torino* makes us aware of the inevitable demise of Eastwood himself, after almost fifty years of acting, and of the old star system itself. Perhaps Freeman's triumphant decade, climaxed with *Invictus*, promises a more positive prognosis for the star system. Putting aside for the moment the potentially reductive classification of the Magical Negro, one can see that the sheer number of roles Freeman has had in his twenty-eight narrative films of this decade encompasses everything from absolute goodness to absolute evil. If anything, this variety reminds us of what transpired at the height of the Hollywood star system, when an actor like Humphrey Bogart could star in over twenty films in the 1940s, playing everything from America's hero Rick in *Casablanca* (1942) to a psychotic killer in *The Two Mrs. Carrolls* (1947). Granted, in those days stars were subject to the dictates of their studio contracts whereas Freeman has had much more freedom, first by not being bound to a long-term studio deal and also because his own production company has been the power behind some films. The encouraging news is that Freeman is still going strong. Maybe he hasn't "grown up" and will continue acting until he's almost eighty and thus "be like Clint."

NOTES

1. For a biography of Freeman, see Tracy.

2. Schickel has published both a biography of Eastwood (*Clint Eastwood*) and an attractive coffee-table tribute book (*Clint*). Eastwood successfully sued Patrick McGilligan in 2002 for his unauthorized biography's claims about the star.

3. This comment is suggested by the argument of Brian Henderson regarding Ethan Edwards (John Wayne) in *The Searchers* (Henderson 9–23).

3 ★★★★★★★★★★★★

Jennifer Aniston and Tina Fey
Girls with Glasses

VICTORIA E. JOHNSON

As figures who initially rose to prominence on television in the mid-1990s, Jennifer Aniston and Tina Fey starred in top box-office features in the 2000s, each receiving prestigious industry awards, serving as a high-profile spokesperson, driving magazine sales records, and being hailed as, respectively, "the one woman who we find most compelling" ("Aniston Joins the Guys," *USA Today*, 15 November 2005, 3D), "wise, culture-shaping" ("Why I Love Chick Flicks," *Entertainment Weekly*, 20 February 2009, 41), and thoroughly "connected to the zeitgeist" ("The Accidental Movie Star," *Entertainment Weekly*, 18 April 2008, 26). Aniston and Fey challenge us to reconsider the typical historic opposition between film stardom and television celebrity. While "the (successful) film appearance" arguably "remains pivotal to 'stardom proper'" ("The Television Personality System: Televisual Stardom Revisited after Film Theory," *Screen*, Spring 2008, 34), Aniston's

---

Jennifer Aniston, Tina Fey. Both photographs courtesy of Photofest New York.

and Fey's multi-mediated stardom encourages us to analyze ways in which the "hierarchy once headed by cinematic stars has apparently shifted as glamorous names from film, TV, and other arenas feature alongside one another as equal objects of desire and public interest" (Jermyn 73).

While industrial transitions and economic factors are integral to their construction and emergence in a given era, stars in their popularity and cultural resonance do not reflect purely market-based desires, but are social phenomena whose primary value is ideological. Stars thus emerge and flourish in dialogue with broader cultural shifts and struggles over questions of identity and selfhood. While stars function to reinforce shared cultural values, Richard Dyer notes that such "reinforcement may be achieved not so much by *reiterating* dominant values as by concealing prevalent contradictions or problems" (*Stars* 27). Aniston and Fey are icons of a "synthetic media" era (Caldwell, "Welcome" 92)—an era distinguished by a synthesis or convergence and co-dependence of media forms, particularly television and film—across which each actress symbolizes related yet individuated versions of the post-millennial independent woman who "is very much a *woman's* star, a woman championed, admired and desired most predominantly" but not exclusively "by other women" (Jermyn 78).

As expressed both in their characters and in publicity reports, Aniston and Fey are girls with glasses. Aniston's career mythology symbolically positions her as such through repeated narration of her rise from purported ugly duckling to swan while remaining down-to-earth. Fey is a literal girl with glasses whose career mythology charts revenge of the "nerd." Both women's star personae represent independent, smart, career-oriented women whose ambition and intelligence are softened by their perceived "girl's girl" relatability, their "reluctant" stardom, and their search for love and balance between career and home.

For Dyer, the "independent woman" was a distinct "type," exemplified by, among others, Bette Davis, Katharine Hepburn, and Barbara Stanwyck. With Aniston and Fey emerging from television comedy into film, contemporary critics and journalists typically associate them with a legacy of independent screen comediennes, including Jean Arthur and Carole Lombard from classical Hollywood and Mary Tyler Moore and Sally Field from the 1970s and 1980s. While Aniston and Fey each embody elements of Dyer's classic "independent woman" type, each also melds or hybridizes that type with a distinctly "non-threatening," accessible, "warm," and/or comedic iteration. Specifically, Aniston melds the independent woman with the classic "girl next door," while Fey melds the independent woman with contemporary "geek chic."

Aniston's and Fey's particular resonance with female audiences is correlated to each star's timely but also savvy and self-conscious fit as an icon of a neoliberal era characterized by an ongoing struggle to successfully negotiate feminist commitments and "investment in the rehabilitation of masculinity" (Negra, "Structural" 62). Aniston's independent woman/girl next door and Fey's independent woman/chic geek each model relatable and appealing strategies for making "the self a *conductor of power*" in the contemporary era (Ouellette and Hay 15). They imagine their heroines "as someone *empowered* to take charge of one's life, and also as someone who can effectively conduct a charge . . . or who can deliver what is *expected*" (15), balancing feminist ideals with acceptance that it's "a man's world."

★★★★★ Synthetic Media Stardom: Theory and Context

A crucial element in the foundation and growth of academic film studies was to define film as a worthy object of study in its own right. In this process, film was often aligned with texts and fields of study that had existing disciplinary value and scholarly methodologies, gaining analysis through theoretical models from, for example, literary studies (aligning films with canonical works of literature or their directors with great authors); or it was linked with art-historical approaches to studies of aesthetic form. An additional strategy to distinguish cinema's uniqueness and scholarly importance has been to theorize it in opposition to television. John Caldwell has written that this "extreme dualism between film and television—this mythology of 'essential media differences'" (*Televisuality* 25) continues to have surprising traction in present-day discussions of these media.

A rough outline of this essentialist dualism might be summarized as follows. Film viewing is theoretically characterized by the concentrated involvement of a spectator who, surrounded by strangers in a darkened public space, is sutured into the action onscreen through an undistracted dream- or hypnotic-like gaze, into a larger-than-life narrative universe that offers an exceptional experience, uncharacteristic of our daily lives. Cinema features "auratic" stars who exist at a distance from the audience as the focus of erotic spectacle. The formal properties of film (the characteristic shots, camera movements, editing, and scoring techniques) place the larger-than-life star at the center of the photographic frame and of the film's narrative world, allowing the spectator to admire her idealized form—a cinematic image that offers audiences "the synthesis of" the star's "voice, body and motion" which, offscreen, "are less complete, less stunning" (Ellis 93). Conversely, television viewing has been argued to be characterized by the distracted attention of a viewer who, with lights on at home, is typically busy doing other domestic things, only intermittently cued, by sound, to return her "glance" to the small-screen world whose market-based, commercial "segmentation and flow" mimic the work-day and work-week rhythms of everyday life itself. Television is not populated by untouchable, auratic stars, but by approachable, friendly "personalities" who are as familiar to us as our next-door neighbors (and, often, more beloved).

Within this schema of media specificity, John Ellis is credited with the most thoroughgoing early conceptualization of the distinction between film stardom and television celebrity. For Ellis, the star can *only* exist in cinema through its realization of the "photo effect." While images (such as photo spreads in magazines and the like) offer "incomplete" representations of actors, "the film performance," displaying the star larger than life in sound and motion, is necessarily "more complete" (93) in ways that no other medium can achieve. The cinema star remains distanced from the day to day, thus "auratic," because her film performance remains relatively rare. True stars thus remain objects of desire because they seem untouchable and "extraordinary," at a distance from the everyday world of the viewer (98). Simultaneously, however, a key thrill of cinema is that it potentially offers spectators a fleeting glimpse of the "real" person behind the star, in those moments onscreen in which the star "is caught unawares" and "seems to be feeling the emotion of the role at that point as his or her own emotion" (99). These appear to be moments in which the "star is not performing . . . so much as 'being'" (99), implying access to the "real" and ordinary, beyond the untouchable, overtly constructed extraordinary auratic illusion.

While Ellis's model is arguably limited by his focus on particular types of television to the exclusion of others, he is also careful to point out that the mythology of essential media differences he theorizes is not inherent to the media of film or television themselves. That is, the distinction between film star and television celebrity is not determined by film or television technology, per se. Instead, these distinctions are indicative of "the typical uses to which these technologies have been put" (13) and their broader social and cultural functions. For Ellis, the social function of television is to be a quotidian marketplace, directly addressing its audience's immediate, pragmatic needs (what toothpaste to buy, which beer to drink) in the privacy of the home, through personalities who are "distinguished for their representativeness, their typicality, the 'will to ordinariness' to be accepted, normalized, experienced as *familiar'*" (Bennett 32, quoting John Langer). Film, on the other hand, seems transcendent of the market (even as stars themselves are key marketing strategies) and is exceptional to our everyday routine—going to the movies requires our active choice and engages our desire to step outside our familiar "lacks" and to have them momentarily forgotten, if not resolved. Ellis wrote his work on television just prior to the transition from the broadcast era to a multi-channel era of TV, however, and well in advance of the explosion of paparazzi/tabloid culture, twenty-four-hour news cycles, or bloggers with mobile phone cameras and Internet access, able to post a star's every move for a global audience, thereby effectively diminishing (if not destroying) "aura" and "democratizing" the distance between "us" and stars.

As Susan Murray's *Hitch Your Antenna to the Stars* outlines, stardom's "centrality to the larger economic, aesthetic, and cultural structuring" of television cannot be underestimated (185). Through the 1950s, "the relationship between the broadcast and film industries was becoming more synergistic" (103), with formal production affiliations between networks and film studios including, for example, ABC's merger with United Paramount Theaters and that network's later collaborations with Warner Bros. and Disney studios. In this context, radio and television stars carried economic clout and cultural prominence that often exceeded that of film stars throughout the 1950s, while film stars themselves often guest-starred or had cameos on TV series in this period and beyond. However, according to several scholars, two characteristics of TV stars purposefully mitigated their power in relation to cinema stars: comedy stars were the biggest stars on television; and, television "strategically manipulated connotations of authenticity *relative to* film-dom glamour" (Becker 6; see also Anderson; Desjardins; Hilmes; Mann; and Mellencamp). Through this crucial introductory decade, television's "reliance on connotations of authenticity" effectively implied that TV's "ability to transmit unfettered *reality* into the home was superior to Hollywood's version of *constructed* glamour" (Becker 7). In this way, TV stars used the medium's "essential" liveness and intimacy as a self-conscious "strategy of distinction . . . to lend prominence and prestige to the programs" (8).

Significant to historicizing the contemporary phenomena represented by Aniston and Fey, principal TV stars of the 1950s such as Gracie Allen and Lucille Ball were "idiosyncratically powerful *female* stars, usually in their late thirties or forties" (Mellencamp 319). Each "brought to their programs predetermined images (images in circulation in several media and thus genuine '*star*' images)" (316). But also, as stars whose roles mimicked their lives offscreen, each, on a weekly basis, "brought with them significant components of their publicly available private lives" (316). The identity of the star and her "real" "authentic" self—of *role* and autobiography—were meshed. Television stars of Gracie's and Lucy's stature significantly promised the very glimpse that Ellis theorizes to be essential to cinema—the glimpse of the "real" person behind the star, feeling her "own emotion," and "being" rather than performing. Jennifer Aniston and Tina Fey have each been hailed as this tradition's contemporary progeny.

Industrially, by 2010, DVD and television sales revenues for a given feature film now outstrip its box-office profits. Home theater technology, personal computing with high-speed Internet connections, and hand-held "smart" media devices began to reach "affordability" for a sizable percentage of U.S. consumers. Such institutional shifts were simultaneous with (and encouraged by) the radical conglomeration of media across platforms of profit and ownership that actively discouraged thinking of media forms as discrete from one another. An entire generation of audiences has now always been able to watch "films" on demand, at home. This same generation has never gone to movie theaters without seeing television advertising prior to the feature. Finally, much recent popular and academic critical press has been dedicated to a perceived uptick in "quality TV" series, with particularly "sparkling comedy and compelling drama" opportunities for female film actresses in their forties ("Why TV Is Better for Carrell and Fey," *Los Angeles Times*, 13 April 2010, D1).

Thus, "a new conceptualization of the relationship *between* TV stardom" (Jermyn 82) and cinematic stars is required—one that takes into account that not all TV stars become film stars and that not all TV celebrities (or film actors) are stars. As "Friends" co-creator David Crane once said, "There needs to be some *special* element to make people want to pay money to see people they've been getting every Thursday night for nothing" ("The Good Couple," *Entertainment Weekly*, 25 April 2003, 32). Synthetic media stars are stars due, in large part, to their outsized industrial/economic clout across media. Aniston and Fey, for example, are each stars in TV and film who in addition function as advertising spokespeople, are featured in web productions, and helm production companies with multi-picture "first-look" studio deals (Aniston's Echo Films and Fey's Little Stranger, Inc. are both housed at Universal). Fey also has a book deal with Little, Brown. Aniston has been listed in *Forbes* as the number one "most powerful celebrity" and "opened" five hit films in the 2000s. Fey was named AP's "entertainer of the year" in 2008 and *Baby Mama* (2008) opened at number one at the box office, as well.

However, the real power of stardom in a synthetic media era is, arguably, its rare ability to coherently, if paradoxically, cut through the "clutter" and "noise" as we navigate the media landscape. Fey and Aniston effectively unify an otherwise disparate media environment. They offer us an emotional locus of predictable reward.

Jennifer Aniston's romantic comedy heroine banters with Vince Vaughn in *The Break-Up* (Peyton Reed, Universal, 2006). Courtesy Photofest New York.

★★★★★ Every Inch the Movie Star and Still the Girl Next Door

First introduced to television audiences on NBC's "Friends" (1994), by the 2000s Jennifer Aniston was an undeniable phenomenon. From being the "most featured person on magazine covers" for the year 2000 to making *Forbes*'s list of top paid female actresses in 2009, Aniston's public prominence and box-office clout through the decade allowed her to work in a range of large-budget Hollywood releases as well as smaller independent films. Five of her nine major studio films released in the period opened at number one at the box office. Three of these five films (*Bruce Almighty* [2003], *The Break-Up* [2006], and *Marley & Me* [2008]) attracted audiences that skewed heavily adult (with more filmgoers over twenty-five years of age than not) and female. During the same period, she was also recognized for her work in independent films (including *The Good Girl* [2002], *Friends with Money* [2006], and *Management* [2008], with Independent Spirit Awards and Online Film Critics Society Awards nominations for Best Actress for *The Good Girl*). She was also named "Film Actress of the Year" in 2002 by the Hollywood Film Festival, acknowledging both her work in *The Good Girl* and her box-office success to that point in her career. Simultaneously, Aniston continued to be critically hailed and recognized internationally for her work on "Friends," receiving Emmy nominations for supporting actress (2000, 2001) and for lead actress (2002, 2003, 2004), winning in the latter category in 2003. Also notable here is Aniston's ritual presence and recognition in popular awards venues voted on by fans—such as the People's Choice, Teen's Choice, Kid's Choice, TV Land, and MTV Movie Awards, across which Aniston owned the categories of "Favorite Female Television Performer" from 2001 to 2004 and was nominated for (2010) or won (2007) "Favorite Female Movie Star." Between 2000 and 2010, Aniston also became a producer active in development of future projects, launching her own production company (with business partner Kristen Hahn, in 2008), and investing in and producing content for a web site (voxxy.com) "about empowering girls from all backgrounds." In 2007 she was named spokeswoman for Smart Water, featured in glossy advertising campaigns that emphasized her "openness" and physical fitness. While such market and critical accomplishments indicate Aniston's extraordinary industrial and economic stardom, they do not explain her fundamental appeal and her particularly synchronous fit, in this decade, with broader cultural desires for familiarity, "normality," and self-transformation without structural change.

"Every inch the movie star and still the girl next door" is the phrase with which ABC's Diane Sawyer introduced Aniston in a 2005 interview on "Good Morning America." The line encapsulates the star's powerful yet paradoxical iconicity, suggesting that in spite of—or ultimately overriding—the above extraordinary successes, ordinariness *is* Aniston's distinctiveness. Interviews and features across the decade thus emphasize Aniston's "refreshing" and unusual "good girl"-ness, her comfort as "one of us," and her down-to-earth normalcy. The cornerstone of this narrative is the story of how through self-determination Aniston "blossomed from virtual unknown to Hollywood golden girl":

> She trimmed 30 pounds from her now-taut figure, . . . and married a major movie-star sex symbol, all of which could have made the average woman envious, if not a little cranky. But—maybe because she confessed that Wonderbread and mayonnaise sandwiches are her favorite food; or because she grew up being told her butt was too big and her eyes too close together . . . we can't help rooting for her. . . . We're all that girl at heart. She's our very own Cinderella.
>
> ("The Friend She Really Is," *Good Housekeeping*, February 2002, 66)

And, according to director Glenn Gordon Caron, "she's not the most beautiful girl in the world. She's, like, the second most beautiful girl . . . the one you'd go after once you realized you weren't going to get the most beautiful girl" (Marshall 107).

Further mainstreaming her persona, even though Aniston grew up exclusively in Los Angeles and New York City, she is recurrently portrayed as surrounding herself with friends who are not in "the business." As she notes, "Some of my best times happen outside New York or L.A." where "you're just a human. It's really nice" ("Jennifer Aniston," *People*, 28 December 2008, 64, 67). Preferring to be a "homebody," she nonetheless "seems wholly unconcerned" to disguise herself or perform when "she's in public" ("Jennifer Aniston," *Rolling Stone*, 27 September 2001, 52). This "human" quality—Aniston's expressed preference to live as a "normal" person and to value the perceived lack of pretension and straightforwardness between the coasts—is underscored in press and fan literature about Aniston that consistently emphasizes her unaffected "deep, deep likeability and relateability" ("Aniston Remains Our Favorite Friend," *USA Today*, 15 November 2005, 1D). As Courteney Cox, her co-star from "Friends" and reported "real world" best friend, sums it up, "She's a real girl's girl. Guys love her but women *really* love her and are not threatened by her. It's a really good sign when someone has a lot of good girlfriends" (Marshall 64). Aniston is thus portrayed as generous of spirit (allied with community rather than self-interest), a woman who is not competitive with other women yet who remains desirable to men.

Aniston's offscreen persona as "our" "relatable" girl next door was first forged onscreen, through her iconic television role as Rachel Green on "Friends." According to series co-creator Marta Kauffman, Rachel was originally conceived to be "someone who was not prepared to deal with the world as an adult" (Jennifer Armstrong, "Rachel Green: The Girl Next Door Who'll Be Our Best Friend Forever," *Entertainment Weekly*, 4 June 2010, 46), but, as Aniston settled into the role, it was tweaked to resonate more with the actress's own personality—to make the character more self-sufficient and sympathetic. The more the boundary collapsed between the "real" Jennifer Aniston and Rachel, the more "authentic" Aniston became. Her series character's perceived well-roundedness, normalcy, and relatability were seen to pave the way for mainstream, big-screen roles in which she could be "completely at ease and entertaining" ("7 Days: The Observer Profile—Jennifer Aniston," *Observer*, 22 January 2006, 41) and "characteristically warm and adorable" ("Aniston's Break-Ups Help Vince Break Out," *National Post*, 1 June 2006, A14), exuding "the confident nonchalance of an attractive young everywoman" ("A Romance Battles the Odds: Risk Assessor Woos Daredevil," *New York Times*, 16 January 2004, E6).

The majority of Aniston's films during and since the run of "Friends" have featured her playing to type, as a supportive girlfriend or spouse (*Rock*

Star [2001], *Bruce Almighty* [2003], *Along Came Polly* [2004], *Marley & Me, Love Happens* [2009]) or as a romantic comedy heroine (*Rumor Has It . . .* [2005], *The Break-Up*, and as part of the ensemble cast of *He's Just Not That Into You* [2009]). A handful of other films (including her best reviewed work) has played "against type," "sublimating" Rachel Green entirely (*The Good Girl, Friends with Money, Management*). The analysis below focuses, specifically, on *The Break-Up* and *The Good Girl* as respective representatives of the Aniston/Rachel "type" and of the Aniston/anti-Rachel type to further explore the "collapse" between actress and character that promotes ordinariness (both its promise and potential pitfalls) as Aniston's distinctive brand of stardom.

In the 2000s, Aniston's film career was marked by box-office success in every film save one in which she arguably played "Rachel all but in name" (Ryan Gilby, "7 Days: The Observer Profile—Jennifer Aniston," *Observer*, 22 January 2006, 41). While several of her films also earned critical acclaim (particularly *The Break-Up* and *Marley & Me*), Aniston's best reviews were for two independent features (*The Good Girl* and *Friends with Money*) in which she was hailed for sublimating herself "to the material with professional grace. You believe her, and you don't think about 'Friends' or Brad [Pitt] or anything like that. . . . That, ladies and gentlemen, is called 'acting'" ("'Girl': Too-Simple Twist of Fate," *Washington Post*, 16 August 2002, C1). In this period, Aniston also had two disastrous outings in which she played both against type (*Derailed* [2005]) and to type (*Rumor Has It*). These last two films, released just after her marriage to Pitt dissolved, led to speculation about her future as a leading lady in either the public or private realms. However, *The Break-Up*, released in June 2006, led the box office and garnered reviews that particularly noted her "team" approach, in underplaying her role to showcase her co-star (and, briefly, real-life love interest), Vince Vaughn.

This "support" role is prominent across Aniston's films wherein, even as she receives above-title billing, the film itself places her in a secondary role—as Mark Wahlberg's/Chris Cole's conscience in *Rock Star*; as Jim Carrey's/Bruce Knowland's conscience in *Bruce Almighty*; as Ben Stiller's/Reuben Feffer's repressed id in *Along Came Polly*; as both Owen Wilson's/John Grogan's sounding-board and Marley the dog's caretaker in *Marley & Me*; and as Aaron Eckhart's/Burke Ryan's "therapist" in *Love Happens*; as well as part of a secondary couple within the large ensemble cast of *He's Just Not That Into You*). While it could be argued that this motif of "support" would seem contrary to Aniston's star billing, star power, and the public perception of her independent self-determination, Diane Negra's analyses of post-2001 "chick flicks" put this paradox into generic and cultural context and point to its *social* function.

According to Negra, "There is a clear paradox at work in the way that women's interests and pleasures are simultaneously commercially privileged and pejoratively conceptualized." While women can drive box office fortunes, Negra argues, once in the theater they are generally confronted with "concession narratives" wherein they "find their femininity through acts of consumption." Further, "Professional achievement for women has to be accounted for, as it is automatically understood to be a compensation activity of some kind. In order to earn romance, the female protagonist must repudiate her profession, downsize her ambition, or retire," and/or she must embrace "the procreative epiphany" which "speaks to a culture unwilling to surrender the belief that motherhood is female destiny" ("Failing" 92).

For Negra, such "chick flick" narrative investments and conventions point to a conflation of cultural anxieties in an era of "post-feminist," "neoliberal" discourses of self-help. Sociologist Samantha King argues that post-1990 U.S. culture—as visualized and communicated, largely, through its popular films, TV series, and iconic stars—is characterized by women's and women-centered social movements distancing themselves "from explicitly feminist agendas" while "the emergence of an enormously popular self-help movement during the same period created an environment much more conducive to struggles geared toward *internal* reflection and transformation than toward external or *structural* change" (King xi). While *He's Just Not That Into You* is overtly about this reality, Negra proposes that most "women's films" of the 2000s effectively conceal the fact that "self-improvement culture in general has the contradictory effect of undermining self-assurance by suggesting that all of us are in need of constant, effortful (and often expensive) improvement" ("Eat, Pray, Spend," bitch-magazine.org/article/eat-pray-spend).

While the heroine thus finds her femininity through acts of consumption (as evidenced in the chick flick's shopping, eating, or beauty-ritual montages), ultimately, resolution and happiness are found in a "female retreatism" (Negra, "Structural" 62) that reveals "the centrality of gender archetypes and anxieties to the current cultural climate" (Negra, "Brangelina" 60). "In place of a full-fledged female subjectivity," these films "are likely to display a trenchant interest in the rehabilitation of masculinity while frequently emplotting the heroine in a drama of 'miswanting' that requires professional ambition and intimacy to be cast as two opposing states" ("Structural" 62). *The Break-Up* is an interesting film in these respects. It fits Negra's formulae but its ambivalent conclusion partially defies the "concession narrative" in ways that simultaneously affirm and qualify Aniston's "real" ability to be independent.

The Break-Up features Aniston as Brooke Myers, a smart, witty, career-oriented yet relatable and funny "domesticated" girl next door who is living with her boyfriend, Gary Grobowski (Vince Vaughn). The film's pre-credits opening scene reveals how the couple met as Gary interrupts Brooke's date with an uptight preppy to buy her a hot dog at a Chicago Cubs game. The opening credits sequence then presents a photo montage of Gary and Brooke's first full year together, encapsulating their courtship, their purchase of a condo, their friendship and family circles, and their general comfort and ease together (scored to the sound of Queen's "You're My Best Friend"). *The Break-Up* then opens on the "present day" by offering parallel glimpses of Gary's and then Brooke's professional/public lives: Gary is the public face and emcee for "Three Guys" tours of Chicago, while Brooke is an art dealer for the swank Marilyn Dean Gallery. Costuming, performance, and setting thus immediately establish that brash, always-"on" Gary and subdued, politic Brooke occupy different worlds that come together, at the end of the day, in their shared condo. The break-up—precipitated by Brooke's concern for appearances before hosting a combined family dinner, followed by Gary's inattentiveness and unwillingness to help with dinner-related domestic tasks—concludes the first act of the film, after which the remainder presents an escalation of Brooke's attempts to make Gary realize that "losing me would make him want to stay." Gary is slowly confronted with examples of his self-centeredness that, cumulatively, encourage his epiphany, after which he proclaims his love and willingness "to do whatever it takes" to be with Brooke.

The Break-Up posits Brooke as a "girl's girl," through her close relationship with her best friend, Addie (Joey Lauren Adams) (who also represents the "dream" of placid family life, with her attentive, if docile, husband and two kids), and as the focus of male attraction through her easy inclusion and banter with Gary's poker buddies and the couple's bowling team. Brooke literally "buys in" to consumer strategies to try to keep Gary: she subjects herself to a feminine waxing technique nicknamed the "Telly Savalas" in a wink to Aniston's offscreen godfather; she purchases tickets to a rock show to "casually" get Gary to join her on a post-break-up date; and her boss offers her a blank check to go to Europe to "find" herself, promising that Brooke's job will remain "right here, waiting" for her return. However, when Gary awakens to his "true" feelings for Brooke, she meets his confessional, apology, and proposal to get back together with an untraditional romantic comedy response—but one that meshes with the star's autonomy. Brooke states, "I don't feel the same way. I don't think I have anything left to give." The film then cuts to the following Christmas season to have its heroes run into each other on the street. Based on her cell phone conversation, and sleek new wardrobe and hairstyle, Brooke appears to now have a "high-powered" career. Gary is newly trim while his business has expanded exponentially. The film thus overtly denies a "concession narrative," keeping Gary and Brooke apart, if in a place of hopeful détente. However, the film does imply a different *type* of "miswanting" (Negra, "Structural" 53) by suggesting that the heroine cannot "rehabilitate" Gary for domesticity until she, herself, is rehabilitated and prepared to have even more to give. While the break-up did rehabilitate Gary for a mature, adult dedication to class ascent through entrepreneurial success in the masculine, public sphere, it led Brooke to conduct work upon herself instead through travel abroad and amassing external signifiers of success. The film closes to the strains of "I Can See Clearly Now," with the audience able to read into the couple's concluding encounter whichever future it is most predisposed to believe—that, now that each is a fully-fledged, self-actualized adult of a certain professional class standing, the two have something to build upon together; or that each now moves onward, having learned from the past relationship to work on self-awareness through more "appropriate" consumption.

Although Aniston's film career has been staked overwhelmingly on romantic, Rachel-type roles, thanks to her synthetic media stardom she can oscillate between high-cost features and smaller, independent projects. Her most praised role came in one such film about which Aniston has stated, "Doing *The Good Girl* extended my visa on the acting planet by a couple of years. . . . The romantic comedies did not" (Miller 32). *The Good Girl* and Nicole Holofcener's *Friends with Money*, along with the Aniston-produced *Management*, represent, perhaps, Aniston's least viewed work but clearly support her claim to "credibility" as an actress who can successfully play against Aniston type "to go out there on a limb" ("Jennifer Makes Good," *Time*, 19 August 2002, 58). According to *The Good Girl*'s screenwriter Mike White, noting the purposeful irony of the title and the consciousness with which the film was cast: "Who wouldn't want to see America's sweetheart get blackmailed for sex and try to institutionalize her boyfriend and cheat on her husband?" (58). With a performance hailed as brave, gimmickless, "inventively morose . . . sodden and exhausted" ("The Catcher in the Texas Chain Store," *New York Times*, 7 August 2002, E1), *The Good Girl* suggested to critics that "it will no longer be possible to consider [Aniston] the same way" ("Lead Actress: Jennifer Aniston," *Daily Variety*, 8 January 2003, 36).

While *The Good Girl* allows Aniston to sublimate Rachel, in doing so the film poses a meta-critique of both her "good girl" persona and her typical film roles. Specifically, the film interrogates the very desirability and viabil-

Aniston sheds her sitcom persona in *The Good Girl* (Miguel Arteta, Fox Searchlight, 2002), with Jake Gyllenhaal. Courtesy Photofest New York.

ity of heterosexual romance, marriage, and family. It also criticizes "mainstream," small-town, everyday life (from the hypocrisy of a Bible-study leader to the petty larceny of "Retail Rodeo's" law-and-order store manager). Aniston's performance is largely effected through physical and vocal transformation. While in "real" life and as Rachel she talks with her hands a good deal, Aniston and director Miguel Arteta worked to keep her hands fused to her side, with her shoulders slumped. Aniston's gait follows suit. With little to no flexibility in her arms and hands, she lumbers and shuffles as if weighted and sinking. Her costuming throughout the film features oversized, "big box" retailer, off-the-rack clothes. Equally deglamorized through minimal makeup and unkempt hair, Justine Last's morose daily routine is ordinary without distinctiveness, down-to-earth but dark, self-made but spiraling downward. In contrast to Aniston's romantic comedy heroines, Justine seems to already understand that if "work on the self" can only rehabilitate others and not lead to structural change, why work on the self to begin with?

The Good Girl's release was followed by *Bruce Almighty*, which was a blockbuster but primarily a vehicle for Jim Carrey. Aniston next played "against type" in three successive films, each of which was shot during the year of the dissolution of her marriage to Pitt. Of these, only *Friends with Money* was well reviewed, though it was limited in its release. Significantly, however,

Friends with Money featured an otherwise all-indie-star cast of acclaimed female actresses (including Catherine Keener, Frances McDormand, and Joan Cusack) that tapped into Aniston's "women's star," "girl's girl" strengths while also bolstering her critical credibility.

Just prior to *Friends with Money*'s release, the "Brangelina" phenomenon exploded, to shape much of the coverage of Aniston's career since. Married in July 2000, Pitt and Aniston were hailed as an extraordinary Hollywood coupling of golden stars at the height of their powers. This status was only enhanced by the relative rarity of images of them together. By 2005, however, the relationship ended in a flurry of rumors that Pitt had had an affair with co-star Angelina Jolie. Aniston, pre-positioned as "our" girl next door, immediately became the heroine in a real-life saga of marital infidelity that opposed her in stark contrast to Jolie's presumptive Jezebel. Aniston's "involuntary" iconicity seemed all the more down-to-earth by reference to Jolie's historic willingness to shock and to perform or actively put on various identities for the media. Aniston's preexisting good "girl's girl" persona calcified her comparative position and public reception as the "everywoman" scorned—the "second prettiest" good girl, jilted for the mean girl rebel.

The Brangelina incident appeared to crystallize a broader public and committed fan perception that Aniston was a down-to-earth friend in need of support. T-shirts proclaiming one's loyalty to "Team Aniston" were available all over Los Angeles and online. However, the split also threatened to make visible the fact that, though Jolie apparently enjoyed creating and projecting her persona while Aniston was, ostensibly, "an involuntary icon" (Marshall 76), both of these star personae were actively constructed. Following the Brangelina moment, both film critics and popular magazine features were inflected by new criticisms of Aniston's film choices, the nature of her star appeal, and its "authenticity," particularly around her own purposeful mitigation of her star persona as a legacy of her emergence from and continuing association with television. "Brangelina" became a moment from which the potential contradictions of Aniston's ordinariness-as-exceptionalism were now open to invigorated scrutiny and debate.

Such scrutiny took two tacks. The first interrogated the value of mainstream ordinariness, suggesting that Aniston had, instead, become bland and her success bewildering ("Everyone's Best Friend," *Evening Standard*, 26 June 2003, 8). The second posed a broader, institutional critique about stardom, suggesting the possibility that, rather than being larger than life and achieving the "photo effect" of auratic plenitude on the big screen, Aniston may be a star "everywhere except where it counts: onscreen" ("Breaking Up Is Hard to Watch," *Maclean's*, 12 June 2006, 65). Critical consensus, from

2006 forward, seems to be that Aniston's stardom—newly inflected by narratives of the single-woman-over-forty's "constant 'search for love'"—increasingly challenges public notions of ordinariness. Hadley Freeman of London's *The Guardian* perhaps sums up best this strain of criticism: "On what planet does marriage to a Hollywood A-List millionaire, followed by shacking up with a comedy genius, an international male model and an undeniably pretty singer count as 'unlucky'?" ("Lost in Showbiz—Pity Jennifer Aniston? It Must Be Awful Having a String of A-List Dates," *Guardian*, 22 August 2008, 2). With Jolie newly "domesticated" and iconic of "the wealthy celebrity family . . . symbolically positioned to solve economic and social justice problems" (Negra, "Brangelina" 60), Aniston was available to be repositioned as an unhappy combination of self-centered and bland.

Aniston's status as spokesperson for Glaceau's Smart Water may, paradoxically, reinforce this critique. Featuring glamorous black-and-white photos of a nearly nude Aniston (one campaign features her as if "caught unawares" in bed; in another, she directly addresses the camera, post-workout, displaying her no-more-mayo-sandwiches abs), the ad copy plays on her openness ("My Secret Revealed . . . I've got nothing to hide . . . I'm not afraid to spill") and her relatability ("working out feels great . . . afterwards, that's why I drink smart . . . it's the one part of my routine I never sweat)." And yet, it is hard to escape the irony that what she's "not afraid to spill" and what she embraces as her workout "partner" is invisible, essentially substance-less, and widely available for free. Aniston's star continues to flourish, however, particularly as she appears in prominent television roles and develops feature projects as a producer. In 2008 she was nominated for an Emmy for her guest-starring role on Tina Fey's "30 Rock," reinforcing the ongoing viability of the "woman's star" as a team player.

★★★★★ The Highly Successful Professional Mess

Between 2000 and 2010, the phrase "geek chic" entered into everyday use to describe a broad set of cultural phenomena. Previously a term of derision aimed at the exceptionally smart but socially unsavvy, "geek" became "chic" in reference to fashion trends, "prompting a run on thick black-rimmed glasses" (Westman 21); marketing appeals (Best Buy's tech-support division was branded "The Geek Squad"); entertainment industry transformations (from the growing influence of audience testing at ComicCon, to phenomena such as "Lost" and geek heroines from Rory Gilmore to Juno MacGuff and Ugly Betty); and as a political sensibility (with the Obama campaign's embrace of YouTube and the administration's promise to prioritize science and technology). Within this context, "geek chic" was also embraced by a new generation of young women who, according to a 2008 *Newsweek* cover story on the "Revenge of the Nerdette," have "modeled themselves after icons such as Tina Fey" ("Revenge of the Nerdette," *Newsweek*, 16 June 2008, 44). Like Fey, the article argues, these women "are challenged in striking a balance between the presumed dichotomous traits of femininity and nerdiness . . . they're smart . . . and they're hot" (44).

While Fey has tapped into the zeitgeist of geek chic, her stardom is also premised on her connection to the legacy of "idiosyncratically powerful" female stars discussed above. Like Aniston, Fey's reputation is that of a woman who likes women, is supportive of her friends, and who is even "better at sharing the screen than dominating it" ("Tina Fey Is a Master at Playing a Real Mess," www.latimes.com). While she is smart, funny, and sophisticated, she remains, like Aniston, unthreatening. Specifically, according to journalist Betsey Sharkey, Fey is "driven and accomplished sans the teeth-baring side. . . . As a feminist who isn't angry, she supports a brand of peaceful coexistence that leaves men feeling she won't judge them too harshly." Further, she is considered a "real" woman: "It all begins with the face. . . . It's a face . . . more comfortable with no makeup, stacking up laugh lines. . . . It's exactly the right touch for the times. . . . She can seem comfortable and uncomfortable at the same time, a 21st century Lucy with a high-powered job. If anything, Fey's at her best when she's at her worst. . . . We can relate" ("Playing a Real Mess").

Here Fey's relatability is connected to her authenticity (that she ages naturally; that she is endearingly awkward) and to the collapse of any distinction between Fey's onscreen personae (particularly, Liz Lemon of "30 Rock") and her offscreen self. However, this aspect of her star persona—the idiosyncratic geek—depends upon a concealment of her pioneering status and power within the entertainment industry and on covering over her real personal successes (balancing marriage and motherhood with her career). Fey joined "Saturday Night Live" as a writer and performer in 1997 and became the show's first female head writer in 1999. In 2004 she co-produced, wrote, and co-starred in the successful film *Mean Girls*, based on Rosalind Wiseman's best seller, *Queen Bees and Wannabees*. By 2006, she had a long-term production deal with NBC/Universal and launched "30 Rock," for which she is executive producer, writer, and star. Between 2000 and 2010, Fey won two Emmys for "SNL" and two for "30 Rock," a Golden Globe, two Gracie Allen Awards for Outstanding Female Lead in a Comedy Series, and two Screen Actors Guild Awards, in addition to nominations and wins for People's Choice and Teen Choice Awards.

Fey's star is still clearly on the ascendant. Indeed, even given her work in years prior, it was not until 2008 that her presence in television, film, publishing, and as a spokesperson for American Express launched her to star status. Her transformation from industrial pioneer to cultural phenomenon was, arguably, pegged to her 2008 "Saturday Night Live" appearances in which she impersonated Republican vice-presidential nominee Sarah Palin. This brought additional attention to her role and typing as Liz Lemon. By late 2009, Fey was "recognized by 6 of 10 Americans" according to celebrity-market researchers, by whom she was identified to have a quality summarized as "positive edgy" ("Can Brand Fey Get Any Bigger?," *Advertising Age*, 18 May 2009, n.p.).

Just prior to 2008's presidential convention season, Fey's first starring feature film, *Baby Mama*, was released, opening at number one at the box office while attracting an audience that was 68 percent female ("Tina Fey's Baby Outing a Hit with Women," *Globe and Mail*, 28 April 2008, R3). Kate Holbrook, Fey's character in the film, was generally interpreted as "performing a variation on her successful-but-unfulfilled '30 Rock' persona" ("Baby, It's Garbage," *Toronto Sun*, 25 April 2008, E2). Although reviews were notably mixed, those who embraced the film did so in terms of its perceived departure from the standard "chick flick" dynamics of materialism and competition. Many critics associated *Baby Mama*'s strengths with Fey's *adult* sensibility. Ann Hornaday's review in the *Washington Post* (18 September 2009, C10) is representative here, calling the film "quiet-chuckle-funny . . . [an] observant, if uneven, comedy of 21st century manners," in which Fey shows a "gratifying decision to underplay," creating a "recognizable human being" whose "unforced warmth" offers "a welcome alternative to the desperation and self-loathing" characteristic of the Judd Apatow comedies or the other "mama" movies out at that time, *Juno* or *The Waitress* (both 2007).

While Fey has compassion for her characters in the way Hornaday suggests, the "edgy" element of her positive edginess is also central to critics' interpretation of *Baby Mama* as more "mature" than other comedies and to Fey as a "sophisticated" star even when she's a "mess." Specifically, Fey—while in character and in interviews offscreen—is consistently, self-consciously critiquing the "dream" pursued by her characters. While sympathetic to Kate Holbrook's desire to have a baby via surrogacy, Fey's performance (particularly in her scenes sparring with surrogacy provider Chaffee Bicknell [Sigourney Weaver]) deftly critiques her character's uncomfortably race- and class-based privileges and conviction that consumerism can "solve" personal traumas. *Baby Mama* is thus itself an idiosyncratically powerful "women's" picture in its display of the promises of

Tina Fey's "geek chic" in action (l.), with Amy Poehler in *Baby Mama* (Michael McCullers, Universal, 2008). Courtesy Photofest New York.

neoliberal self-governance and "proper" consumerism, only to reveal the impossibility of consumer solutions to personal, familial, and broader communal "lack." Indeed, *Baby Mama* resolves with joyful revelry at this failed "logic," illustrating that, best-laid plans of white, upper-class consumer ideology aside, more often, life is a mess.

As female stars with sizable female audiences, Aniston's and Fey's examples emphasize that analysis of stardom must also be linked to questions of gender and social capital, whereby "women's stars" in "chick flicks" or emergent from the "everyday" medium of television historically have been accorded lesser value in scholarship that focuses on presumptively "masculine," "high-toned," exceptional cinematic texts. Aniston emerged as a star on, arguably, one of the last "mass"-audience TV series and has continued to be a mass-appeal star at the box office. While Fey's stardom did not come to full fruition until 2008, her prominence as an iconic star of the post-2000 synthetic media era points to a possible new iteration of stardom itself in the coming decades, with television fighting hard against film for "niche" status. Not only is Fey's "30 Rock" a successful niche-appeal show whose rather dismal weekly ratings are counterbalanced by the tech-savvy, middle-to-upper-middle-class, urban- and coastal-skewing audiences of viewers twenty-nine to forty-five who consume the show; but her *Baby Mama* revealed her power to also draw mass (if predominantly adult and female) audiences to movie theaters and her ability to sell these iterations of "Liz Lemon" back to TV-viewing/home audiences on DVD. Fey's stardom thus suggests the possibility that mass iconic stardom may be following the path of other "branded" phenomena in contemporary media.

Caldwell's call to understand that we *already* occupy a synthetic media era should be taken up by film and media scholars to address phenomena such as Aniston's and Fey's ongoing multi-mediated star presence; it might also encourage broader consideration of the historically multi-mediated nature of stardom across venues including popular music (see, for example, Beyoncé or Justin Timberlake), professional sport (for example, Serena Williams, Anna Kournikova, Lance Armstrong), or fashion (Michael Kors, Tom Ford). As media-specific boundaries become fuzzier, if never obsolete, an additional concern arises regarding the status of stardom itself, particularly in relation to shifting understandings of "fame" and "celebrity" (Holmes and Redmond) and to technologies such as those on display in *Avatar* (2009), whose "stars" were both real actors and computer-generated images. Yet it is clear that television and film still carry different resonances. As Ellis notes, perceived distinctions between media are deeply and powerfully ideological ones that—regardless of market realities—effectively reinforce cinema's status as an auratic art, consumed at a rational (if rapt) "masculine" distance, representative of cultural capital in contrast to television's intimate, "feminine," everyday status. When Aniston or Fey flop (in 2010's *The Bounty Hunter* or *Date Night*, respectively, for instance), reviews emphasize that their stardom, after all, belongs on television. It is thus important to question what investments this mythology of essential difference serves and why it continues to be so central to our thinking about stars and their effect.

4 ☆☆☆☆☆☆☆☆☆★

Puerile Pillars
of the Frat Pack

Jack Black, Will Ferrell,
Adam Sandler, and Ben Stiller

BRENDA R. WEBER

In June 2004, *USA Today* gifted a group of comedic actors with a name and bankable identity, the Frat Pack. Comprising a set of primarily television-turned-movie actors, including Jack Black, Will Ferrell, Adam Sandler, and Ben Stiller, the "Frat Pack" gained its currency from starring in a series of films that largely deploy fraternity-type puerile humor in stories geared toward adolescent male audiences (Susan Wloszczyna,

Jack Black, Will Ferrell, Adam Sandler, and Ben Stiller.

"Wilson and Vaughn: Leaders of the 'Frat Pack," *USA Today*, 15 June 2004). The Frat Pack strikes the viewer as a bunch of disaffected and directionless men who happen to be in movies, yet their likable and seemingly authentic affability is as much a carefully constructed persona as that of any other entertainment celebrity.

Much of their comedic fare is a peg lower than low-brow. Diarrhea jokes and a pet ferret as toilet paper up your comedic alley? Then check out Ben Stiller in *Along Came Polly* (2004), in which the hapless comedian plays an uptight insurance adjuster whose persnickety need to control contingency makes him, according to the Internet Movie Database, "the most cautious man on earth." Philip Seymour Hoffman's symphony-of-sweat basketball scene in the same film is a masterpiece of gross-out humor, and his boorish bravado in contrast to Stiller's germophobia is comedic genius.

Viewers more inclined to enjoy the thinly disguised homophobia of male-on-male physicality could watch the first ten minutes of Ferrell's *Blades of Glory* (2007)—ten minutes is plenty—where the mano-a-mano challenge between fierce ice-skating competitors played by Ferrell and Jon Heder, of *Napoleon Dynamite* (2004) fame, sets the rink on fire. A small sampling of their "witty" banter:

> *CHAZZ (Ferrell):* This guy could not hold my jock sweat.
>
> *JIMMY (Heder):* I could hold it all day long, try me!
>
> *CHAZZ:* Maybe I will.
>
> *JIMMY:* Maybe you should.
>
> *CHAZZ:* You challenging me, princess?
>
> *JIMMY:* I'm not inviting you to the Skating Federation's annual Christmas party.
>
> *CHAZZ:* Then bring it on!
>
> *JIMMY:* It is on!

Viewers with a more cosmopolitan humor palette could partake of Adam Sandler playing an Israeli elite forces agent, who fakes his own death so that he might smuggle himself to New York City and become a hairdresser with a penchant for sexing up incredibly and uncomfortably old ladies in *You Don't Mess with the Zohan* (2008). (Oy, my osteoporosis!) While in New York, Sandler discovers that Palestinians and Israelis are quite capable of living side by side, given the right material incentives (in this case, stereo equipment and microwave oven stores). One strains to believe the multiple uses to which hummus can be put or how often it's possible for Sandler to appear either naked or wearing what are fondly referred to as electric banana hammocks.

Finally, it was always possible to turn to the reliably out-of-control Jack Black, who somehow seemed to explode off the screen even when playing an overweight and adorable panda trying clumsily to master an ancient martial art or make noodle soup in *Kung Fu Panda* (2008). Black's Panda is remarkably similar to the overweight and obnoxious music teacher he plays in *School of Rock* (2003), posing as a prep school substitute teacher with hopes of earning enough money to launch his own fledgling rock 'n' roll career. In both movies, Black's character is mocked, challenged, and ultimately championed as he triumphantly moves from chubby underdog to portly victor.

Neither exclusively concerned with sight gags and gross jokes nor completely adverse to them, the Frat Pack trades in a sort of cheerful and benign masculine moralism in which the male characters build new values, suture their ties to one another through a form of homosocial bonding endearingly termed bromance, learn lessons about themselves, life, and relationships, and become "better" men, often (and incredibly) getting the pretty girl in the end. How else could Black's repulsive character in *Shallow Hal* (2001), who despises "fat chicks," redeem himself to such a degree that an audience would buy his romantic connection to Gwyneth Paltrow? Her three-hundred-pound fat suit notwithstanding, she is a beautiful Academy Award–winning actress and he's something of a schlubby guy. And how might it be possible for the goofy-faced, frizzy-haired Ferrell to end up with the dark-haired British beauty Anna Friel in *Land of the Lost* (2009), were it not for the relentless feel-good outcomes that permeate Frat Pack films?

In the huge number of movies put out by these four actors alone—nearly one hundred in this decade—there is great diversity. Neither are these actors carbon copies of one another nor are their films endless remakes of the same comedic formula. In fact, I would credit the members of the Frat Pack, these four in particular, with an amazingly fecund filmic imagination that has led them to star in a diversity of fare. So, while Ben Stiller plays the jerky jock or the washed-up male model or out-of-date movie star in, respectively, *Dodgeball* (2004), *Zoolander* (2001), and *Tropic Thunder* (2008), he also shrewdly parodies himself in appearances on Larry David's "Curb Your Enthusiasm" (2000) and Ricky Gervais's "Extras" (2005). Further, Stiller has done the occasional star turn in serious fare with a droll edge, like the sleep-around drama *Your Friends & Neighbors* (1998) or the drug rehabilitation film *Permanent Midnight* (1998), in which a comedy writer develops a $6,000-a-week heroin habit. Not a whole lot of chuckles in those scenarios.

The other actors under consideration here also dabble in more serious art-house fare that is often attached to auteur directors: Jack Black plays the

Jack Black (l.), Robert Downey Jr. (c.), and Ben Stiller as mock action heroes in *Tropic Thunder* (Ben Stiller, DreamWorks SKG, 2008). Digital frame enlargement.

ne'er-do-well fiancé in Noah Baumbach's dysfunctional family melodrama *Margot at the Wedding* (2007) as well as an intrepid and overly ambitious film producer in Peter Jackson's epic *King Kong* (2005). Adam Sandler plays the leads in Paul Thomas Anderson's *Punch-Drunk Love* (2002), about a sweet but simple man dealing with his own childhood abuse and fears of attachment; and in James L. Brooks's *Spanglish* (2004), he is a celebrity chef who becomes fascinated with his Spanish-speaking maid. In Mike Binder's medium-budget *Reign Over Me* (2007), Sandler portrays a man grieving the loss of his family after the September 11 terrorist attacks, and in Judd Apatow's *Funny People* (2009) he is a stand-up comedian with cancer. Even Will Ferrell has the occasional serious/quirky film, as evidenced by a star turn in Marc Forster's *Stranger Than Fiction* (2006), in which he plays an IRS agent whose regulated life becomes punctuated by an internal narrator telling him that he will soon die. Although no one would confuse the Frat Pack actors with the more serious Method acting offered by Daniel Day-Lewis or Robert De Niro, they are the men who frequently and memorably fill our lives and movie screens. They have become familiar figures, like an obnoxious cousin at a family reunion or our hapless college friends. These are not just guys who like to sit around laughing at fart jokes, although flatulence is no small part of their humor—see the DVD extras to *I Now Pronounce You Chuck & Larry* (2007) or most any Jack Black film, *Tenacious D in The Pick of Destiny* (2006), and the fake trailer for *The Fatties: Fart 2* in *Tropic Thunder*. Even in the context of all that foul wind, the more serious, fantastic, and farcical star turns that Black, Ferrell, Sandler, and Stiller choose show that as entertainers they are deeply invested in the process of acting out the complex tragic-comedy that is living.

Ivan Reitman, who has directed many of the Frat Pack films as well as those by a different comedic troupe comprising Dan Aykroyd, John Belushi, and Bill Murray, notes, "Every generation has their own particular comedic voices. Bill Murray had a very iconoclastic voice that spoke to the baby-boom generation and just beyond. The new X and Y generations are looking to these guys" (Susan Wloszczyna, "'Frat Pack' Splits," *USA Today*, 13 July 2006). In true America-loves-an-underdog fashion, these men tend to get attached to films where they are constantly depicted as losers who, as in the case of Black and Ferrell, elicit laughs by displaying their chubby bodies in ill-fitting underwear, or, as with Sandler and Stiller, play likable but often incompetent and clueless men trapped in low-status jobs. As their singular fame and currency as stars has ascended, each of these men has managed the terms of his star status in a way that does not allow professional savvy and marketplace dominance to undo the puerile humor on which his fame is based.

★★★★★ The Frat Pack Is Dead. Long Live the Frat Pack

The Frat Pack officially earned its moniker in 2004. The group had formerly been named the Slacker Pack by Joshua Rich of *Entertainment Weekly*, but Susan Wloszczyna at *USA Today* balked at the term, since the "phrase implied a lack of drive and initiative" clearly not possessed by this cadre of comedians. "This Frat Pack," she declared, "is all about the work" ("Wilson and Vaughn"). And work they have done. Indeed, in this decade the Frat Pack so dominated film production that Jessica Winter, writing for the *Village Voice*, speculated that by 2008, nearly one quarter of all studio-produced comedies would contain some permutation of the collection of actors loosely grouped here (13 July 2005, 41). She was right. Black, Ferrell, Sandler, and Stiller—on their own or together—appeared in more than ninety films between 2000 and 2009, each man having more than twenty feature films to his credit (Black had twenty-two, Ferrell twenty-seven, Sandler twenty-one, Stiller twenty-five) while also spearheading other projects including Broadway plays (Ferrell's one-man send-up of George W. Bush called *You're Welcome America*), rock bands (Black's Tenacious D and Sandler's solo music gigs), nonprofit foundations (Stiller's Stillerstrong), video games (Black's "Brutal Legend"), and comedic web sites (Ferrell's "Funny or Die").

It is practically impossible to miss these comedians clowning around either at the Cineplex or across an intermedial range of viewing options that includes Netflix, pay-per-view, YouTube, premium cable, or the no-man's-land of expanded cable where they must compete with the randy housewives and *über*-adventurers of reality TV. (Ferrell opted to join them rather then beat them, adventuring with "Man vs. Wild"'s Bear Gryllis in 2009 for a survival experience in the remote north country of Sweden. Classic Will Ferrell line: "I know I keep asking you this, but is there some sort of signal you can give me when it's time to drink our urine?") Turn on the TV at any time of the night or day, and you are sure to find one of these four goofy faces contorted to make you laugh or grimace (since their comedy is often more scattershot than surgically precise comedic critique). At one point in the writing and researching of this essay, I actually had a seventeen-day streak going, during which time I was able to catch up on the Frat Pack's back catalog simply by watching TV at odd times. This viewing experience included a giddy three days where I toggled back and forth between Stiller in *Flirting with Disaster* (1996), Stiller in *Meet the Parents* (2000), Ferrell in *Old School* (2003), Ferrell in *Land of the Lost*, Sandler in *The Longest Yard* (2005), Sandler in *Bedtime Stories* (2008), and Black in *Be Kind Rewind* (2008).

Along with their particular brand of humor that is equal parts gross-out and male-coming-of-age stories, the Frat Pack also marks its identity through a signature ensemble of male comedic actors who have been simultaneously cast to anchor big films. It's hard to watch a movie with one of these men in it without also seeing traces of another of them, either in a secondary role or in a memorable cameo performance. A pretty-girl romantic interest is almost, but not always, part of the narrative, but she is virtually unnecessary to the major plot line of the films, since the real point in these movies is the relationships between men. Further, the "frat" as so construed constitutes a larger draw to audiences than any one man alone might provide, since movies like *Dodgeball: A True Underdog Story* or *Old School* or *Night at the Museum* (2006) or *Anchorman* (2004) or *Funny People* (or pretty much any of the films in which any of these four appear) can be relied on for a one-two (and sometimes three-four) team of wise-cracking buddies whose easy rapport makes laughs a sure thing. Watching them clown around onscreen is like suddenly being admitted to the inner sanctum of the fraternity party or the board room, the seat of boys'-club power booby-trapped with a whoopee cushion.

Other comedic actors, such as Steve Carell, Paul Rudd, Vince Vaughn, Owen Wilson, and Luke Wilson contribute to the phenomenon that is the Frat Pack, but it is Black, Ferrell, Sandler, and Stiller who have achieved the greatest popular recognition, earning power, and star status, as often aided by director/producer Judd Apatow. I should note as a matter of full generic disclosure, however, that Adam Sandler is not always—or even usually—cited as a member in good standing of this club. Indeed, according to The Frat-Pack Tribute web site, Sandler leads his own group of merry men dubbed "The Bad Boys of SNL/Happy Gilmore Gang" (the-frat-pack.com). The Frat Pack has its own Facebook page (not necessarily created by any of the men within the group), and it pointedly creates hierarchies of belonging, with Stiller at the center and other "core" members (Vaughn, the Wilson brothers, and Ferrell) grouped around him. Jack Black is here depicted as being on a second rung, a friend "between Ben and Will." If you do a little more engaged scholarship into the Facebook page, you will soon find Adam Sandler included as a "real" Packer, while other actors (like Will Arnett, Bill Murray, and, bizarrely, Stiller's own father, Jerry) are labeled "junior varsity" Frat Packers. Pack bonafides are clearly hard to come by, but with Sandler's *You Don't Mess with the Zohan*, written by Apatow, and *Funny People*, which was directed, produced, and written by Apatow, he strikes me as pretty clearly Frat Pack material. If not a brother in good standing, he is at least a pledge, and I hereby shoehorn him into the mix, recognizing that Frat Pack purists may take umbrage at his inclusion.

Yet it's not only Sandler's questionable right to Frat Pack membership that can make writing about Jack Black, Will Ferrell, Adam Sandler, and Ben Stiller a bit like playing that "Sesame Street" game, "One of these things is not like the other." Many other odd-man-out elements apply. For example:

Three are shortish and one is pretty tall. Sandler is 5' 9", Stiller is 5' 7", and Black is 5' 6", while Ferrell is a towering 6' 3".

All reference ethnicity boldly and unmistakably, but not in the same way. Black, Sandler, and Stiller play up Jewish schtick in their comedy, while Ferrell references a pasty WASP-y whiteness.

Black, Ferrell, and Sandler frequently rely on gratuitous scenes of them in their underwear and jiggly bare-bottom comedy, while Stiller has bulked up his chest and arms even as he plays nebbishy characters; we should not forget, however, that one of the more classic comedic scenes showcasing Ben Stiller as a fledgling star was the excruciating moment in which his penis is caught in a zipper in *There's Something About Mary* (1998).

They are all children of television, yet differently. Three started their early careers on "Saturday Night Live" (Ferrell and Sandler as actors, Stiller as a writer), while Black began his career on 1980s television shows including "Life Goes On" (1989) and "Northern Exposure" (1990).

Three are self-made celebrities whose families do not work as professional comedians (Black, Ferrell, Sandler), while the fourth (Stiller) is son to the comedic duo Jerry Stiller and Anne Meara. It should be noted that Ferrell's father, Ray Lee Ferrell Jr., was a guitarist for the Righteous Brothers, which he joined in 1967, the year Will was born.

All have acting and writing SAG cards, but only Stiller can also claim directing credits for feature films (*Reality Bites* [1994]; *The Cable Guy* [1996]; *Zoolander*; *Tropic Thunder*).

All have tried their hands at voice acting: Ferrell with *Curious George* (2006); Sandler with *Eight Crazy Nights* (2002); and Stiller with *Madagascar* (2005) and *Madagascar: Escape 2 Africa* (2008). But only Jack Black has a veritable and viable additional career doing the voices for animated feature films, as evidenced by *Ice Age* (2002), *Shark Tale* (2004), and *Kung Fu Panda*.

All have had an impact on the world of art and culture in their own way, but only Stiller has been named to *Time* magazine's "100 Most Influential People" list, largely due to the benevolent work performed through his foundation, Stillerstrong.

More important than their differences, however, is what their collective celebrity and industrial-strength influence meant for comedic film in the 2000s. These men, all of whom were born in the 1960s (Stiller 1965, Sandler 1966, Ferrell 1967, Black 1969), have come of age in a fashion that has allowed them collectively to dominate the contemporary comedic film industry. On the model that the closed fist is mightier than the open hand, they've saturated the entertainment marketplace by sticking together. Ross Douthat observes that in combination with the films produced by the Farrelly brothers (*Dumb & Dumber* [1994], *There's Something About Mary, Me, Myself, and Irene* [2000], *Shallow Hall*, etc.), Frat Pack productions hold the kind of Hollywood clout that allows them to "get just about any production green-lit, and to induce just about anybody to star in it. If you're a friend of Stiller or a protégé of Apatow, you can do whatever the heck you want" (Ross Douthat, "Hit and Miss," *National Review*, 15 September 2008, 72).

The Frat Pack has remained solid through the early decade of the twenty-first century, even in the context of a 2006 *USA Today* report that the "comedy cabal" had "split" since individual members of the group were appearing in films without the others ("Splits"). Susan Wloszczyna ruminated that the likely cause for the Frat Pack's purported fracturing was actually their increased individual popular appeal. "Popularity also breeds bigger paychecks," she notes; "With both Ferrell and Vaughn in the $20 million club, it's financially wiser to hire a supporting cast from outside the pack." Jon Favreau, another Frat Pack regular who has acted in and directed several of the signature films done by the Pack, makes the case for casting and cost: "Before, they were all sort of at the same level and price range. Filmmakers could afford to pull together two or three of them. You could hire one Jim Carrey, or you could mix the Jack Blacks with the Owen Wilsons and the Ben Stillers. Now, they are too expensive" ("Splits"). Yet Frat Pack nice guy Owen Wilson suggests the way that the Frat Pack identity functions as a trustworthy insurance policy. "If the challenges [of carrying his own film] prove too much," Wilson says, "the pack can always count on each other. It might be a bit selfish of me, but I know if my brother's [Luke Wilson's] movie does great, I can always get him to be in a movie with me. A rising tide lifts all boats" ("Splits"). The success or failure of individual members of the Pack thus assures the continuity and recognizability of its core, or so they would have us believe. Indeed, their public reinforcement of a band of brothers helps solidify the brand that is the Frat Pack.

★★★★★ Leader of the Pack: Ben Stiller

The heart and undeniable ringleader of the Frat Pack is Ben Stiller. Stiller purportedly dislikes the Frat Pack moniker, a label he considers weird and unnecessary. Hate it or love it, Stiller spawned the group's identity, and his continued high-profile career helps keep the Frat Pack a dynamic commercial success. Stiller stands ahead of the other three performers in terms of his bankability. As actor, writer, and director, he has contributed to nearly one hundred separate productions in the 2000s alone, these including feature films, television series, and music videos, often pulling his friends into the mix. Stiller's acting repertoire covers four basic categories: (1) the nerdy nebbish who is basically a decent guy: *Meet the Parents*, *Meet the Fockers* (2004), *Along Came Polly*, *Envy* (2004), *Night at the Museum*, *Night at the Museum: Battle of the Smithsonian* (2009); (2) the body-centric clueless buffoon: *Zoolander*, *Dodgeball: A True Underdog Story*, *Tropic Thunder*; (3) the semi-serious quirky misunderstood man in crisis: *The Royal*

Tenenbaums (2001), *The Heartbreak Kid* (2007); and (4) the seemingly self-parodic high-strung actor with aspirations to greatness ("Curb Your Enthusiasm," "Extras").

Some of his films delight in noting Stiller's shortness of stature. *Night at the Museum: Battle of the Smithsonian* features the Lincoln Memorial, now come to life, scrutinizing Stiller's character and saying, "You are small, even for a normal-sized human." Although Stiller has the physique of a man who has spent considerable hours in the gym, in films his body is typically covered so that he might more convincingly play the beset everyman, the type on which his celebrity is grounded. Indeed, in *Meet the Parents*, his characterization of the male nurse Gaylord "Greg" Focker, who struggles to impress the parents of his girlfriend, is so convincing that when he appears in a bright blue Speedo at a pool party, his toned body plays for laughs rather than for admiration. There is perhaps no better quote to sum up Stiller's celebrity than that offered by J-Man (Christopher Walken) in *Envy*: "You, my little dumbbell friend, are like everyman, and you don't even know it, which makes you like the Grand Turbo, Mr. Everyman."

Jessica Winter has described Ben Stiller as "the tightly coiled workaholic, pecs and brain muscles rippling in rhythm; he's both the Idea Man and the Body" (41). But in media interviews, Stiller himself eschews both his top-dog status and his six-pack props. In 2001, *People* identified Stiller as the world's sexiest funnyman, even while their commentary on him belied such status: "He calls his overblown alter ego 'the world's most famous really, really good-looking male supermodel,'" *People* wrote, "but *Zoolander*'s 5' 7" writer, director and star is one reluctant pinup. Ben Stiller claims he's 'lucky just to get through life and feel okay with how I look some days'" (26 November 2001, 109). In an extended interview with the actor that also focused on his doubts, Gil Pringle, writing for the Australian magazine *Filmink*, noted, "Ben has described his own childhood as a 'show business upbringing,' with 'a lot of traveling, and a lot of late nights. I didn't mature until later in life, and if I could do it all again, I would just chill out. I was very fixated on what I wanted to do, and I wasn't that well adjusted socially. . . . I wasn't very popular in high school. I had bad skin and I was a little overweight" (June 2009, 39).

This production of Stiller's own everyman status occurs even in the context of his phenomenal success. In 2005 *New York* magazine termed him "Billion-Dollar Ben," when the five movies he had released in 2004—*Along Came Polly, Envy, Starsky & Hutch, Dodgeball,* and *Meet the Fockers*—surpassed the billion-dollar mark for worldwide profits ("Billion-Dollar Ben," 21 May 2005). In 2007, *Forbes* ranked the comedian twenty-eighth on their Celebrity

100 list, anointing him the "king of comedy" when *Night at the Museum* earned $572 million worldwide (www.forbes.com). *Forbes* was particularly titillated by the rumor that Stiller had been tapped to "rehabilitate" Tom Cruise's "bruised career" by starring with him in the comedy *The Hardy Men*, an updated version of *The Hardy Boys*. (For more laughs related to the Stiller/Cruise connection, see Stiller's parody of the 1986 Martin Scorsese–Cruise collaboration *The Color of Money* called *The Hustler of Money*, or Stiller playing Tom Crooze, Tom Cruise's stunt double, both available on YouTube). But even with all his success, Stiller speaks of having difficulty getting the projects he wants to produce green-lighted. Logan Hill notes that Stiller has struggled unsuccessfully "to adapt Budd Schulberg's Hollywood novel *What Makes Sammy Run?*, and he's been unable to find funding for the film he'd most like to direct: *CivilWarLand in Bad Decline*, a theme-park fantasy from short-fiction master George Saunders." Unable to resist the opportunity, Hill threw in the zinger: "Apparently, once you've zippered your scrotum, dangled sperm off your ear, been Tasered, faked explosive diarrhea, and filmed yourself in an orgy involving a donkey and a Maori tribesman, some studios just won't trust you with serious material" ("Ben").

Given the number of projects Stiller has been able to finance during the decade, one has to assume that his frustration about not being taken seriously is a bit disingenuous. At least, it's difficult to believe he is obstructed making a picture about a Civil War theme park. After all, *Envy* concerns a magic spray that makes dog poo disappear! So while comics are generally on a lower rung of the talent hierarchy, the fact remains that Stiller often provides the engine that gets work made. Neal Conan put this question to him in an interview on NPR's "Talk of the Nation" on 30 March 2010:

> *CONAN:* You are regarded, I would think, as somebody who is, what they call, a bankable star. Were you brought into this project [*Greenberg*] to say, boy, if we can get Ben Stiller, we can get this made? Or were you part of this project and say, I'm going to join this and we're going to get it made.
>
> *STILLER:* I would hope the latter. I mean, I think it was, you know, I was just happy to get the call from Noah [Baumbach], because I'm such a huge fan of his movies.

In this discursive gesture, Stiller the artistic fan wins out over Stiller the power broker, but the fact remains that Stiller's celebrity stature affords a particular visibility not only to him but also to projects in which he takes interest. As Hill puts it:

> The odd and ugly truth of this particular Hollywood moment is that bottom-line pandering may in fact be the easiest way for a smart comic actor to buy

into artier opportunities. Jim Carrey got his shot in *Eternal Sunshine* after taking a pay cut—but only because he'd proved, beyond a doubt, his bankability. "It's at the point where you need a star to get an independent film made," John Waters recently told me. According to this curious, circuitous logic, doing a bad blockbuster like *The Grinch* will not only pad your bank statement—it may actually help you get a tough role in a Michel Gondry film. "It started in the past decade that even the smallest parts are being taken by celebrities," says Philip Seymour Hoffman. The shift, he says, "will make it even easier for Ben to get good roles."   ("Ben")

★★★★★ Tenacious JB: Jack Black

Jack Black is famous as much for his movie roles as for being half of the music group Tenacious D, a "rock band/standup routine that Black has described as 'a Smothers Brothers for the Dungeons and Dragons misfits set,'" says the *New York Times* (movies.nytimes.com). I'd actually describe the band less as the Smothers brothers and more like a middle-aged tribute duo to Black Sabbath, minus the big hair and spandex pants. All of the screaming, hyperbolic intensity, random medieval iconography, and surreal lyrics about devil's horns and magical mushrooms are very much in evidence. Also, it can be problematic in some venues to reproduce any of Tenacious D's lyrics, since most of them rather hilariously throw around vulgarity and drop the F-bomb with abandon, as in "Kickapoo":

> Oh, the dragon's balls were blazing
> As I stepped into his cave,
> Then I sliced his fuckin' cockles
> With a long and shiny blade!
> 'Twas I who fucked the dragon
> Fuckalize sing fuckaloo!
> And if you try to fuck with me
> Then I shall fuck you, too!

Suffice it to say that *Tenacious D in The Pick of Destiny* (produced by Ben Stiller's Red Hour production company) is the sort of film a young professor might be likely to show the undergraduates in a gender and popular culture class to demonstrate just how quickly gender stereotypes are expressed through mainstream movies, since the male bonding is as intense as the homophobia in this film.

In both *Tenacious D* and Black's other film work, JB's celebrity persona comes alive as the exuberantly over-the-top scene-stealer in what Yahoo! Movies calls Black's signature role: "an overconfident, smart aleck loser with an arsenal of expressive faces and a gung-ho attitude towards the most absurd plans of action" (movies.yahoo.com). It seems more than fitting to rely on this anonymous posting to a generalized web browser site, if only because its author, who goes by the posting number 1800180457, so firmly accounts for the appeal of Black's celebrity cachet. Said anonymous author writes (oddly in past tense), "He was at his most memorable when he was portraying just the type of person he might have become if he had not found a lucrative niche for his unique persona—the bitter record store clerk, the failing musician conning his way into easy day jobs, the pontificating 'artist' of no discernable creative output, the guy who works the late shift thanks to fists full of speed." And there you basically have it in a nutshell. Jack Black is not the highest paid member of the Frat Pack (although he does pretty well, commanding healthy salaries and reportedly sitting on a net worth of $40 million). Black is also not the Frat Pack member of longest standing or with greatest industry influence (Stiller occupies both of these statuses). But he is without question the silliest, loudest, and most joyously raucous of the Frat Pack boys, leading the charge where charges must be led, doing the heavy lifting on the inane intensity that is life in the comedy lane. Jack Black is always the one to get the kick to the groin in the name of comedy; he's the one who will vomit, belch, and eat excrement for laughs; he's the go-to guy for both ridicule and the ridiculous.

Jack Black's body seems to make him fated for comedic excess. Small of stature, round of belly, and shaggy all over, if he weren't playing an out-of-control comedian he'd be prime makeover material on reality TV. If Ben Stiller's characterization as the neurotic everyman requires that he cover his chiseled frame, Jack Black's volcanic eruptions seem to necessitate that he bare his body multiple times in any film in which he appears, including, somewhat enigmatically, the animated children's comedy *Kung Fu Panda* for which only his voice is present. In *Tenacious D* the viewer bears witness to repeated scenes of Black's rotund form, including a ridiculous butt-baring sequence in which his character Jables (or JB) reveals the mysterious birthmark on his right butt cheek that says "Tenac," and his band mate, the equally rotund though not equally outrageous Kyle Gass, reveals the birthmark on his left butt cheek that says "ious D"—all adding up, of course, to the predestined name of their band. Even and especially in Baumbach's *Margot at the Wedding*, where Black is not playing a comedic role per se, the sight of his bared derriere is de rigueur and a bit frightening. Black himself told MTV at the release of the film that he was somewhat horrified when he saw his own butt onscreen. " 'I've had a lot of ass work,' he said, remembering movies where he's dropped trou for comedic effect. 'But this one was a dramatic ass—and it's a full moon rising. . . . Oh man, when I saw the screening of this I was like, "Dude, mix in some crunches! Some ass

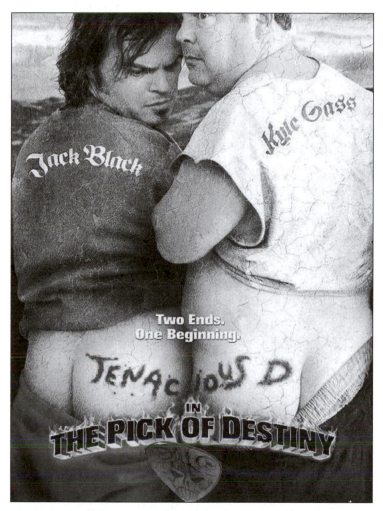

Buns of Truth. Jack Black and Kyle Gass in *Tenacious D in The Pick of Destiny* (Liam Lynch, Red Hour Films, 2006). Digital frame enlargement.

crunches!" Sit-ups are good for the abs, but what's good for the back fat? Power squats?'" (Larry Carroll, "Jack Black Grows a Mustache, Drops Trou, for Margot at the Wedding," *MTV News*, 21 November 2007).

This delighted shame in his own excess of behavior and body seemingly accounts for much of Jack Black's popular appeal. In May 2008, he appeared on "The Tonight Show with Jay Leno," telling the host that his twenty-three-month-old son, Sammy, had confused Black's gut with his wife's pregnancy of eight months. The moment was picked up and broadcast through the blogosphere. *People*'s niche site, Moms&Babies, featured respondents praising Black as "hilarious" and "genuine" (celebritybabies. people.com, 13 May 2008). Wrote one Amanda, "You gotta love Jack! He's so funny and seems a genuinely nice guy." Racheal Taylor agreed, "I love Jack Black he's so hilarious." Susan chipped in, "Talk about a house that is filled with laughter!!!" So, it seems, living large is working well for JB, since his hyperbole is so outrageous that it doesn't appear to be constructed.

★★★★★ Funny or Die: Will Ferrell

Much like Ben Stiller, Will Ferrell's persona hinges on the idea of his being average, not so much the put-upon everyman that Stiller plays to such perfection, but just a normal guy somehow caught on big, medium-sized, and little screens, since Ferrell is as much a television and Internet phenomenon as he is a movie star. Ferrell told Barry Koltnow that his normalcy is the key to his success: "That's the whole setup. A lot of what I do works because of the way I look" ("Will Ferrell Says Growing Up in Irvine Made Him Funny," *Orange County Register*, 25 July 2008). And how does he look? He's a tall guy with frizzy hair and a bit of a gut, a bit pasty in the face but sort of sweet overall. Jessica Winter describes him as "the galvanizing force of nature, macho-suave yet thrumming with reserves of sugarsmacked hysteria, hairy of chest and manner yet unafraid to cry like a girl or scream like a woman" (41).

Much like Jack Black, Will Ferrell often strips down to his skivvies (and beyond) to trigger laughs, and iconic comedic scenes of Ferrell include jogging naked down a city street in *Old School*, spazzing out with John C. Reilly as they jump into a swimming pool arms akimbo and revealingly swimsuit-clad in *Step Brothers* (2008), and re-creating Burt Reynolds's 1970s *Playgirl* pose in full-frontal recline in *Semi-Pro* (2008). The baring of his less-than-classically beautiful body has also inspired the nation's journalists to new heights of descriptive prose. Here's one of my favorites, from movie reviewer Richard Corliss of *Time* magazine:

> Will Ferrell appears topless onscreen more frequently than any current movie actress. So to think of him for more than a second obliges one to contemplate, with a kind of cringing pleasure, his torso. The chest is large, white and flabby, suggesting a beached sea otter, and it's pocked with what looks like dozens of tiny, imperfectly attached hair-implant tufts. It might be a helicopter's-eye view of merino sheep stranded on a tundra. For Ferrell to expose this slab of flank might be deemed inappropriate at best, sadistic at worst. But because he does it without the requisite shame, it's funny, since the actor is usually playing guys who are cocooned in, and sustained by, an utterly unwarranted belief in themselves. Ferrell knows, as surely as his characters don't, that his body is nothing to boast about. So to display it as if it were worthy of a *Muscle & Fitness* cover is to tell us that they are as unself-conscious as they are self-unaware.
> (*Time*, 30 March 2007)

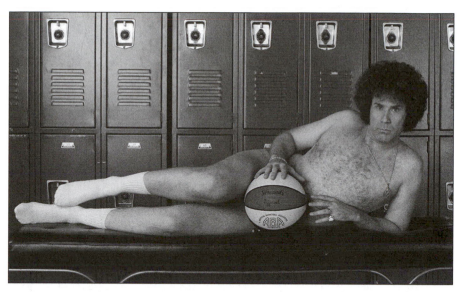

Homage to Burt [Reynolds]. Will Ferrell in *Semi-Pro* (Kent Alterman, New Line Cinema, 2008). Digital frame enlargement.

Like Adam Sandler, Ferrell's rise to fame started on and became meteoric due to "Saturday Night Live." In Ferrell's case, his seven-year run on the comedy sketch program from 1995 to 2002 allowed him to develop an arsenal of insane and memorable characters, including the inappropriately dressed office worker who comes to staff meetings in a G-string, and the ebullient Craig, who joined with Cheri Oteri's Arianna to compose the spastic Spartans cheerleading squad. One of their more memorable cheers?

> Taco! Burrito!
> What's coming out of your speedo?
> You got troubles, whooo!
> You're blowin bubbles, whoo!!
> Float, float, float, float.
> Your puttin' around like a motor boat.
> Troubles, whooo!
> You're blowin bubbles, whoooo!
> YOU STINK!!

(Incidentally, amateur versions of people acting out Craig and Arianna's routines are legion on YouTube.)

In addition to these characters, Ferrell also generated multiple celebrity spoofs, including James Lipton, the bald-domed *über*-serious host of Bravo's "Inside the Actors Studio"; Alex Trebek, the long-suffering face behind the game show "Jeopardy"; Neil Diamond, the tough-talking, gravelly voiced singer with a penchant for violence; Gene, the zealous cowbellbeating member of the Blue Öyster Cult; and, of course, George W. Bush, then the much-reviled president of the United States. Ferrell's best line? "I'm George W. Bush, and I approved this message. In fact, I think it is awesome." Ferrell's characterization of Bush earned him a one-man show on Broadway and an HBO special, *Will Ferrell: You're Welcome America* (2009).

Of the four men under consideration here, Ferrell is perhaps the one who makes best use of the Internet. In 2007 he launched Funnyordie.com, a web site devoted to streaming short comedic vignettes that often feature—you guessed it, Jack Black, Adam Sandler, and Ben Stiller (among countless others). Anyone is eligible to submit videos to the web site, but only celebrities get top ranking. Probably the biggest splash on Funnyordie.com has been Ferrell's "The Landlord," which depicts him disputing his overdue rent with his foul-mouthed alcoholic landlord Pearl, a two-year-old toddler. Two months after "The Landlord," Ferrell released "Good Cop, Baby Cop," using the same toddler as a loose cannon cop who forces a confession from Ferrell as felon. Both videos went viral immediately, and though the ethics of coaching a baby to "get her drink on" were hotly debated, the controversy itself secured the long-range reach of Funnyordie.com.

All this exposure has been good for Ferrell on financial grounds. He is reportedly paid between $5 million and $20 million for his feature film work. Although his films do not always do well at the box office, they obviously earn enough for Ferrell to be a top player in Hollywood—not bad for a guy who grew up in Irvine, California, where the city life was so boring that Ferrell credits the birth of his comedic self as a necessary remedy to break the boredom.

☆☆☆☆★ The Sandman: Adam Sandler

Adam Sandler is not commonly grouped among the Frat Pack. Indeed, he has scarcely ever shared big-screen time with the three actors I've discussed here, the closest being uncredited parts for Ben Stiller in *Happy Gilmore* (1996) and *Pauly Shore Is Dead* (2003). Given that this group is made legible by its nepotistic repeat casting of a select group of actors, what is the logic of including Sandler in the mix? Mostly because he strikes me as the missing brother in the fraternity house, the guy who isn't there but should be, the lost pledge. Sharing precious few acting credits with other Frat Packers, Sandler is often grouped with the Frat Pack boys by association. Google their names together, and there is a veritable feast of chatter in the blogosphere about which actor is the funniest, whose films are the best, and who could win in a kick-ass smack down (funniest: Sandler; best: Stiller;

kick-ass king: Black. Sorry, Will Ferrell). There are never more than two degrees of separation between people like Black, Ferrell, Sandler, and Stiller, whether through fellow co-stars like John C. Reilly or Jennifer Aniston or in terms of competing film release dates. Even entertainment journalists are prone to these comparisons, as evidenced by David Edelstein's observation: "Like Will Ferrell, Sandler has layers of tenderness under layers of irony under layers of tenderness—plus a floating anger like Jupiter's great red spot" ("Israeli Stud, Aspiring Hairdresser," *New York*, 5 June 2008).

Even though Sandler excels in starring in films built around somewhat ridiculous premises, he, like the rest of the Frat Pack, holds a celebrity largely grounded on being a regular Joe, an unpretentious, straight-shooting class clown who is in constant need of learning a lesson. Roger Ebert has described Sandler's characters as "almost oppressively nice, like needy puppies, and yet they conceal a masked hostility to society, a passive-aggressive need to go against the flow, a gift for offending others while in the very process of being ingratiating" ("Punch-Drunk Love," *Chicago Sun-Times*, 18 October 2002). Manohla Dargis put things a bit more bluntly: "Sometimes he makes you laugh, sometimes he makes you wince, though usually he makes you wonder how many times and in how many different permutations he will recycle his obnoxious Everyman" ("Dude [Nyuck-Nyuck], I Love You [as If!]," *New York Times*, 20 July 2007). Yet, that recycled and familiar Everyman is the precise ingredient that stands at the core of Sandler's appeal. Writing for Fandango, an Internet movie site, Chuck Walton summarized Sandler's star power in three ways. First, he's the "loveable all-American man-boy," not too threatening to other men, not too repulsive to women. Second, he's not overly serious, even in grim films. And finally, he's genuine, offering the audience a slice of "what-you-see-is-what-you-get" authentic pie with every trip to the Cineplex (20 July 2007). These attributes are somewhat debatable since Sandler's everyday-Joe averageness is as constructed as any other celebrity's public image. Even "backstage" comments about Sandler are part of the mediation of his identity. For instance, there is a clip of him on "Late Night with David Letterman" where he is pretending to be a movie star diva on the set of *Funny People*, but the boorishness of his elitism only reinforces the idea that he is "actually" quite affable. The only thing that one might point to as more "real" are the YouTube fan videos of him less-than-exuberantly signing autographs. Authentic earnestness remains central to Sandler and the Frat Pack. We have the sense that these guys are earnestly eager to make us laugh, ostensibly not for the money they will make but for the sheer joy those guffaws can bring to our lives.

Adam Sandler learns from a remote control that spending time with your family really does matter in *Click* (Frank Coraci, Columbia, 2006). Digital frame enlargement.

Even so, Sandler's earning power is enormous and stands at the heart of his Hollywood influence. Throughout this decade, all the films in which he starred, except for the more serious *Reign Over Me*, earned close to $30 million. Some, like *The Longest Yard, Anger Management* (2003), and *Click* (2006), toppled into the $150 million range. Although he earned raves as the sweet but volatile protagonist of *Punch-Drunk Love*, prompting film critics such as Ebert to urge the actor to leave his string of "moronic comedies" behind, the industry seemed firmly committed to keeping him in his perpetual man-child role by recycling films where Sandler's raucous but basically decent characters had to learn lessons of heteronormative humility and domestication (a lothario meets the girl of his dreams and commits to monogamy, a perpetually adolescent man finally gets a job and seeks a family, a disgruntled father realizes the important things in life: family relationships). This recycling of themes has helped to give Sandler his cachet and to make him a critical element in the idea factory that perpetuates the celebrity of the Frat Pack. Indeed, all members of the Pack participate in a form of seeming self-parody that capitalizes on the fantasy of a perpetual adolescence punctuated with penis jokes, marijuana, and beer kegs. And yet, all four of the Frat Pack pillars I've discussed here are poster boys for American heteronormative adult capitalist triumph, highly successful multi-millionaires, married, and fathers.

★★★★★ Conclusion: Let's Hear It for the Boys

For all their box-office clout during the 2000s, the guys in the Frat Pack are still and will always be underdogs, the class clowns trying to compete with the popular football players. "You can think of Hollywood as high school," says Owen Wilson. "TV actors are freshmen, comedy actors are maybe juniors, and dramatic actors—they're the cool seniors" ("Splits"). Jack Black and Will Ferrell put the matter a bit more succinctly in their tongue-in-cheek song at the 2008 Academy Awards ceremony: "A comedian at the Oscars, the saddest man of all," sings Ferrell mournfully, playing straight man to his own unruly hair. "Their movies may make millions, but their name, you'll never call." Jack Black then rushes onto the stage in a fireball of intensity: "What did you think when you took off your pants, and you ran around the race track and did that silly dance, what did you think?!" We may not win this battle, encourages Black, but we'll win the larger fight! In this case, his words are literal since he threatens to beat up all the Best Actor nominees after the show. But the point here is really that the enduring celebrity of the Frat Pack puts them in a league of public consciousness that certainly parallels the cultural currency held by more august actors. The comedians of the Frat Pack may never win an Oscar, but then, Oscar will never be a varsity player in the Frat Pack.

5 ☆☆☆☆☆☆☆☆☆☆★

Javier Bardem and Benicio Del Toro
Beyond Machismo

MARY C. BELTRÁN

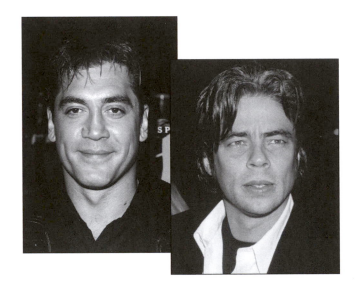

When Benicio Del Toro was awarded the Oscar for Best Supporting Actor in 2001 for his role as Mexican police officer Javier Rodriguez in Steven Soderbergh's *Traffic* (2000), he dedicated his award to the people of Nogales, Arizona, and Nogales, Mexico. (The sister cities, divided by the U.S.-Mexico border, provided locations for the production of *Traffic*, a crime drama focused on the 1990s "war on drugs" and drug trafficking across the border.) In doing so, Del Toro called attention not only to the importance and concerns of Mexican Americans, other Americans, and Mexicans living near the border, but by extension also to his own unique status as a Puerto Rican and Latino star within the predominantly white realm of the Hollywood star system. He was only the fifth Latino actor and the third Puerto Rican to be awarded an Oscar for his acting—the first two being José Ferrer

---

Javier Bardem and Benicio Del Toro.

(in 1950, for the title role in *Cyrano de Bergerac*) and Rita Moreno (in 1961, for *West Side Story*).

Javier Bardem, already an established and highly acclaimed film star in Spain when he was awarded the Academy Award for Best Actor for his performance as a sociopathic villain in the Coen brothers' *No Country for Old Men* (2007), similarly made his status as a Latino actor, more specifically as a Spanish actor, central to his acceptance speech in 2008. Concluding the speech in Spanish, he dedicated his Oscar to his actor mother, a film and television star in Spain, to the rest of his family (which includes several other successful actors and filmmakers), to the actors of Spain, and to Spain itself. In Bardem's case, he was the sixth Latino actor to achieve the Academy Award and only the second to be awarded the Oscar for Best Actor.

It should be noted that it is debatable among scholars of Latina/o stardom whether Javier Bardem and other Spanish actors should be considered "Latino" in the U.S. context, as the racialized grouping "Hispanic/Latino" in the United States does not always include Spaniards, given their geographic roots in Europe rather than Latin America or the American Southwest. However, the Hollywood film industry has historically constructed its imagined version of *Latinidad* (Latin-ness) in relation to Spanish-speaking abilities, Hispanic accents, and "Latin looks" (to use Clara Rodriguez's term) as opposed to geographic ties, with Spanish actors embraced among other Hispanic performers and sometimes even privileged in the processes of casting and star promotion; Angharad Valdivia and other scholars have documented this tradition. Because Spanish actors need to conform to the prevailing preference for U.S. films to be shot in English, and must also face the challenge of appealing to audiences in Latino roles that may be limited in scope, they often face an equally daunting task in breaking into the U.S. film industry.

Latino stars were few and far between in Hollywood film until the 2000s, in large part because until recently, compelling roles portrayed by Latino actors, which might encourage audience identification with, and thus attention to, the actors' performances, have been rare. As film scholars such as Charles Ramírez Berg have documented, Latino and Latina characters often were presented in fairly one-dimensional roles as especially sexual, childlike, or aggressive. In addition, as I note in my study of Latino film and television stardom, *Latina/o Stars in U.S. Eyes*, and as Adrienne McLean has noted in a book-length study of Rita Hayworth, Latina/o film actors who did not mask their *Latinidad*, even as late as the 1990s, were less likely to be cast and promoted as potential stars; and if they were, it was typically through emphasis on tropes that reinforced racialized stereotypes. The growth of the

U.S. Latino audience, surpassing African Americans as the largest non-white audience domestically, and the success of popular performers and actors such as Selena, Ricky Martin, and Jennifer Lopez in the 1990s, set the stage for greater opportunity and promotion experienced by Latino actors in the 2000s. In this regard, the performances, critical acclaim, and stardom achieved by Del Toro and Bardem in the 2000s illustrate a broadening horizon of imagined possibilities for Latino and Spanish actors, particularly regarding notions of Latino masculinity and machismo that might historically have been attached to stars such as these. Del Toro and Bardem emerged as Hollywood film stars, in complex and critically lauded roles in which they embodied a nuanced masculinity and in promotional texts in which they were presented as intelligent *and* sexy icons for American and global fans.

Both born in the late 1960s, Del Toro and Bardem have broadened expectations of Latino roles and possibilities for Latino stardom through their nuanced and impassioned acting and daring choice of film roles, as well as in relation to their popularity with American and global audiences and critics. In the 2000s, as their star images became increasingly complex and their performances were acclaimed by critics with regularity, a notably sophisticated sensibility was etched by these two actors on the big screen.

★★★★★ Benicio Del Toro: Don't Box Me In

Benicio Del Toro became a major film star in 2000s Hollywood through transcending industry tradition and acting his way out of the box that was the long history of cinematically typecasting Latino actors—and Anglo actors performing in Latino roles—as macho thugs (such as Al Pacino's Cuban mobster Tony Santana in *Scarface* [1983]), comic buffoons (as in Leo Carrillo's recurrent role as Pancho, the dim-witted sidekick of the Cisco Kid in *The Valiant Hombre* [1948], its sequels, and its television adaptation), or sultry romantic figures (such as Zorro, portrayed most recently by Antonio Banderas in 1998 and 2005). This ascent was arguably facilitated by Del Toro's sheer talent and determination, as well as by his perceived versatility for bringing to life characters of a variety of ethnicities and from widely varying backgrounds in committed, Method-style performances. He also benefited from partnering with talented and broad-thinking directors from a variety of countries who have been interested in showcasing his unique abilities, among them Terry Gilliam, Alejandro González Iñárritu, Susanne Bier, and Soderbergh.

According to biographies of the star, Del Toro—of Spanish and Italian Puerto Rican heritage—was born Benicio Monserrate Rafael Del Toro

Sanchez to Gustavo Del Toro and Fausta Sanchez in 1967 in a suburb of San Juan, Puerto Rico, where he spent the first thirteen years of his life. After a long period of illness, his mother died of hepatitis when he was nine, a loss that Del Toro has described in recent interviews as powerfully affecting his life and work. After his father remarried a few years later and some family conflicts ensued for him, he was eventually allowed to attend boarding school in Mercersburg, Pennsylvania. He later attended the University of California, San Diego, ultimately changing his major from business to acting, despite a lack of support from his father. He trained for several years in New York and Los Angeles, with a focus on Method acting, most notably at the Stella Adler Conservatory in Los Angeles. Del Toro got his first acting job on the West Coast in a small role on the television series "Miami Vice," followed by the lead in a theatrical production, *The Orphans*.

Throughout the early 1990s, Del Toro appeared in a range of small film roles and established himself as an offbeat and intelligent character actor who fully researched his roles and threw himself into them. The role of mumbling, eccentric, small-time criminal Fred Fenster in Bryan Singer's *The Usual Suspects* (1995) was Del Toro's first break as a film actor, his performance garnering an Independent Spirit Award for Best Supporting Actor, elevating his visibility with both audiences and film producers. He followed with a memorable performance in a small role as artist Jean-Michel Basquiat's longtime friend Benny Dalmau in Julian Schnabel's *Basquiat* (1996), which earned him a second supporting actor award from the Independent Spirit Awards. In a differing turn, he played a car thief turned unwilling kidnapper turned love interest in Marco Brambilla's romantic caper *Excess Baggage* (1997), opposite then-reigning teen star Alicia Silverstone, who as a producer of the film hand-picked Del Toro for the role (during a period when the two were reportedly dating). While *Excess Baggage* did not do well at the box office and was panned by critics, Del Toro received positive reviews (Roger Ebert, writing for the *Chicago Sun-Times*, stated that "Benicio Del Toro steals [the film] with his performance" ["Excess Baggage," 29 August 1997]), while Timothy M. Gray, reviewing for *Variety*, claimed, "The most interesting acting [in the film] comes from Del Toro, an offbeat leading man whose oddball line readings and quirky charm give the film most of its energy" (6 September 1997). Perhaps in relation to Ebert and others noting that Del Toro performed "with a dash of Brad Pitt," Del Toro began to be promoted as a young star, to the extent that he was described as the "Latino Brad Pitt," and so on. Del Toro himself typically brushed off such references, however, preferring to keep his private life out of the public eye and to stay focused on his work as an actor.

Many consider Del Toro's next performance, as "Dr. Gonzo" (the nickname of Oscar Zeta Acosta), the job that illuminated his potential as an actor. Acosta was "gonzo" journalist and author Hunter S. Thompson's lawyer friend and sidekick in drug-related mayhem in the late 1960s, as Thompson shares in his book *Fear and Loathing in Las Vegas*; Del Toro played the role in Terry Gilliam's 1998 film adaptation alongside Johnny Depp as Thompson. To embody Acosta, Del Toro did extensive research, put on over forty pounds, and delved deeply into the dark corners of the role in what was viewed by most critics as a convincing and troubling portrayal. In one scene, for instance, he repeatedly burned himself with cigarettes, as Acosta was known to have done (the scene was cut from the final version of the film). Shot and edited in deliberately surrealistic style to echo the drug-addled perspectives of its protagonists, the film did poorly at the box office and garnered mixed reviews from critics. Del Toro has speculated in interviews that a decline in roles he was offered after the film's release may have been due in part to producers having a hard time separating him as an actor from the dark, drug-ridden character he had portrayed. Others in the Hollywood film community took notice of Del Toro's talent, however. As Gilliam described him in later years: "Del Toro is an exciting actor. He's obsessed with his work. He draws the camera like a magnet because he keeps coming up with things that are dark, brooding, dangerous and sexy" (*Fear and Loathing* Production Notes, *The Terry Gilliam Fanzine* 1).

While opportunities may have slowed for Del Toro in the next year, this quickly turned around. Influential in this regard was the actor's popularly and critically acclaimed performance in *Traffic*, an intricate crime drama that explores the 1990s "war on drugs" from a variety of vantage points, that of law enforcement, politicians, users, and traffickers. In the film, Del Toro plays a Mexican police officer who finds himself struggling in the face of organized Tijuana drug trafficking that is slipping by, aided by corruption on both sides of the border. His Rodriguez is a man of integrity, though with human imperfections, who wants to do something to help the people and particularly the children in his impoverished city to have a better life. But he finds his hands tied by larger forces. Rodriguez arguably serves as the conscience of the film, in which there are few redeeming individuals. The performance is nuanced and at times appears luminous in relation to the sad realities of the complicated, interwoven storyline; for the role he also spoke most of his lines in Mexican-inflected Spanish, having diligently studied the region his story was set in and having worked for many months with a dialect coach. While the film earned mixed reviews, critics roundly praised Del Toro for his performance. Representative was Owen Glieberman's critique for *Entertainment*

Benicio Del Toro as Tijuana police officer Javier Rodriguez in the crime drama *Traffic* (Steven Soderbergh, Bedford Falls Productions, 2000). Courtesy Jerry Ohlinger Film Archives.

Weekly in which he enthused, "Haunting in his understatement, [Del Toro] becomes the film's quietly awakening moral center" (25 November 2005). Del Toro was subsequently named Best Supporting Actor at the Golden Globes, Best Actor by the Screen Actor's Guild, and Best Supporting Actor by the Academy of Motion Picture Arts and Sciences. *Traffic* was named one of the top films of the year by many film critics and earned Oscars for Best Director, Best Adapted Screenplay, and Best Film Editing, in addition to a range of Best Picture and Best Director awards elsewhere. Notably, Del Toro was also lauded by Steven Soderbergh for his input during the film's production. The director noted in interviews that Del Toro had made several useful suggestions on the script and in the shooting of scenes, and gave him due credit for his contributions, illuminating the formation of a creative partnership between the two that was to continue and grow with *Che* (2008).

Del Toro has reported that winning the Oscar for *Traffic* helped him get better offers, and soon he was working with many of the most respected directors in the industry and demonstrating his range in a variety of roles. In the few years after *Traffic* he had small but memorable roles as diamond thief and gambler Franky Four Fingers in English director Guy Ritchie's crime caper *Snatch* (2000), as a mentally retarded American Indian falsely accused of murder in Sean Penn's *The Pledge* (2001), and, in a starring and darkly compelling role, as a former military special operations soldier who has become a psychologically unbalanced killer after suffering a breakdown in William Friedkin's dark thriller *The Hunted* (2003). While these last two films were box-office failures, Del Toro's acting was uniformly praised.

The star received further acclaim for his portrayal of a hyper-religious former convict forced to face an ultimate test of his faith in *21 Grams* (2003), alongside Sean Penn and Naomi Watts and directed by Mexican filmmaker Alejandro González Iñárritu. A complex, interwoven narrative about their characters' choices in the face of life-changing catastrophes, *21 Grams* earned multiple film and acting nominations and awards, including several for Del Toro's performance. To include a few representative reviews, J. Hoberman's critique for the *Village Voice* found Del Toro's performance "powerfully restrained" (18 November 2003). And Manohla Dargis summed up many critics comments in describing *21 Grams:*

> To watch these three [Penn, Del Toro, and Watts]—working alone and in tan-
> dem—is to experience the strange, at times frightening alchemy of screen act-
> ing. No matter how occasionally wobbly the story, the three are something
> fierce. Not only because they throw themselves headlong into the fray, but
> because there are moments—as in a scene between Del Toro and the actress
> who plays his wife, Melissa Leo—when you wonder how actors shake off the
> heartache when they go home at night.
>
> (*Los Angeles Times*, 2 November 2003)

Through such critiques, Del Toro's star image was becoming fused with awe for his skill as an actor.

Adding to his impressively wide body of work, each of Benicio Del Toro's subsequent roles was vastly different from work he had done earlier. In *Sin City* (2005), a series of loosely connected narrative vignettes based on the neo-noir graphic novels by Frank Miller and directed by Miller, Robert Rodriguez, and Quentin Tarantino, the actor plays Lt. Jack "Jackie Boy" Rafferty, a once honest but now corrupt police officer, with convincing hard-hearted cruelty. In his vignette "The Big Fat Kill," Jackie Boy threat-ens and eventually hits his ex-girlfriend and mistreats a prostitute, ulti-mately meeting a justifiably deadly end. In Susanne Bier's *Things We Lost in the Fire* (2007), Del Toro played Jerry Sunborne, a diametrically different character. In this family-oriented drama and love story, Jerry is a recover-ing addict who turns his life around after his best friend is murdered, leav-ing a grieving widow (Halle Berry) and children who need his support. Del Toro garnered praise from Bier for his work as a meticulous actor, and from many film critics who remarked about his powerful and nuanced perform-ance. Writing for the *Chicago Sun-Times*, Roger Ebert noted, for instance, that the central performance in the film is by Del Toro, "who never over-plays, who sidesteps any temptation to go over the top (especially in scenes of his suffering), and whose intelligence as a one-time lawyer shows through his street-worn new reality" (19 December 2007). Some reviews, however, criticized the film as overly melodramatic and panned Bier's propensity for extreme close-ups and hand-held camerawork. While the film, shot on a very small budget, was a financial success, given its mixed reviews it did not substantially add to Del Toro's star image.

In promotions during these years, Del Toro came to be framed as a talented and compelling actor and producer. Interviews in the late 2000s typically focused heavily on the subject matter of his film projects. Earlier in his career, by contrast, he had typically been asked primarily about being a Latino actor. In response to such a question in 1997, for instance, he had replied:

> Logically, I feel a great responsibility for being a Latino actor working in Hollywood. . . . [But] the fact that my name is Benicio Del Toro should not imply that I must be thought of only as a Hispanic actor. Logically, I don't have a problem with playing Latino characters, and would play them more frequently if they were better written.
>
> (Gabriel De Lerma, "This Is My Life," *Miami Herald*, 10 October 1997)

Del Toro noted in later interviews that while his fame had brought him acting opportunities, he still hoped to be offered a greater range of roles, and particularly to be considered for romantic and comedic roles. For the time being, he noted, he was trying to perform the roles he was offered to the best of his abilities.

While comedy and romantic parts have eluded Del Toro, in recent years he has taken on the highest profile roles of his career. In 2008, working again with Soderbergh, he played the title role in the two-part biopic *Che* (now released commercially as two films, *Che Part 1: The Argentine*, and *Che Part 2: Guerrilla*). The films follow revolutionary leader Ernesto "Che" Guevara first over a period of two years when he helped Fidel Castro and an army of Cubans to overthrow the Fulgencio Batista government in 1957, and then during his unsuccessful attempt to lead Bolivian peasants to overthrow their government in 1968 and in the last years of his life that followed. Notably, Del Toro also served as one of three producers of the film, working for many years researching and developing the project and raising financing prior to working with Soderbergh on *Traffic* and Soderbergh's coming on the project as director. Faced with decisions about what language in which to shoot the film, Soderbergh and the producers ultimately chose to make *Che* a noncommercial film by keeping the dialogue in Spanish with English subtitles. This greatly restricted its distribution but preserved the integrity of the film, according to Soderbergh ("Got 4 Hours to Kill? Steven Soderbergh Can Help," CNN, 23 May 2008). Working with a low budget for

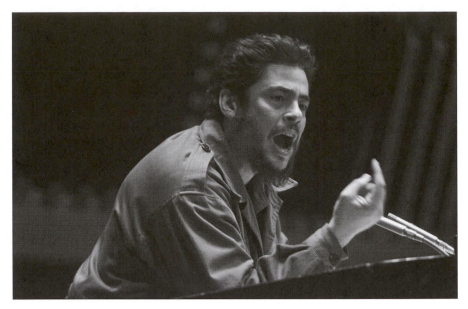

Benicio Del Toro as political leader Ernesto "Che" Guevara in Part One (*The Argentine*) of Steven Soderbergh's two-part biopic *Che* (Steven Soderbergh, Wild Bunch, 2008). Courtesy Photofest New York.

a film of this magnitude, the production crew completed shooting in just seventy-nine long, hard days in Campeche, Mexico, and Puerto Rico (travel embargoes prevented filming in Cuba).

The two films were screened as one at the Cannes Film Festival in 2008; Del Toro received the festival's Best Actor award for his performance and *Che* received praise from audiences. The film received limited release, however, and did not recoup its costs. Although Del Toro received strong positive reviews from critics, the film itself generally did not. Roger Ebert in the *Chicago Sun-Times* described Del Toro's acting as "heroic" and self-effacing, and noted that he seemed to simply disappear into the role (14 January 2009)—indeed, Del Toro reproduces Che's progressive, hacking cough with almost distracting verisimilitude. A. O. Scott, writing in the *New York Times*, described his performance as "technically flawless" and infused with Del Toro's considerable charisma, but declared that the film itself was limited in emotional scope ("Che: Saluting the Rebel Underneath the T-shirt," 12 December 2008). Many in the film community felt that *Che* and Del Toro should have received more recognition. Sean Penn, for instance, during his acceptance speech for the Best Actor award he received at the Screen Actors Guild for his performance in *Milk* (2008), lamented that Soderbergh and Del Toro were not awarded for *Che*, and wondered whether it was because the film was in Spanish or because of its length or politics.

In 2001, Del Toro noted to *New York Times* journalist Anthony DeCurtis that he wanted to perform in more films like *Traffic* "that deal with big themes" ("Hot Actor of the Moment Can Also Play Cool," 21 January 2001). Years later, asked by another journalist about his motivation for producing *Che*, Del Toro responded, "I think I understand Che. . . . It's a piece of history that I felt needed to be explored and, as I learnt about Che and the way his life came to an end, that put the final flame under my desire" ("Benicio Del Toro Gets to the Man Behind the T-Shirt Myth in *Che*," *London Sunday Times*, 4 October 2008). In another interview, he shared that as a young man he had learned about Che Guevara and found him a powerful role model, particularly regarding Guevara's wish to put an end to poverty around the world. While Del Toro chose not to overtly identify his politics, he mentioned that his upbringing on the island of Puerto Rico and his continued interest in the struggles of the people there played a role in his identification with Guevara. "And you see bad things," he concluded. "And it just reminds you of the capacity for good and change" (Simon Hattenstone, "Dammit, This Guy Is Cool," *Guardian*, 29 November 2008).

Del Toro also played the title role in his next film, *The Wolfman* (2010), a gothic thriller about a man doomed to become a werewolf. Critics considered it a poorly constructed narrative with Del Toro miscast, and largely panned the film. The demand for Del Toro as an actor, however, continued with his role as a celebrity in Sofia Coppola's *Somewhere*, in Italian director Christian Filippella's crime caper *White Widow* (2011), and in *Lunar Park*, cowritten by Bret Easton Ellis and adapted from Ellis's novel of the same name (and in which the main character is in fact Bret Easton Ellis).

In addition to his work as a producer on *Che* and *The Wolfman*, Del Toro was the executive producer of *Maldeamores* (*Lovesickness*), a 2007 Spanish-language feature film set in Puerto Rico about love as experienced at various ages. The film has been recognized as part of a new wave of Puerto Rican filmmaking spurred by the activity of the Puerto Rican Film Commission since the late 1990s. It's possible that in the future Del Toro will be recognized as a force to be reckoned with as much behind the camera as in front of it.

☆☆☆☆☆ Javier Bardem: A Career of Transcending Expectations

With a storied career in Spanish and now Hollywood cinema, Javier Bardem easily fills the shoes of the sensitive, romantic leads as in *Eat Pray Love* (2010). Like Benecio Del Toro, however, he has instead become a successful star through taking risks, playing against type, and regularly transforming his looks and persona in a wide variety of film roles. With respect to his star image, fans typically know him not only for his brooding good looks and urbane image as a modern-day Renaissance man but also for the seriousness with which he approaches his work. He has often mentioned in interviews that he sees himself as a worker rather than a star, even after his acting opportunities, critical recognition, and fame in the United States have grown to match his Spanish stardom throughout the 2000s.

Notably, given his Spanish heritage and status as a film star in Spain, Bardem's experience in relation to Hollywood's construction of *Latinidad* and Latino stardom is unique. Based on his looks and Spanish-speaking abilities, Bardem has been embraced and promoted as a Latino star by U.S. film producers while facing fewer of the casting limitations typically experienced by Latino performers in Hollywood. Whether because of his physical appearance, his European heritage, his proven bankability, and talent in Spanish films, or, most likely, a combination of these factors, Bardem has had the opportunity to demonstrate his acting range and charisma in a wide variety of Latino and non-Latino roles in U.S. films, an opportunity that is broadening as he becomes more comfortable acting in English. He has also managed to underscore his talent and dedication to the craft of acting in idiosyncratic character roles while still occasionally playing romantic leads with ease, a feat that has resulted in a complicated but appealing star image.

Bardem was born Javier Ángel Encinas Bardem in Las Palmas de Gran Canaria, the capital city of one of the Canary Islands, in 1969; his parents are Carlos Encinas and Pilar Bardem, she a successful actor in Spanish film and television. His mother's family, in fact, has a long history in Spanish cinema that can be traced back to its earliest days; many of his relatives, including his grandparents, uncle, and older brother and sister have established careers as actors and filmmakers in Spain. Bardem himself dabbled in acting as a child, first as a young boy in the television series "El Pícaro" ("The Scoundrel," 1974–75) and later as a teenager in other television roles. He played rugby for the Spanish amateur rugby team, participated in an independent theatrical troupe, and studied painting. Bardem has noted in interviews that he initially began working as a film actor to support his painting, a circumstance that is turned on its head in Woody Allen's *Vicky Cristina Barcelona* (2008), in which he paints as part of his work as a film actor.

As a handsome man of athletic build, Bardem's earliest film roles tended to play on his good looks and sexual appeal. He performed in a number of small film roles, but most notably became known to Spanish audiences in a trio of dark comedies directed by José Juan Bigas Luna that examined and poked fun at the machismo of Spanish men in various ways.

These included a small but showy role as a sexy working-class stud in *Jamón, jamón* (*Ham, Ham*, 1992) and his first starring role in *Huevos de oro* (*Golden Balls*, 1993), which he reprised in a cameo in the coming-of-age comedy *La Teta y la luna* (*Teté and the Moon*, 1994). In *Huevos de oro*, Bardem plays the central role of Benito González in the story of the rise and fall of an arrogantly confident and chauvinistic man who is extremely attractive to women and uses them to make his fortune. Notably, these roles and the Spanish context presented a distinctly unique *macho* in relation to the Spanish imagination quite distinct from Hollywood's images of Latin males.

Bardem chose not to take similar roles so that he might not be typecast. He broke out of the mold in a variety of Spanish films, including the fantasy thriller *El Detective y la muerte* (*Death and the Detective*, 1994); *Éxtasis* (*Ecstasy*, 1996), a dark drama in which he portrays a young grifter posing as a wealthy man's long-lost son; and the lighthearted sex comedy *Boca a boca* (*Mouth to Mouth*, 1995), in which he plays a struggling actor who takes on the job of telephone sex operator, only to find himself embroiled in a married couple's romantic troubles. Bardem was later seen by global art house audiences in Pedro Almodóvar's *Carne trémula* (*Live Flesh*, 1997), in which his character, a wheelchair basketball star (after an accidental shooting has left him paraplegic), is part of an emotionally wrought, complicated love triangle. Bardem also began to act in films with production connections outside Spain at this time. He appeared in perhaps his darkest role to date in *Perdita Durango* (1997), released in the United States as *Dance with the Devil*, a Spanish-Mexican co-production directed by Spanish horror and dark comedy director Álex de la Iglesia. In Roger Cormanesque farcical style, Bardem and Rosie Perez play Romeo Dolorosa and Perdita Durango, devil-worshipping psychotic criminals and lovers who travel from the United States to Mexico and kidnap a young American couple with the intention of sacrificing them. Reviewers typically had more to say about De la Iglesia's construction of what they considered a Quentin Tarantino–inspired Bonnie and Clyde than about Bardem's or Perez's acting. Bardem also appeared in *Los Lobos de Washington* (*The Washington Wolves*, 1999), a Canadian film, directed by Mariano Barroso and produced by Bardem, about two brothers who are struggling financially and decide to steal from an old friend.

Bardem's next role in a U.S. film was his clear breakthrough as a performer. He came to the attention of the Hollywood film community and global audiences in the demanding role of persecuted Cuban writer Reinaldo Arenas in Julian Schnabel's *Before Night Falls* (2000), based on Arenas's autobiography of the same name. It debuted at the Venice International Film Festival, with its North American debut at the Toronto Film

Javier Bardem (l.), as persecuted Cuban writer Reinaldo Arenas, with Johnny Depp in *Before Night Falls* (Julian Schnabel, El Mar Pictures, 2000). Courtesy Photofest New York.

Festival, both in 2000. While the film was not seen widely outside art cinema circles, Bardem received overwhelming popular and critical acclaim for his performance, including the Best Actor award at Venice, the Independent Spirit Award, and an Oscar nomination for Best Actor.

In lyrical and often visually arresting style, *Before Night Falls* relates the story of Arenas's life as a young man growing up in Cuba and his later years there and in the United States. A strong-willed man who became a writer of novels and poetry and who came to identify and live as a homosexual, he found himself persecuted and ultimately imprisoned by the Cuban government for his refusal to censor his writing with respect to his homosexuality and his criticism of government policy. After many years he took the chance of asylum in the United States, where he lived in New York City until the age of forty-seven, when he committed suicide while losing a battle with AIDS. Bardem brings Arenas to life in powerful fashion in the film, in a performance that was lauded as incredibly rich and subtle. Reviewers were almost universal in their high praise for the poetic direction and aesthetic style that Schnabel, a successful painter, brought to the film, and were particularly enthusiastic about Bardem's ability to present the passion with which Arenas, an openly gay novelist and poet in Castro's Cuba, made difficult choices and openly lived his life in a politically and socially repressive culture while still maintaining his dignity and masculinity. For instance, Rita Kempley described Bardem's performance as "extraordinary" and uniquely as "a tender, accessible depiction of the character as a gifted intellectual, cruelly punished for his passions, his heedlessness and his courage. Never once does the actor diminish the man with a swish, a lisp or a limp wrist" ("*Before Night Falls* Tells of Gay Writer's Struggle," *Washington Post*, 2 February 2001). Owen Glieberman noted how Bardem's performance possessed a grace and restrained intensity that was remarkable:

> Wearing a melancholy half smile as ambiguous as the Mona Lisa's, he carries himself with a mournful, catlike tentativeness that is rare to see in an actor with so much physical magnetism. Bardem's every action appears haunted, tragically downsized, and this gives the movie, which sprawls through Arenas' life as if it were a crystal of pristinely hallucinated memory, a unique psychological suspense: It invites us to focus not just on what Arenas shows us but on what he's concealing, and why.   (*Entertainment Weekly*, 5 January 2001)

While *Before Night Falls* performed only moderately at the box office, it was screened in many countries and received almost universally positive reviews in addition to earning multiple awards, including for Bardem's performance; the actor's career experienced an upswing as a result. He began to have more opportunities for starring roles in Hollywood films that could showcase his versatility, discipline, and talent as an actor. He went on to perform in a number of popular and critically lauded roles in American and Spanish films in the 2000s. In *The Dancer Upstairs* (2002), the directorial debut of actor John Malkovich, he portrayed a police detective in an unnamed Latin American country who is tracking a delusional revolutionary (a story inspired by the real-life capture in 1992 of revolutionary Abamiel Guzmán in Peru). Initially a solid family man, he gets sidetracked by a romantic entanglement with his daughter's ballet instructor. While critics typically waxed more about the film in relation to Malkovich's prior acting career than about Bardem's performance, the actor earned respectable reviews.

Bardem also earned universally positive reviews the same year for the lead role in the bittersweet Spanish comedy *Los Lunes al sol* (*Mondays in the Sun*, 2002), about a group of friends in a northern Spanish port city who are now unemployed shipworkers. Bardem stars as Santa, the rebellious leader of the group, which gathers daily at a friend's bar. The film went on to earn multiple Goyas, the Spanish equivalent of Oscars, for Best Film and other categories, while Bardem was awarded Best Lead Actor. The film premiered in the United States at the Sundance Film Festival and the Palm Springs Film Festival in 2003, where it was a strong audience favorite; according to Bardem, during screenings it had to be stopped several times because of audience applause.

Bardem also portrayed the historical Spanish figure Ramon Sampedro in *Mar adentro* (*The Sea Inside*, 2004), helmed by Spanish director Alejandro Amenábar. Bardem's performance as Sampedro, who became quadriplegic and fought a thirty-year campaign in favor of euthanasia and his own right to die while simultaneously inspiring those around him to live fuller lives, was viewed as tour-de-force. He followed this with a starring role in the historical drama *Goya's Ghosts* (2006), directed by Czech American director Milos Forman, set during the 1790s and the Spanish Inquisition. Shot in Spain, *Goya's Ghosts* was a joint U.S.-Spain co-production, but was performed in English. In the complicated storyline, Bardem portrays a Roman Catholic clergyman, Brother Lorenzo, who defends painter Francisco Goya when his muse, Inés, is arrested by the Church for heresy. The film was not well received by critics.

Notably, Bardem has thus far received the most visibility and highest critical recognition in the United States in his portrayal of Anton Chigurh, a sociopathic criminal for hire in *No Country for Old Men* (2007), adapted from Cormac McCarthy's novel of the same title and directed by Joel and Ethan Coen. The story is set along the U.S.-Mexico border and focuses on the consequences of one man's chance finding of a suitcase full of money related to the illegal drug trade and his choosing to keep it. The Coens created an atmospheric retelling of old western tales aimed to highlight issues of morality, fate, and the unpredictability and tenuousness of luck. Chigurh, hired to bring the money back with its temporary owner dead or alive, brings elements of the horror genre and gallows humor to the film as an unhinged individual who coldly tracks his prey throughout a long cat-and-mouse journey, idly killing individuals based on coin tosses along the way. Audiences and critics alike found his performance both convincing and chilling, and Bardem as Chigurh was often described as the heart of the film. Todd McCarthy praised Bardem's "diabolically effective performance" (*Variety*, 18 May 2007), while Richard Schickel noted that "caught in the movie's grip, you are simply hypnotized by the damned thing. Especially, I think, by Bardem. . . . Whenever Bardem appears, something nasty starts twisting in your gut. He's about as perfect a representation of unambiguous evil as the movies have lately offered" (*Time*, 9 November 2007). Unsurprisingly, the film's promotional poster also capitalized on the verisimilitude and passion of Bardem's performance through an outsized image of Chigurh against the background of the Texas landscape, a shadowy but ever-present reminder of the horror the character represents.

No Country for Old Men did well at the box office and received strong praise from critics; only a small percentage of reviewers were less than impressed. It was included among many critics' lists of the top films for 2007. It also dominated the Academy Awards the following year, winning top honors for Best Picture, Best Director, and Best Screenplay Adaptation, in addition to the Best Supporting Actor award earned by Bardem.

Bardem followed this performance with a very different role in *Love in the Time of Cholera* (2007), adapted from the popular novel by Colombian writer Gabriel García Márquez and directed by English director Mike Newell. In the film, set in Colombia from the 1880s through the 1930s (but performed in English), Bardem performs in the showy role of Florentino Arizia, a man who sets about trying to heal his heart, after being spurned by the woman he loves, through embarking on decades of purely carnal experiences. Fifty years later, he tries to court her again after learning that her husband has died. The film was not well received by critics or particularly popular with audiences in the United States. It cast no shadow on Bardem's career, however, given that *No Country for Old Men* swept the Oscars in February 2008, and Bardem's eloquent and ebullient dedication to his family and to the actors and country of Spain furthered his star image as both intelligent and sexy idol and family man.

In Bardem's most recent films he has repeatedly taken on a role that he might have avoided prior to the 2000s: that of the handsome and romantic lover, albeit with subtly nuanced shadings. He played Juan Antonio in *Vicky Cristina Barcelona*, a U.S.-Spanish co-production written and directed by Woody Allen. Juan Antonio, a charismatic and freewheeling but troubled artist, becomes romantically involved with two American women (Scarlett Johansson and Rebecca Hall) who are visiting Barcelona, while he is still enamored of his emotionally volatile and charismatic wife (Penelope Cruz). While American film critics for the most part found the film quite engaging, many naming it among the top films for 2008, it is arguably an American fantasy of Spanish life and people that moves only slightly from traditional stereotypes of *Latinidad*. Nevertheless, the film, shot on a low budget, performed respectably at the box office. Bardem was praised for his performance, as in a comment by *Entertainment Weekly* that his Juan Antonio "turns out to be the wittiest of leading men" (Owen Glieberman, 15 August 2008).

Bardem's status as a Hollywood film star was reinforced in his recent role as Julia Roberts's love interest in *Eat Pray Love* (2010). Here he plays a sensitive Brazilian divorcé who is the true love at the end of an American woman's sojourn through Italy, India, and Indonesia. While the film received mixed reviews, Bardem's performance was not panned. This film will likely be forgotten in Bardem's oeuvre in the wake of his performance in the crime drama *Biutiful* (2010), written and directed by Alejandro

González Iñárritu. In the film he plays the lead role of Uxmal, a flawed but well-meaning father in the slums of Barcelona who is involved in small-time criminal activities. At the film's premiere at Cannes, Bardem's acting received mostly lavish praise from international film critics, while the film itself has garnered mixed reviews.

Bardem's star promotion in North America has typically centered on his sexy looks, his urbanity, and his commitment to his craft as an actor. As he noted in an interview he gave for *Dancer Upstairs*, in comments that he has echoed with variation in the years since:

> Well, I just try to be honest in what I do, no matter what it is. If I'm an actor, I try to be honest as an actor. If I were a plumber, I'd try to be an honest plumber (laughing). . . . I believe the acting job is a way for people to watch themselves. It's some kind of a mirror where we can see the best and the worst of the human condition. That's my duty, to find that material and make it happen in front of an audience.
>
> ("Javier Bardem Talks about 'The Dancer Upstairs,'" www.about.com, 2003)

Bardem speaks little about his private life in interviews. In 2007 he reportedly started dating fellow Spaniard Penelope Cruz; they married in a private ceremony in the summer of 2010.

★★★★★ Del Toro and Bardem: Beyond Machismo

The success of Benicio Del Toro and Javier Bardem in Hollywood films of the 2000s, their casting in subtly shaded roles much unlike those they might have been offered in the 1980s or 1990s, and their rise to the status of bankable draws around which film projects can be developed is evidence of subtle but perceptible shifts in the U.S. film industry with respect to Latino actors and perceptions of how U.S. and global audiences will receive them. While the decision as to whether to shoot films in Spanish continues to be controversial for Hollywood film producers, Del Toro and Bardem have proven the lucrative potential of Latino stars and set the stage for new expectations as highly talented, versatile, and successful performers in roles that take them far beyond the stereotypical *machismo* expected in previous decades.

This is not to imply that casting and character development for Latino roles in Hollywood films is universally shifting, however. In this regard, it should be remembered that both Del Toro and Bardem appear to have sufficient ethnic ambiguity, with respect to their fair appearance, height, and ambiguously European rather than indigenous facial features, and that both have played characters of a variety of ethnicities, including Anglo/European as well as characters of indeterminate ethnicity. The ability of both stars to play white American and European characters in addition to Latino and Latin American characters no doubt has facilitated some of their opportunities in the Hollywood film industry and offers an important factor to consider regarding how their performances have pushed audience expectations of Latin *machismo* in film roles. Moreover, this is a dynamic that also applies to Spanish and Latin American cinema. As Hector Amaya has noted regarding constructions of masculinity in contemporary Mexican films, "racialized masculinities" typically play out in loosening notions of Latino masculinity in recent films: fair-skinned "white" men are afforded a greater flexibility in this regard, while men of darker hue still are required to perform traditional *machismo* in film roles.

Finally, notable in relation to the stardom of both Benicio Del Toro and Javier Bardem is the instrumental role of the auteur directors who provided them with acting challenges and cast them in breakout roles in the last decade. In the case of Del Toro, these directors in the 2000s included Steven Soderbergh, Alejandro González Iñárritu, and Bryan Singer; while in Javier Bardem's Hollywood film career, directors who have provided important opportunities include Julian Schnabel, Joel and Ethan Coen, and John Malkovich. The impact of the film roles these forward-thinking directors offered to Del Toro and Bardem underscores the continuing, powerful impact of the director in relation to contemporary stardom.

6 ☆☆☆☆☆☆☆☆☆☆☆

Philip Seymour Hoffman
Jesus of Uncool

JERRY MOSHER

"The only true currency in this bankrupt world is what you share with someone else when you're uncool," declares music critic Lester Bangs, played by Philip Seymour Hoffman, in *Almost Famous* (2000). I am, by Bangs's rather unforgiving standards, uncool. And if you're reading this, it's a good bet that you are, too. Critics, after all, are inclined to be spectators, perched on the sidelines of art and experience. When the opportunity to participate beckons, our thoughts tend to run wild with possibilities until the precarious moment of indecision has safely passed, so we can be left again to observe the feats of others—and to take solace at the movies, where time stands still. And perhaps that is why the screen persona of Philip Seymour Hoffman, ripe with intelligence and sensitivity, affects us so powerfully. Again and again, his socially awkward characters have made the hesitant leap into wisdom and experience that we would dare not endure. The results might be painful, disturbing, funny, enlightening, or sublime, but they are always electrifying.

Philip Seymour Hoffman.

In Hoffman's performances, looking and acting uncool has never seemed so—cool. Even the most loathsome of his personae manage to convey a sense of vulnerability and humanity, whether the film is a low-budget character study or a Hollywood blockbuster. Working constantly, Hoffman is a throwback to the physically distinctive character actors of classical Hollywood as well as a post-classical, independent star who takes only the roles that interest his peculiar sensibility, no matter their size, monetary reward, or potential audience. Lacking matinee-idol looks and any trace of vanity, the actor's astounding ability to subsume himself within a role and still remain recognizable makes his artistry seem largely *sui generis* and difficult to pin down. But it is certain that Hoffman takes great pains to reveal the worst in his characters, which he believes constitutes artistic truth: "I think deep down inside, people understand how flawed they are," the actor told David Edelstein. "I think the more benign you make somebody, the less truthful it is" ("Pervert, Vampire, Lout. Perfectly Nice Guy, Though," *New York Times*, 15 January 2006, 22). This warts-and-all approach to acting, however, can sometimes look like self-martyrdom when Hoffman's talent and sacrifice so outshine that of his colleagues. Indeed, Hoffman's need to strip his characters of any phony "movieness" can be so fiercely uncompromising that he appears at odds with the idea of movies themselves and why audiences enjoy them.

The stage-trained and self-effacing Hoffman would be the first to deny that he is a movie star, and his apparent lack of interest in box office returns or celebrity makes me inclined to agree with him. Yet Hoffman's classical ideals, work ethic, and eagerness to astonish also make me suspect that he is attempting to remind us what it means to be a great *actor* at a time when "stardom" is so cheaply conferred upon the hapless participants of reality shows and viral videos. What follow, then, are some thoughts about the conflicted film stardom of Philip Seymour Hoffman, whose screen roles in the 2000s have provided legions of the uncool with true currency to share in an increasingly bankrupt world.

★★★★★ The Scene Stealer

As the year 2000 began, it seemed Hoffman was everywhere, poised on the cusp of stardom. He had significant supporting roles in three films playing in U.S. theaters in 1999: Rusty the drag queen, who sings and spars with Robert De Niro's stroke-ridden NYPD officer in Joel Schumacher's *Flawless*; the preppy bully Freddy Miles, who taunts Matt Damon's duplicitous Tom Ripley in Anthony Minghella's *The Talented Mr. Ripley*; and the sensitive nurse Phil Parma, who cares for a dying Jason Robards in Paul Thomas

Anderson's *Magnolia*. Acclaim was immediate and came from some of the most esteemed members of his profession. "I remember seeing Philip in *The Talented Mr. Ripley*," Meryl Streep told Lynn Hirschberg. "I sat up straight in my seat and said, 'Who is that?' I thought to myself: My God, this actor is fearless. He's done what we all strive for—he's given this awful character the respect he deserves, and he's made him fascinating" ("A Higher Calling," *New York Times Magazine*, 21 December 2008, 45).

In these three films Hoffman not only held his own with veteran actors De Niro and Robards, but also showcased his ability to shape-shift from role to role. His physical appearance, speech, and countenance were so strikingly different in each film that it was hard to believe it was the same actor. "I don't know how he does it," said Mike Nichols, who has directed Hoffman on the stage (*The Seagull*, 2001) and in film (*Charlie Wilson's War*, 2007). "Again and again, he can truly become someone I've not seen before but can still instantly recognize. Sometimes Phil loses some weight, and he may dye his hair but, really, it's just the same Phil, and yet, he's never the same person from part to part" (Hirschberg 41). By the end of the 1990s, Hoffman's knack for leaving an indelible impression with a supporting role was becoming widely known; seeing the actor pop up in a film, one critic noted, was like "discovering a prize in a box of cereal, receiving a bonus, or bumping unexpectedly into an old friend" (David Kamp, "Have You Seen This Man?" *GQ*, January 2001).

Hoffman earned a BFA in drama from New York University's Tisch School of the Arts in 1989. After graduating and completing a stint in rehab for drug and alcohol addiction (he has remained sober), the actor landed a few bit parts before getting noticed as a spoiled prep schooler in Martin Brest's *Scent of a Woman* (1992). After working with Brest, who taught Hoffman to never treat acting as a job, the twenty-five-year-old actor resolved to avoid type-casting and not repeat himself; to work with only the best directors and actors possible, no matter how small the role; and to keep his career grounded in stage performance. A likely model was Streep, well known for her immersion in character, theater background, avoidance of celebrity, and attachment to the East Coast (Hoffman grew up in Fairport, New York). Soon, Hoffman was getting punched by Paul Newman in Robert Benton's *Nobody's Fool* (1994); rolling craps with Philip Baker Hall in P. T. Anderson's feature debut *Hard Eight* (aka *Sydney*, 1996); chasing tornadoes with Helen Hunt and Bill Paxton in Jan de Bont's *Twister* (1996); and incarnating a pudgy crew member who harbors a crush on a porn star in Anderson's *Boogie Nights* (1997).

The following year, Hoffman continued to plumb the depths of geek-dom as the officious, easily embarrassed assistant to multimillionaire Jeffrey

Lebowski in the Coen brothers' noir parody *The Big Lebowski* (1998), and as the pasty, sweating office worker who makes obscene phone calls in Todd Solondz's misanthropic comedy *Happiness* (1998). Both films have gained considerable cult followings since their release, and Hoffman's character in *Happiness* is now widely regarded as one of the most memorable perverts in screen history. In an embarrassingly raw performance, Hoffman simulates masturbation and ejaculation after making one of his obscene phone calls. The actor worried about the scene, but had no regrets. "I was pretty heavy, and I was afraid that people would laugh at me," he recalled. "Todd said they might laugh, but they won't laugh at you. He saw what we were working for, which was the pathos of the moment" (Hirschberg 45). The actor's degradation was so convincing, however, that some industry executives and critics began to question Hoffman's self-image and career motives. In Hollywood, one writer noted, Hoffman is "hot enough that everyone suddenly wants to party with him, even if they're not quite sure what to make of him" (Simon Dumenco, "Family Affair," *New York*, 9 December 2002, 44). In *The New Biographical Dictionary of Film* (2002), David Thomson wrote that Hoffman "is so good that only the best material is going to help build our sense of him," and worried that the actor has a "very dangerous talent at work—astounding, yet so pronounced it could help make its own prison" (404). Hoffman's ability to steal scenes was undeniable, but many wondered whether it would lift the actor to stardom or condemn him to a life of character parts.

★★★★★ At the Crossroads:
State and Main and *Almost Famous*

On the brink of film stardom as the 2000s began, Hoffman confounded industry expectations by returning to the stage: he co-starred with John C. Reilly in a revival of Sam Shepard's *True West* at the Circle in the Square Theatre in New York, completing 154 performances between March and July 2000. (The two co-stars received Tony nominations for Best Actor in the roles of Austin and Lee, which they alternated.) Hoffman appeared in only two films that year: David Mamet's lighthearted movie-industry satire, *State and Main*; and Cameron Crowe's autobiographical paean to seventies rock 'n' roll journalism, *Almost Famous*. Both were supporting roles and both involved playing writers, but the similarity ended there. The dichotomy between puppy-doggish Joseph Turner White and world-weary music critic Lester Bangs revealed Hoffman's interests, strengths, and career direction; the actor's uniqueness and intensity were better served in the latter role.

In *State and Main*, a Hollywood movie crew on location in New England descends upon a small Vermont town, mingling cynical industry types with the dazzled townsfolk. The eager playwright-turned-screenwriter White, however, is just as naive as the locals when it comes to the ways of location shooting and Hollywood deal-making. Ordered to do rewrites by a caustic producer (William H. Macy) and propositioned by the film's neurotic leading lady (Sarah Jessica Parker), White falls into the arms of a spunky local bookseller (Rebecca Pidgeon). For the role, which represented the closest Hoffman had come to playing a traditional romantic lead, the actor appeared thin and clean-cut and exhibited an appealingly boyish charm. Hoffman was undoubtedly eager to work with a major American playwright, but *State and Main*, regrettably, was "Mamet light"; despite its many stinging one-liners and fine ensemble acting, the amiable film often looked and sounded like a television sitcom. Hoffman proved himself capable of engaging in a wholesome screen romance, but the role was too one-dimensional to showcase the depth of his talent.

In *Almost Famous*, Hoffman's Lester Bangs, editor of the freewheeling music magazine *Creem*, mentors high-schooler and aspiring rock 'n' roll writer William Miller (Patrick Fugit), a stand-in for writer-director Cameron Crowe. Pontificating on the failure of rock 'n' roll to combat a corporate culture that thrives on mediocrity, the mercurial Bangs emerges as the film's conscience and center of gravity with just a handful of scenes. Sensing the star-struck teenager's eagerness to please the band he's writing about, Bangs offers this advice: "You wanna be a true friend to them? Be honest, and unmerciful." William will make a half-hearted attempt to follow his mentor's admonition, but this genial character, as written by Crowe and played by Fugit, is by nature too nice and too compliant to ever be unmerciful.

Almost Famous is admittedly a coming-of-age film, not a rock 'n' roll film. Its repeated insistence that rock 'n' roll writing should be "about the music," however, never acknowledges that the kind of reportage to which William aspires is merely another form of celebrity journalism, whereas Bangs's ideal of rock *criticism* (reviewing albums and concerts) is, in fact, truly focused on the music. William's failure to be critical is also Crowe's failure: they produce palatable, crowd-pleasing work because they simply want too much to be liked. "When Crowe has Bangs inform William that there's 'fuckin' nothin' about you that's controversial,'" noted critic David Edelstein, "it's like the filmmaker's (endearing) admission that his work will always be *Rolling Stone* and not Bangs' *Creem*. Where Bangs would compulsively rip the fabric of his own work, Crowe wants to make the fabric stronger. . . . *Almost Famous* could use some rips. Its smoothness makes it

Music critic Lester Bangs (Philip Seymour Hoffman) mentors his teenage protégé (Patrick Fugit) in *Almost Famous* (Cameron Crowe, Columbia/DreamWorks SKG, 2000). Courtesy Photofest New York.

feel smaller than it is" ("Sentimental Journey," *Slate*, 21 September 2000). Indeed, the curmudgeonly Bangs can proselytize about journalistic integrity because he's at home writing honest and unmerciful music criticism; he would rather be uncool than chase after rock stars in hotels and parking lots, groveling for a good quote. "*Almost Famous* is a movie that defuses its own bad conscience," noted *Village Voice* critic J. Hoberman. "As suggested by *Jerry Maguire* (1996), Crowe's specialty is the principled sellout." After being forced to swallow this sugar-coated valentine to classic rock's hedonism, many critics agreed with Hoberman's assessment: "Hoffman and his character should have been the movie" ("Generational Tastes," *Village Voice*, 19 September 2000, 115).

In *Almost Famous* Hoffman revealed a newfound maturity that channeled Bangs's authority, conviction, and complexity. The task of playing not just a character but a historical person and hence "a body too much" seemed to rein in some of Hoffman's uglier physical instincts. (The actor's corporeal restraint playing a real person would become even more focused when he uncannily portrayed writer Truman Capote several years later.) "When you're playing someone who really lived, you carry a burden, a burden to be accurate," Hoffman said. But after establishing historical authenticity, he noted, "It's [a burden] that you have to let go of ultimately"

(Megan O'Rourke, *Slate*, 31 January 2006). Notoriously self-destructive, the real Bangs died of a drug overdose at age thirty-three, but Hoffman, undoubtedly motivated by writer-director Crowe's hopeful worldview, instead portrayed the lucid, articulate Bangs who had written so beautifully about Van Morrison's *Astral Weeks* (1968). "When I read that [essay] I knew that this was a guy I could key into," Hoffman said. "I saw him as kind of lonely" (Walter Chaw, "Love Notes," *Film Freak Central*, 2 March 2003).

After the lonely critic advises the young journalist to avoid befriending the hipster rock stars he writes about ("friendship is the booze they feed you"), Bangs delivers a sermon on art and life that could very well have served as a manifesto for Hoffman and the many conflicted, socially awkward characters he has chosen to play: "We are uncool. Women will always be a problem for guys like us. Most of the great art in the world is about that very problem. Good-looking people, they got no spine. Their art never lasts. They get the girls—but we're smarter. Great art is about conflict and pain and guilt and longing and love disguised as sex, and sex disguised as love." As the decade progressed, Hoffman's acting interests would indeed gravitate toward the pursuit of great art and the portrayal of "conflict and pain and guilt and longing" that his character in *Almost Famous* so eloquently elaborated. After *State and Main*, the actor would not play such a clean-cut, romantic character again during the decade of the 2000s. Hoffman had amply demonstrated his ability to steal scenes with a quirky supporting role, but whether this heavy-set, self-effacing character actor could carry a movie—and attract a mass audience—remained an open question.

☆☆☆☆☆ Leading Roles: *Love Liza* and *Owning Mahowny*

"Even if I was hired into a leading-man part, I'd probably turn it into the non-leading-man part," Hoffman told Jasper Rees ("A Real Actor's Director," *Daily Telegraph*, 20 March 2002, B1). Indeed, when the actor finally agreed to play lead roles, his starring projects—Todd Louiso's independently produced *Love Liza* (2002) and Richard Kwietniowski's *Owning Mahowny* (2003)—only confirmed industry fears about Hoffman's oddball, uncommercial instincts. In *Love Liza*, written by Hoffman's brother Gordy, the actor plays Wilson, a widowed web site designer who cannot bear to read the suicide note left by his recently deceased wife and thus begins huffing gasoline to numb his pain. Avoiding his concerned mother-in-law (Kathy Bates) and co-workers, Wilson frequents gas stations, often blacks out, and, in pursuit of higher octane fuel, inadvertently falls in with a group of model-airplane enthusiasts who begrudgingly tolerate his erratic behavior.

Critics appreciated the film's hypnotic, minimalist depiction of bereavement, but most found *Love Liza* too deliberately aimless and quirky—familiar indie-film strategies that had quickly become clichés. "What should have been a twenty-minute short," noted *Village Voice* critic Michael Atkinson, "is distended by repetition and loads of standard indie-film time-killers . . . always returning to the spectacle of Hoffman huffing gasoline, an activity even he can't make interesting" ("The Mourning After," 1 January 2003, 89). The absence of any backstory or climactic revelation reduces Hoffman's character to a cipher; in spite of the actor's gut-wrenchingly poignant performance, Wilson remains as ethereal as the fumes he pursues. *New York Times* film critic A. O. Scott applauded Hoffman's ascension to leading roles but noted that the actor's "omnipresence is something of a mixed blessing," largely due to the fact that the film's protagonist is "more a state of feeling than a character" ("A Prisoner of Grief Binges on a Deadly Diet of Sympathy," 30 December 2002, E1). *Variety* critic Todd McCarthy suggested that Sony Classics market *Love Liza* "as Hoffman's decisive transition from much-admired supporting character actor to heavyweight topliner," but Hoffman's new status was not enough to attract audiences to such a meandering, downbeat film (22 January 2002). After a very limited release, *Love Liza* quickly disappeared, grossing a mere $210,000.

Owning Mahowny, another story of addiction that premiered a year later at Sundance, recounts the true story of a Toronto bank employee who embezzled ten million dollars to feed his gambling habit in Atlantic City. Sweating and twitching in his nerdy glasses and cheap suits, Hoffman looks very much like the heavy breather in *Happiness* as he single-mindedly indulges his gambling obsession to the exclusion of his dowdy fiancée (Minnie Driver) and everything else—he even turns down the free liquor, food, and hookers offered to high rollers at the casino. Like *Love Liza*, *Owning Mahowny* provides little glimpse into the mind of its central character, turning Mahowny into an automaton who joylessly plays the tables under the numbing glare of fluorescent lights until his ruse collapses.

"Can this repressed, depressed, adenoidal schlub hold the movie?" asked J. Hoberman. Despite Hoffman's "relentlessly self-effacing performance," the answer was negative ("Risk Management," *Village Voice*, 30 April 2003, 125). Some critics, paradoxically, tended to praise the actor's steadfast refusal to be a "movie character" while noting that the movie suffered as a result. "This is a case of an actor making the perfect choice for a character and following through to the letter, only to end up with exactly the effect he wanted: a character who squirms right out of our grasp," noted critic Stephanie Zacharek. "He's the movie's anchor, but he's such a vaporous one, he leaves *us* feeling adrift" (www.salon.com, 2 May 2003). David Edelstein concurred: "Total immersion can have its downside. You could argue that it's a mark of Mr. Hoffman's integrity that he does nothing to leaven his characters' obsessions. But this can also result in monotony—in a lack of drama" ("Pervert" 22). While some critics noted that the film made trenchant comparisons between the predatory business strategies of casinos and banks, most wondered why such an unpleasant and unengaging film—which cost $10 million and grossed only $1 million—had even been made. And again, many critics questioned Hoffman's choice of roles.

When asked in interviews why he tends to play such strange and unpleasant characters, Hoffman has consistently stated that life is far stranger than anything on the screen or stage. Living near the World Trade Center when it was destroyed on 11 September 2001, however, certainly darkened his worldview. "We learnt something that day that a lot of people on the planet already knew," Hoffman said. "It was shattering. It screwed me up good. Saying that, I feel that whatever you think up is going to be no weirder than what's actually happening. . . . Whatever image you have of a normal human being doesn't exist'" (Brian Viner, "Further Tales of Hoffman," *Independent*, 15 May 2002, 17).

In the wake of 9/11 and the commercial failures of *Love Liza* and *Owning Mahowny*, Hoffman spent more time on the stage, where he still seems most comfortable with himself. He became increasingly involved in the artistic direction of the New York–based LAByrinth Theater Company, a multicultural collective that produces an average of five American plays each year, and in 2003 he appeared on Broadway with Vanessa Redgrave and Brian Dennehy in 127 performances of Eugene O'Neill's *Long Day's Journey into Night*, an experience Hoffman still considers the most demanding acting role of his career (he received another Tony nomination). That year, the actor also fathered the first of his three children with his girlfriend, costume designer Mimi O'Donnell. Although Hoffman's film work during this period was limited to small supporting roles that could be worked into his busy schedule, they nevertheless revealed his continued interest in performing acts of discomforting self-revelation.

★★★★★ The Rules of Attraction

"Philip Seymour Hoffman Is Irresistible," declared the headline on the January 2001 cover of men's lifestyle magazine *GQ*, which featured a slim, dapper Hoffman perched on a stool in a designer suit. Since his romantic role in *State and Main*, however, it seemed like the actor had gone out of his way to make himself unappealing in the movies. In addition to playing the self-destructive main characters in *Love Liza* and *Owning Mahowny*, between 2002 and 2004 Hoffman appeared in a handful of supporting roles that showcased his characters' unattractiveness and physical anxiety: an arrogant tabloid reporter who is stripped to his underwear and tortured by the titular serial killer (Ralph Fiennes) in *Red Dragon* (2002); a foul-mouthed phone-sex entrepreneur who blackmails a client (Adam Sandler) in *Punch-Drunk Love* (2002); a frumpy, withdrawn high-school teacher who is frightened by his desire for a female student (Anna Paquin) in *25th Hour* (2002); a fornicating southern preacher who complains about his constipation in the Civil War drama *Cold Mountain* (2003); and a buffoonish former child actor who craps in his pants ("I sharted") at a party in the romantic comedy *Along Came Polly* (2004).

In these roles Hoffman repeatedly demonstrated his ability to mold his doughy physique into distinctive characterizations, deftly maneuvering his girth so it floats him when he's happy and sinks him when he's sad. But it was also becoming apparent that the corporeal anxiety exhibited by so many of Hoffman's characters likely originated with the actor himself. He had been an athlete in high school until a wrestling injury forced him to give up sports and take to the stage, and as he grew older Hoffman's proclivity for playing social misfits appeared to manifest in his increasingly puffy face, expanding waistline, and hangdog posture.

"I'm grateful for the way I look," Hoffman has said. "I'm grateful for the fact that I have a body with which I can do what I need to do and I can come off as—anybody" (Hirschberg 44). Film industry casting practices are rarely so flexible, however. Hoffman possessed a body that could be molded into many social types, but in terms of casting it was also an "in-between" physique that was neither particularly fat nor thin. Hollywood history is littered with tales of gifted actors, especially as they softened in middle age, who found themselves in this corporeal no man's land, obliged to either reduce or gain weight to obtain roles. Some, like Laird Cregar and Mario Lanza, attempted to slim down in order to play romantic leads and literally killed themselves with extreme dieting regimens and surgery; others, like Edward Arnold and Eugene Pallette, bulked up and accentuated their physical eccentricities to obtain steady work in character roles. Hoffman had shown little interest in playing heroes or romantic leads, and as he approached middle age (he turned forty in 2007), he appeared less willing or able to maintain the traditional good looks required to play such roles. It is thus not surprising that he took the latter route and began to focus exclusively on playing eccentric characters.

Such a choice would have relegated the actor to a lifetime of support-ing roles and bit parts if he had worked in the classical Hollywood era—not that Hoffman would have minded. But the post-classical rise of American independent cinema enabled Hoffman to land leading roles in intimate, lower-budget character studies like *Love Liza* and *Owning Mahowny* while still earning a decent paycheck for supporting parts in studio genre fare like *Red Dragon* and *Along Came Polly*. His next leading role, playing flamboyant writer Truman Capote in *Capote* (2005), would benefit from the best of both worlds: an independent sensibility and the infusion of $7 million from a major studio (United Artists) with modest commercial expectations and the ability to widely promote the film. Hoffman's performance would bring him an Academy Award for Best Actor, and all of the acclaim and expectations that come with it.

★★★★★ *Capote:* Transcending Mimicry

When *Capote* premiered at the New York Film Festival in September 2005, critics agreed that Hoffman had finally found the perfect leading role to display his substantial talent—so perfect, in fact, that it prompted suspicion that the film and Hoffman's performance were too carefully groomed for awards consideration. "Hoffman controls every ges-ture down to the nerve ending, and they all signal 'nominate me,'" wrote critic Nathan Lee ("A Portrait of the Artist as a Monster," *New York Sun*, 30 September 2005). Even praise for the actor's performance was occasionally laced with sarcasm, as evidenced in this observation by David Edelstein: "Watching Philip Seymour Hoffman (big head, big body, big deep voice) embody Truman Capote (small head, small body, bizarre baby voice) in *Capote*, you want to throw every acting award there is at him and maybe a couple of Olympic medals, too. What concentration! What shape shifting!" ("Pervert" 5). Hoffman had finally delivered the commanding lead per-formance everyone knew he was capable of; that performance was now being ridiculed, it seemed, merely for its inevitability.

Capote's release in the fall premiere season—that three-month window from mid-September to Christmas when the majority of "serious" American films are now released in anticipation of awards consideration—also con-tributed to the critical cynicism regarding Hoffman's performance. Playing famous but troubled artists, like playing alcoholics, addicts, and disabled characters, had become a proven strategy for ambitious actors seeking respect from the film industry; radical physical transformation, such as gaining or losing weight, only improved one's chances for recognition.

However, Academy Awards given earlier that year to Jamie Foxx as singer Ray Charles in *Ray* (2004) and Cate Blanchett as actress Katharine Hepburn in *The Aviator* (2004) had fueled complaints that Academy voters were too often rewarding mimicry rather than acting. "No one has bothered to question how much these entertainments rely on the cheap high you get when famous people imitate other famous people," noted Nathan Lee. "Isn't Jamie Foxx the real subject of *Ray*? And how interesting, really, is Jamie Foxx?" ("Portrait"). Critics' skepticism regarding celebrity impersonation only heightened that fall when, in addition to Hoffman playing Capote, David Strathairn appeared as broadcaster Edward R. Murrow in *Good Night, and Good Luck* (2005) and Joaquin Phoenix and Reese Witherspoon played Johnny Cash and June Carter Cash in *Walk the Line* (2005). Like Hoffman, all three would be nominated for Academy Awards.

Much of the cynicism regarding *Capote* abated after critics reflected on the film's avoidance of biopic clichés and its meticulous portrayal of a writer's conflicted motives during the creative process. Even skeptic Nathan Lee was "surprised to discover, if not quite a revisionist example of the genre, an unusually tough-minded movie whose hard, sharp pleasures are incidental to historical fact or thespian showboating" ("Portrait"). Rather than spanning the birth-to-death cycle of a famous person, *Capote* narrowly focused on a troubling and transcendent period in the writer's life: the years 1959–1965, when Capote researched and wrote his "nonfiction novel," *In Cold Blood*. The best-selling book and Richard Brooks's riveting 1967 film adaptation had made the November 1959 murders of the Clutter family in Holcomb, Kansas, widely known, but *Capote* side-stepped the problem of overfamiliarity by focusing on the writer's symbiotic relationship with the killers, which eventually turns parasitic. Despite the compassion and desire the author feels for convicted killer Perry Smith (Clifton Collins Jr.), Capote cannot help but view the condemned man as a literary gold mine. Capote's friend since childhood, writer Harper Lee (Catherine Keener), helps the eccentric author ingratiate himself with the Holcomb locals, but even the good-natured Lee will be viewed with suspicion and jealousy after she attains success with her novel *To Kill a Mockingbird* (1960). Capote finally becomes increasingly alcoholic as he waits for the killers' execution, ignoring their pleas for financial and legal help so he can have an ending for his book.

Recognizing that Capote's literary significance had long been eclipsed by his fame as a queer cultural icon, Dan Futterman's screenplay minimized the author's oft-caricatured flamboyance and instead focused on the writing *process*, and how an author's celebrity both helps and hinders it. "There have been many films about writers writing, and generally they resort to a kind of

Philip Seymour Hoffman as writer Truman Capote in *Capote* (Bennett Miller, A-Line Pictures, 2005). Courtesy Photofest New York.

clichéd visual shorthand to convey the agonies of what people like to call the creative process: pieces of paper being yanked in frustration out of typewriters, crumpled, and tossed into wastebaskets," noted Daniel Mendelsohn in the *New York Review of Books*. "*Capote* is the only movie I know of that comes close to suggesting successfully what the complex process of creating a literary work actually looks like" ("The Truman Show," 17 November 2005, 22–24).

In *Capote*, Hoffman displayed enough of the author's well-known physical and vocal mannerisms to convey authenticity without resorting to caricature. More important, he created a complex *character* who behaves in believable and subtle ways within the cinematic portrait of a writer's process. To play the diminutive author (who stood five foot three), the five-foot-ten-inch Hoffman lost a considerable amount of weight and prepared for more than four months by watching videotapes of the author's many television appearances. In interviews the actor likened his preparation to daily training at the gym, pushing his body and voice into new territories of discomfort. During production, "because I was holding my body in a way it doesn't want to be held and because I was speaking in a voice that my vocal cords did not want to do, I had to stay in character all day," Hoffman said. "Otherwise, I would give my body the chance to bail on me" (Hirschberg 45).

Beyond these technical considerations, for Hoffman the key to unlocking the character was the recognition of Capote as a performer, made abundantly clear in the screenplay by Futterman (who is an actor with numerous screen credits). Many writers can get by with words and imagination, but in his pursuit of a "nonfiction novel" Capote the journalist must continually confront his real-life characters—who are total strangers—and charm and manipulate them to gain access and insight. Hoffman thus portrays a multifaceted *performer* who is at times childish, ambitious, sentimental, entertaining, and ultimately ruthless in his pursuit of literary success.

Despite the screenplay's unflattering portrait of Capote as journalistic predator, Hoffman (who co-produced the film) reportedly fought with director Bennett Miller in the editing room to make his character even more unattractive. "You could easily cut that film and not show him in as harsh a light," Hoffman told David Edelstein. "The harder you are, the more empathy you'll gain, ultimately, by the end . . . you will definitely understand why he would be in the emotional distress he was in, if you really, actually see him act in ways that are reprehensible" ("Pervert" 22).

Miller might have feared that appalling revelations about Capote would appear excessive in such an austere film, but the actor's instincts were proven right when another Capote film chronicling the same events was released the following year. *Infamous* (2006), starring the impish British actor Toby Jones as Capote, offered a wilder and gayer portrait of the writer's life in New York City and Kansas; despite the film's unevenness, some critics noted approvingly that it took more chances than Futterman and Miller's relatively clinical approach. In hindsight, Hoffman's insistence on presenting such an unbecoming portrayal of Capote lent his film some indie credibility, sparing it from further accusations of pandering to awards voters. (*Capote*, produced at a cost of $7 million, eventually earned $29 million after getting a boost from Hoffman's Academy Award; *Infamous*, which cost $13 million, barely cleared $1 million.)

After *Capote*, it was clear that Hoffman viewed physical sacrifice and degrading self-exposure as the most authentic ways for an actor to achieve dramatic truth—they separated "the great actors from the journeymen" ("Pervert" 22). Like Charles Laughton in *The Hunchback of Notre Dame* (1939) and Robert De Niro in *Raging Bull* (1980), Hoffman had demonstrated a deep need to endure physical pain and humiliation onscreen. And, like Laughton and De Niro, Hoffman was now being anointed by some critics as the greatest actor of his generation (see Andrew Sarris, "Head Case," *New York Observer*, 28 October 2008; and "David Thomson's Biographical Dictionary of Film #57," *Guardian*, 30 January 2009). Laughton and De Niro, however, could not sustain their breathtaking level of artistic commitment; later in their careers they would be accused of coasting through roles. Hoffman now faced the dilemma of how to follow up on the most demanding and rewarding role of his film career.

★★★★★ Greater Than the Sum of His Parts

In Sidney Lumet's violent family melodrama *Before the Devil Knows You're Dead* (2007), Hoffman plays Andy Hanson, a real estate accountant embezzling funds from his firm to feed his high-end drug habit. In the course of several days he will learn that his mother is dead (killed in a botched robbery of the family's jewelry store, which Andy organized) and that his wife is cheating on him (sleeping with his younger brother, whom Andy recruited for the robbery). As he gets high in a luxury shooting gallery overlooking Manhattan, Andy reflects on his situation and wearily complains to his dealer about the disconnectedness of his life: "All my parts don't add up."

It is a powerful performance, one of several that Hoffman delivered in the years following *Capote*. His Academy Award brought him larger roles in projects with more substantial budgets and more accomplished directors and actors. Hoffman was widely seen and widely praised, and he received two Academy Award nominations for Best Supporting Actor (for *Charlie Wilson's War* and *Doubt*). Yet there remained an uneasy feeling among critics and audiences that these parts, as strong as they were, did not add up; Hoffman's potential had not been fully realized.

Always one to confound expectations, Hoffman had followed *Capote* with a supporting role in *Mission Impossible 3* (2006), a Tom Cruise franchise film with a budget of $150 million. Hoffman could have been accused of cashing in and slumming his way through a summer blockbuster, but he infused his villainous character, international arms dealer Owen Davian, with a sinister gravitas. Like Jeremy Irons in *Die Hard: With a Vengeance* (1995), Hoffman brought an Academy Award and years of stage training to a big-budget action picture; the actor's cultural capital served to make his character appear even more cunning. In return, the film exposed Hoffman to millions of viewers: its domestic box office of $133 million would be more than the combined total of the remainder of Hoffman's films in the decade.

More than a year passed before Hoffman appeared onscreen again, in three films released in fall 2007: top-billed in *Before the Devil Knows You're Dead*; starring opposite Laura Linney in Tamara Jenkins's dark comedy *The Savages*; and supporting Tom Hanks and Julia Roberts in Mike Nichols's satirical political drama *Charlie Wilson's War*. All three films were well written and acted, and all three were praised by critics, but only *Charlie Wilson's*

War managed to earn substantial box office returns ($67 million), largely due to the marquee value of Hanks and Roberts. With a crackling screenplay by "The West Wing" creator Aaron Sorkin, the film chronicles real-life Texas congressman Charlie Wilson's struggle to covertly fund Afghanistan's resistance to Soviet occupation in the early 1980s. Enlisting the help of a Texas millionaire (Roberts) and a streetwise CIA operative (Hoffman), Wilson's wheeling and dealing brings defeat to the Soviets in Afghanistan, leading to the eventual break-up of the Soviet Union. Hanks and Roberts, who in middle age have seemed increasingly limited by their need to be revered, play against type by being a little naughty as the partying playboy congressman and the flirtatious socialite. Hoffman, as trash-talking, bushy-haired CIA agent Gust Avrakotos, runs circles around them, walking away with the picture and an Academy Award nomination. The film "starts firing on all cylinders once Hoffman shows up," noted *Variety* critic Todd McCarthy. "Whenever he's on, the picture vibrates with conspiratorial electricity" (29 November 2007).

The Savages was set in more familiar territory: Hoffman is modern theater professor Jon Savage, who is writing a book on Bertolt Brecht and teaching at a university in Buffalo; Laura Linney plays his floundering sister, Wendy, who writes plays and applies for grants while working office temp jobs in New York City. Single and still very much unsettled as they lurch into middle age, these highly educated adults who are so knowledgeable about modern drama will be reduced to ineffectual children when confronted by the real thing: news that their estranged father (Philip Bosco), suffering from dementia, can no longer live in a retirement community in Arizona and must be transferred to an East Coast nursing home. The darkly comic and poignant film, which takes an unsentimental look at the aging of America and middle-aged children's inability to care for their parents, provided an acting showcase for Hoffman, Linney, and Bosco. Despite strong reviews and Academy Award nominations for Linney (Best Actress) and Tamara Jenkins (Best Screenplay), the film grossed just $7 million in limited release.

Before the Devil Knows You're Dead was widely hailed as Sidney Lumet's return to greatness, and the film's devastating portrayal of a middle-class New York family destroyed by treachery and greed prompted many critics to deem it an American tragedy of O'Neillean proportions. Lumet's efficient visual style mitigated some of the showiness in Kelly Masterson's fractured narrative, allowing the film's fine ensemble cast (which included Albert Finney, Ethan Hawke, and Marisa Tomei) to shine. Hoffman's pudgy, well-groomed accountant, the eldest son whose robbery scheme plunges the family into a downward spiral, is a bully and a liar who shows little remorse for his crimes. Yet Andy's emotional breakdown after being derided by his grieving father (Finney) reveals a wounded child who never received the parental attention lavished upon his cuter, younger brother (Hawke).

Fraught with fraternal tension, the scenes between the slow-burning Hoffman and the anxious, twitching Hawke revealed Hoffman's vast experience in appearing uncool onscreen. "The problem with actors who think they're way cool," David Edelstein noted of Hawke, "is that they think they have to work really, really hard to look uncool. Wrong." Hoffman, conversely, "knows how to modulate his eruptions—he only lets go when it counts" ("'Devil' Worship," *New York*, 18 October 2007). The actor did indeed let it all hang out in the film's opening shot, which features a naked Andy banging his wife (Tomei) from behind in a Rio de Janeiro hotel room. Their naked passion has a point, for it is the only time during the film that this husband and wife will appear to enjoy each other's company. Most actors with anything less than a well-toned physique would have avoided doing the scene, but Hoffman's fearlessness again revealed the humanity within a deeply flawed character. Andy, whose simmering rage will finally burst into paroxysms of violence, "is a cold, shallow, angry man, one of the least likable guys Mr. Hoffman, a specialist in acutely observed male unpleasantness, has ever played," noted A. O. Scott. "And yet, while never for a moment soliciting our empathy, Mr. Hoffman makes us care about this man" ("Robbing a Mom and Pop Store, Too Close to Home" *New York Times*, 26 October 2007, E1). Produced at a cost of $18 million, Lumet's lauded comeback film inexplicably reached only a few hundred screens, grossing a disappointing $7 million.

A year later, Hoffman appeared in a role that seemed made for him: the thoughtful and articulate Father Flynn, parish priest at a Bronx Catholic school in 1964, who is accused of child molestation in John Patrick Shanley's *Doubt* (2008). Shanley's Tony Award–winning play (2005) had featured Brían F. O'Byrne and Cherry Jones in the lead roles, but the screen adaptation was eagerly anticipated for its pairing of Hoffman and his idol Meryl Streep, who plays Father Flynn's wicked accuser, Sister Aloysius. "What do you do when you're not sure?" asks Father Flynn during a sermon in the film's first scene. It appears that Flynn might be tipping his hand, but the evidence against him will never amount to more than insinuation and coincidence, leaving the audience to wonder whether Sister Aloysius's actions constitute duty or treachery.

The chance to play a priest accused of molestation would seem like the perfect opportunity for Hoffman—who was raised a Catholic—to indulge in self-flagellation and affirm his reputation as the Jesus of uncool. The film's dramatic tension and examination of faith, however, are dependent on the ambiguity of Father Flynn's actions, which required the actor to remain tightly controlled. Critics noted that Hoffman invested the priest with a magisterial elegance that had rarely been seen from the actor. "It's refreshing to see him carrying himself with the confidence of a dancer," observed Stephanie Zacharek, "instead of playing yet another schleppy loser (the kind of character he's too often been saddled with of late)" (www.salon .com, 12 December 2008). It was Streep, ironically, who was critically lambasted for delivering an over-the-top performance. Her tyrannical Sister Aloysius was widely panned as a stock character embodying every cliché about Catholic school discipline. The nun's rigidity even extends to the song "Frosty the Snowman," which "espouses a pagan belief in magic and should be banned from the airwaves." Nevertheless, Streep was nominated for an Academy Award for Best Actress, and Hoffman, Amy Adams, and Viola Davis received nominations for supporting roles. The film, which cost $25 million, grossed a respectable $33 million.

In his final major role of the 2000s, Hoffman played the neurotic playwright Caden Cotard in writer-director Charlie Kaufman's ambitious *Synecdoche, New York* (2008). Chronicling Cotard's struggles to stage a play based on his own life as he is living it (hence its function as a synecdoche, a figure of speech by which a part is put for the whole), the film might also represent Cotard's life as he *imagines* it during the instant his alarm clock awakens him on the first day of fall. Encompassing the issues of time, memory, the representation of reality, and our anticipation of death, Kaufman's dense screenplay is packed with puns and allusions, referencing everything from Schenectady, New York (the filmmaker's home town), to Marcel Proust's *In Search of Lost Time* (1927) to Cotard's Syndrome (a delusional belief that one is dead or decaying).

Known for his distinctive, mind-bending screenplays, Kaufman was one of the few writers in Hollywood to achieve auteur status. In *Synecdoche, New York*, Kaufman the acclaimed "genius" screenwriter was again trying to top himself, but this time there was no one but Kaufman the inexperienced director standing in his way. The result was a wildly ambitious work that felt, oddly enough, like both a debut and a valedictory statement, not unlike Orson Welles's *Citizen Kane* (1941). Kaufman's undisciplined direction, however, too often sacrificed entertainment for postmodern posturing. Although Hoffman appeared in nearly every scene, he and the other actors were straitjacketed by their function as placeholders in Kaufman's philosophical schemata, and were rarely allowed to act like human beings. The

Aging playwright Caden Cotard (Hoffman) and his aging assistant Hazel (Samantha Morton) in *Synecdoche, New York* (Charlie Kaufman, Likely Story, 2008). Courtesy Photofest New York.

film's much-welcomed ambition and originality were enough for Roger Ebert to rank it the best of the decade and Manohla Dargis to rank it the best of the year, but most critics, while respectful, remained wary (*Roger Ebert's Journal*, 30 December 2009; "Dreamer, Live in the Here and Now," *New York Times*, 24 October 2008, C1).

Synecdoche, New York represented both the best and the worst of Hoffman's artistic instincts. On the one hand, the film showcased the actor's intelligence and courage as he endured the mental strain of relentless introspection and the physical demands of exhibiting his body in a continual state of decay. On the other hand, it encouraged the actor's penchant for ugly self-revelation by exhibiting his character's hypochondria and medical problems in excruciating detail. Kaufman's introspective screenplays had already reduced vigorous male stars like Nicolas Cage and Jim Carrey to pathetic schlubs, and the chronically miserable Hoffman certainly didn't need any prompting in that regard. It was feared that Kaufman, after writing himself into his self-reflexive script for *Adaptation* (2002), had nowhere left to go but up his own ass; sure enough, in *Synecdoche, New York*, Hoffman as the writer's stand-in examines his own feces, and his wife (Catherine Keener) will inspect their child's excrement for good measure. "There has long been a strain of sorry lassitude in Kaufman's work, and here it sickens into the morbid," noted critic Anthony Lane. "Although Philip Seymour Hoffman appears in almost every scene, he is seldom given the chance to shrug off his blue mood and demonstrate the dazzling range of which he is capable" ("Let's Put On a Show," *New Yorker*, 3 November 2008, 122).

The full extent of Hoffman's range and capability, regrettably, remained untested at the end of the decade. The actor had impressively played several challenging roles, but he had not delivered another commanding performance on the level of *Capote*. In a 2009 reassessment of Hoffman's career, David Thomson, perhaps the actor's biggest admirer and harshest critic, noted that Hoffman "has not been able to settle in his own mind the question of whether he is meant to be a spectacular, ever-changing support, or a real actor who can take over the emotional center of a movie and dominate it (in the way that Sean Penn dominates *Mystic River* or *Milk*) ("Biographical Dictionary #57"). Hoffman's good nature, leadership of a theater company, and reputation as a team player too often resulted in his willingness to share the spotlight with his colleagues and encourage ensemble performance. It is a practice that makes an "actor's actor," but it does not make a star. As director Joel Schumacher noted, "The bad news is that Philip won't be a $25-million star. The good news is that he'll work for the rest of his life" (Ed Potton, "Scene Stealer," *Times*, 25 November 2000, Play 9).

Disappointment with Hoffman's performances, of course, reveals how demanding we've become as viewers of his exceptional work. So far, the actor's need to stay close to New York City has limited his work to an exclusively American context, in Hollywood genre films and independent art cinema. Perhaps, when his children are older and he is not responsible for a theater company, the actor could find more commanding roles with auteur directors in Europe, Asia, or South America. Still, Hoffman remains one of the most intelligent actors in the American cinema, and the actor has shown no signs of easing up from his self-punishing level of physical sacrifice. "I don't know why I make it so complicated," says his character Caden Cotard in *Synecdoche, New York*. To which his wife responds, "That's what you do."

7 ✩✩✩✩✩✩✩✩✩✩✩

A Postfeminist Primer

Maggie Gyllenhaal, Hilary Swank, and Renée Zellweger

CORINN COLUMPAR

The 2000s were good to Maggie Gyllenhaal, Hilary Swank, and Renée Zellweger. Three of the most active and acclaimed actresses of their generation, they worked continually over the course of the decade, and, in turn, each was richly rewarded for her efforts, be it with largely laudatory reviews, copious attention, or at least one (Gyllenhaal) and as many as three (Zellweger) Academy Award nominations. Moreover, each of the three either attained or consolidated her status as "star" in this same period, even while keeping one foot (or more, in the case of Gyllenhaal) planted in the world of independent cinema, which tends to produce "picture personalities" instead (see de Cordova; Negra "Queen"). As a result, not only their work but also

Maggie Gyllenhaal, Hilary Swank, and Renée Zellweger.

their lives offscreen and in private generated buzz, speculation, and commentary that informed their public personae. While Zellweger's celebrity had already been secured by the start of the decade due to a break-out performance in *Jerry Maguire* (1996), it only intensified as the decade wore on and she honed her skills as a comedienne. Meanwhile, definitive proof of Swank's and Gyllenhaal's arrival among the ranks of A-list actresses came with their inclusion on the cover of the 2004 Hollywood issue of *Vanity Fair*. After that they both rose considerably in profile due to events both professional and personal, and in so doing attained a level of visibility equal to, if not greater than, some of the Hollywood-issue veterans, such as Gwyneth Paltrow and Jennifer Connelly, with whom they posed (March 2004).

What makes the achievements of Zellweger, Swank, and Gyllenhaal all the more noteworthy is the fact that the 2000s were not good to actresses in general, in large part due to the cultural changes wrought by 9/11. By many accounts *everything* changed after that fateful day, and, as Susan Faludi amply illustrates in her book *The Terror Dream: Fear and Fantasy in Post-9/11 Media*, that includes women's presence in the media. Arguing that "we [Americans] reacted to our trauma . . . not by interrogating it but by cocooning ourselves in the celluloid chrysalis of the baby boom's childhood," Faludi charts a profound cultural shift throughout the 2000s, one that depended on a reversion to the traditional gender roles embodied by John Wayne on the one hand and a generic female caretaker on the other (4). As a result of this shift, women's presence in the public sphere, including popular culture, was severely curtailed in the wake of 9/11; registering the cumulative toll this curtailment took on the film industry, Manohla Dargis published a resonant lament in 2008 over what she called "the new post-female American cinema" ("Is There a Real Woman in This Multiplex?" *New York Times*, 4 May 2008). Furthermore, when women did feature in the media, Faludi argues, the roles they typically played were more circumscribed due in part to the revivification of "sex-coded rescue language," which positions men as heroes and women as either damsels in distress or cheerleaders from the domestic sidelines. The result was a reinforcement of certain trends—chiefly, a disregard for feminism and the establishment of a new traditionalism—associated with an already pervasive postfeminist culture.

For the most part, Zellweger, Swank, and Gyllenhaal are exceptions to the rules that Faludi fleshes out. Not only did these three work regularly throughout the 2000s, but the majority of characters they played exhibit a considerable degree of both agency and dimension, even when they functioned as supporting players in someone else's drama. In fact, a number of their films are explicitly concerned with foregrounding certain figures, be they historical personages (Beatrix Potter in *Miss Potter* [2006] and Alice Paul in *Iron Jawed Angels* [2004]) or fictional types (a female masochist in *Secretary* [2002]), so as to grant them gravitas and to complicate facile assumptions about them. As a result, it is tempting to ignore the larger social context at issue for Faludi and even Dargis, one that testifies to ongoing gender inequality in Hollywood and elsewhere. Yet to do so is also to ignore the very conditions that made the stardom of Zellweger, Swank, and Gyllenhaal possible; after all, the ideas these three articulate about not only personhood, as Richard Dyer would have it, but also womanhood clearly resonated within a social context where postfeminism, more than any other influence, had shaped popular opinion on questions of gender and sexuality (*Heavenly Bodies* 10). Thus I begin this star study with a consideration of the postfeminist phenomenon, which both set the stage for and was fueled by the changes Faludi recounts.

As suggested by the word itself, "postfeminism" denotes that which comes after feminism—or, more specifically, after the feminist movement of the 1970s, which is also known in American, Canadian, and British circles as "second-wave" feminism; as such, it denotes the period of time from the 1980s forward. What is connotes, however, is a more complicated issue. As illustrated by scholars ranging from Sarah Projansky to Stéphanie Genz and Benjamin A. Brabon, the term postfeminism has, since its coinage, provoked considerable discussion related to a number of issues, including whether it signals a break with feminism or, alternately, a new phase in the movement's ongoing development; how it dovetails with other "post-" phenomena, such as postmodernism; and what kind of politics, if any, it enables or precludes. Yet despite its status as a slippery signifier, many find it uniquely equipped to describe a particular "sensibility," to use Rosalind Gill's word, that has prevailed in recent decades. For example, in the introduction to their anthology *Interrogating Postfeminism*, Yvonne Tasker and Diane Negra express their preference for "postfeminism" over "backlash" due to the distinctive temporality the former supposes: one that does not rely on a linear chronology of political gains won and then lost, but instead acknowledges that the history—and present—of feminism is one of ongoing struggle between the advancement and containment of an activist agenda. Ever since the 1980s, when women (and men) at a full generational remove from "second-wave" feminism began to come of age as not only consumers but also producers of texts, that struggle has played itself out primarily in the most public of forums, popular culture.

Due to their historical and social location, the relationship that members of this younger generation (as well as subsequent ones) have to feminism is unprecedented: everything from their political rights and social institutions to their sexuality and vocabulary has been shaped, to some extent, by it. Nevertheless, they are largely disinclined to recognize a feminist movement per se (or any social movement, for that matter) as necessary, relevant, or even extant due to the historical moment in which they live, which has been shaped by a wide array of interconnected forces: the relentless expansion of consumer markets under multinational capitalism; the influence of postmodernism with its capacity to blur the boundary between the processes of consumption and critique; and the pervasiveness of neoliberal ideology, which emphasizes the individual self over any collective body and extols consumerism as the primary means of defining and moreover empowering that self. One result of this situation has been the emergence of a paradoxical postfeminist culture, one that depends on, and in the process sustains, aspects of feminism—in particular, those related to the rhetoric of choice, independence, sexual subjecthood, and "having it all"—at the same time that it narrates gender equality as a *fait accompli* and feminism as obsolete. Hence, Tasker and Negra's assertion: "as an idiom, postfeminism popularizes (as much as it caricatures) a feminism it simultaneously evokes and rejects" (21).

Given the topic at hand, three actresses who have come of age professionally amid postfeminist culture, playing more than forty-five characters among them in the 2000s alone, it is noteworthy that much of the debate over the effects of postfeminism has orbited around its various fictional avatars. Of the three female characters most frequently identified as such— Ally McBeal and Carrie Bradshaw, both from television, and Bridget Jones— only one has a direct connection to this chapter: Jones, fleshed out by Zellweger in the character's transition from literature to cinema. Nonetheless, all three of these figures are noteworthy since it is that which they share that epitomizes the postfeminist protagonist and, more broadly, delineates the terms in which female characters are rendered both legible and appealing to a contemporary mass audience. All these characters are defined by not only their professional status, which comes to them relatively easily, but also their unbridled, and largely conventional, desires—for good sex, designer shoes, potent cocktails, and, most important, the man of their dreams. What is more, being white and middle class, they enjoy a considerable amount of privilege, which allows them to prioritize such desires over a more communitarian agenda and to pursue them without prohibitive risk.

To be sure, many of the characters Zellweger, Swank, and Gyllenhaal play in this decade, not to mention popular perceptions of the stars themselves, deviate to varying degrees from this archetype. In fact, some of their performances both onscreen and off bespeak a high degree of political engagement and even contribute to a so-called "third-wave" feminist agenda of building on, rather than repudiating, feminism of the past so as to address those structural inequalities upon which patriarchal culture (still) depends. Nevertheless, an examination of how exactly these three working actresses fit within the cultural field that produced Ally, Carrie, and Bridget, objects of both ready identification and wary ambivalence, yields a sense of the texture and extent of postfeminist culture as well as its alternatives. Thus I devote the rest of this chapter to considering each of them in turn, prioritizing those moments of consonance and contradiction, complicity and resistance both within and across their respective careers.

★★★★★ Renée Zellweger: Where the "Pre" and the "Post" of Feminism Meet

More than any other, the role of Bridget Jones has earned Zellweger the title "perennial post-feminist poster girl," to quote Nina Martin. By playing Bridget repeatedly—in *Bridget Jones's Diary* (2001), *Bridget Jones: The Edge of Reason* (2004), and a forthcoming third installment currently in production—Zellweger has by association become the face of not simply a film franchise but a cultural phenomenon that also includes author Helen Fielding's books (the films' source material), as well as, more generally, the whole genre of "chick lit," of which Fielding's work is deemed emblematic. As a result, Zellweger's image has been shaped in no small measure by Bridget's myriad postfeminist traits, which include everything from her status as, in Angela McRobbie's words, "a self-monitoring subject" who tries desperately to structure her life in isolation from a larger community to the combination of girlish vulnerability, irreverent sass, and benign solipsism that allows her to win the heart of both Mark Darcy and legion fans.

Yet despite being best known for her portrayal of the quintessentially modern woman, Zellweger's career as a whole has her firmly rooted in the past. Out of her twelve live-action films released from 2002 through 2009, eight are period pieces. Of these, *Cold Mountain* (2003), the Civil War–era epic for which Zellweger won a Best Supporting Actress Oscar, and *Appaloosa* (2008), a western featuring the New Mexico Territory of the 1880s, are located in the most distant past; the rest of them position Zellweger in the early- or mid-twentieth century, be it in the immediate wake of the Victorian era, the swinging sixties, or some historical moment in between. Moreover, three of her period pieces—*Chicago* (2002) and *Leatherheads* (2008), set in the 1920s, and *Down with Love* (2003), set in the 1960s—not only take place in the past but also self-consciously hark back, in their style and narration, to a bygone era of filmmaking in order to breathe life into a genre whose heyday has long passed. In the context of these three films, all devoutly nostalgic in their approach, Zellweger is of central importance. In both character and performance she references certain iconic leading ladies of the classical Hollywood era (Ginger Rogers, Carole Lombard, and Doris Day, respectively) and thereby embodies, quite literally, the retrospective impulse that animates the texts in general.

Reviews and media profiles of Zellweger suggest that one significant reason she is the go-to actress for period cinema is that her looks and temperament evoke qualities generally perceived as out of step with our contemporary times. This is best illustrated by two reviews of *Nurse Betty* (2000), which appeared two years before Zellweger's career took a turn toward the past. In one, Edward Guthmann of the *San Francisco Chronicle* identifies Zellweger as "a performer who emanates kindness and a pure heart," a feat worth celebrating "in an era when actors all seem to be experts in the art of withering sarcasm"; and in the other, Charles Taylor of *Salon* concurs by way of the logic of physiognomy: "With her apple cheeks, scrunched up eyes and big smile, Zellweger has possibly the most open face in the movies right now" (both 8 September 2000). As the 2000s continued and commentators had even more reason to view Zellweger through the lens of former decades, others elaborated on the theme sounded by Guthmann and Taylor: they regularly described Zellweger in old-fashioned terms, citing her "kewpie doll looks" and her "moxie" or "pluck," while also ascribing to her even more traits—innocence, sincerity, cuteness, and naiveté— that hardly square with an era that trades on irony and cynicism.

The consistency with which Zellweger has been constructed as an anachronism of sorts is attributable to a number of factors. First, there is a connection between Zellweger's physicality and her character; indeed, so many writers have pointed to this that the correlation between her trademark squint and all things wholesome has been thoroughly sedimented. Although mentioned less frequently by reviewers, the fact that her voice, with its resonant treble huskiness, is as distinctively good-natured as her face has not been lost on the makers of such animated features as *Shark Tale* (2004), *Bee Movie* (2007), and *Monsters vs. Aliens* (2009). Second, in interviews Zellweger comes off as exceedingly thoughtful, humble, and serious-minded. Crystallizing this is her manner of self-presentation during an appearance on "Inside the Actor's Studio." In the course of the questionnaire with which host James Lipton concludes all his interviews there, she distinguishes herself from other guests by taking the high road on every query, earnestly asserting that "honor" is one of her favorite words and that "great expression . . . motivated by passion and truth" turns her on while "dishonesty, gluttony, lack of empathy, lack of compassion, and conditional kindness" turn her off. As much as such sentiments, which recur consistently throughout Zellweger's interviews in the 2000s, construct the star as moral-minded, they also provide her with an out when confronted with questions that are politically charged in any way. Zoe Williams demonstrates as much in a 2003 profile of the actress for *The Guardian*. In it, Zellweger is adamant in her refusal to take up a public position on political issues, for fear that, in Williams's words, "[her] view on larger matters will not just be derided, it will bring the entire standpoint into disrepute." Instead, she defers to a language of individual responsibility, like that illustrated above, and deflects pointed questions about, for example, the politically conservative nature of Hollywood with the deliberately noncommittal response, "I really couldn't say. I just don't know" ("Just the Job," 13 December 2003).

Finally and most important, the very attributes that lend Zellweger credibility in period pieces are the ones she brings to nearly every film in which she stars, no matter the setting. That is, Zellweger typically plays characters who never succumb to cynicism or hopelessness, even when their situation merits such a response—and it usually does. In fact, one thread of thematic continuity that runs through her entire body of work involves the response of individuals to conditions that qualify as less than ideal, be they tragic in proportion (involving, say, poverty or a traumatic experience) or simply unfulfilling (such as being single when one, or one's parents, can only think of marriage). The exception that proves this rule most persuasively is the romantic comedy *New in Town* (2009), which presents Zellweger, at least initially, as a cold-hearted corporate executive. Tellingly, the performance was roundly panned by critics, who pronounced it, among other things, unconvincing, joyless, and lazy (Stephen Holden, *New York Times*, 30 January 2009; Peter Hartlaub, *San Francisco Chronicle*, 30 January 2009).

Confronted with unfortunate circumstances, Zellweger's characters tend to react in one of two ways. As Ruby Thewes, the colorful and capable farmhand who brings levity to an otherwise dour *Cold Mountain*; as Mae Braddock, the devoted wife of the Depression-era boxer known as *Cinderella Man* (2005); and as Anne Deveraux, the fading beauty who searches out a new life for herself and her sons on the heels of a divorce in *My One and Only* (2009), the actress weathers hardship in a valiant manner, never losing her humor, dignity, or can-do attitude. More frequently, however, she plays characters who respond to a dissatisfying reality by taking refuge, and often achieving unprecedented recognition, in an alternate universe of their own design. For this reason Susanne Kord and Elisabeth Krimmer suggest that her films tend to "attack . . . [the] sovereignty of the real world," subjecting it to "virtually limitless manipulation" (76).

In the case of *Nurse Betty*, immersion in a fantasy world is a function of delusion: after witnessing her husband's brutal murder at the hands of two hit men, Betty Sizemore dissociates from reality and sets out on a quest to find a fictional doctor from her favorite soap opera. Other films feature an immersion that is less pathological, but equally absorbing. In *Chicago*, she plays Roxie Hart, whose dreams of becoming a glamorous star provide a pretext for the film's many musical numbers. In *Miss Potter*, she portrays children's author Beatrix Potter as a woman who not only invents but also inhabits the world of Peter Rabbit. And in *Down with Love*, her character, best-selling author Barbara Novak, is ultimately revealed to be an elaborate alter-ego created by one Nancy Brown in order to romantically entrap a charismatic playboy for whom she once worked as a secretary. Even Bridget Jones can be understood as a character cut from this same cloth, especially in light of the fact that what is being negotiated through the traversal of the boundary between fantasy and reality in the above films is competing models of feminine identity. Not only does *Bridget Jones's Diary* feature the occasional fantasy sequence, but in the diary entries that gain expression through her voiceover narration, Bridget imagines herself as any number of idealized women, from a "screen goddess in the manner of Grace Kelly" to a "hard-headed journalist ruthlessly committed to promoting justice and liberty." Yet, as the film stresses, she embodies these paragons only in her mind; immediately after invoking each one, she is shown falling short of it in some flamboyant way.

As has been much discussed, particularly among those taking stock of postfeminism by way of Bridget Jones, the fear that motivates her more than any other as she cycles through this range of ego-ideals is that of remaining a "singleton" forever. Yet as much as this fear belies her formation in a postfeminist culture that supposes women's advances in the public sphere to have come at the cost of their private lives, it also constitutes the common ground that she shares with so many of Zellweger's other characters, including—indeed, especially—those who predate the women's liberation movement. That is, Bridget, like the majority of the characters mentioned above, is spurred on by an impetus that is germane to normative definitions of femininity: the need for love, be it from a single partner or a mass audience; the need to complete, and be completed by, someone else. One noteworthy exception to this formulation, at least at first glance, is Beatrix Potter. Not only does *Miss Potter* construct her as a woman who

Bridget (Renée Zellweger) fantasizes herself as a bride in *Bridget Jones's Diary* (Sharon Maguire, Miramax/Working Title Films, 2001). Courtesy Photofest New York.

willfully defies parental and, more generally, societal pressure by prioritizing her work over the hunt for a husband, but it also delivers a trenchant critique of marriage by way of Beatrix's like-minded friend Millie, who equates the institution with domestic enslavement. Yet as swiftly as a (proto)feminist vision is established, it is subsequently contained, for that which lends the film its dramatic arc is a love affair that Beatrix enters into rather than her career: while her success as an author is secured by the end of the first act, her parents' disapproval of her fiancé and his eventual death provide the film with its requisite conflict. Moreover, when Beatrix nervously breaks the news of the engagement to Millie, the latter recants her earlier objections to matrimony, asking innocently, "What else is a woman on her own supposed to say?"

As much as *Miss Potter* capitulates to certain representational conventions so as to construct its protagonist in terms that resonate with the rest of Zellweger's body of work and, more generally, pre-feminist and post-feminist culture, it does prove unusual on another count. Unlike the majority of Zellweger's characters, Beatrix is not content merely to endure or escape from the hardships she encounters. Rather, by way of the environmental activism she engages in after her fiancé's death, she allows her experiences to fuel commitment to a cause larger than herself. Zellweger's other films, in contrast, tend, like the social context from which they emerge and the actress herself, to dramatize experience in terms of individual choices rather than collective demands. With engaged resistance and community-based struggle beyond their horizon of both narrative and political possibility, they capture the shift in subject matter that postfeminism registers: that from "an unproblematic 'we'" to "a problematic 'she'" (McRobbie 29). In this way, Zellweger shares a fundamental trait with her character in *Bridget Jones: The Edge of Reason*, whose "liberation," *The Observer*'s Phillip French notes, "resides more in its feisty language and permissive attitude towards sex than in its sexual politics" (14 November 2004): she lays bare in dramatic (and comedic) form the difference between pluck and politics, at least those of the social movement variety.

★★★★★ Hilary Swank: Solo Flights, Solo Fights

In 2005, upon receiving the Best Actress Oscar for her performance in *Million Dollar Baby* (2004), Hilary Swank avowed, "I don't know what I did in this life to deserve all this. I'm just a girl from a trailer park who had a dream." With this admission, Swank not only posited the parallels between her life and that of Maggie Fitzgerald, the boxer whose rise from rags to riches the film chronicles; she also crystallized the narrative of her life that most acutely informs her star persona. Expanding on this narrative, while also exploiting its dramatic potential by resorting to crass stereotypes, "60 Minutes" began a subsequent feature on the star this way: "From trailer trash to *Million Dollar Baby* and the Oscars. In short, that's the story of her life. But there's a whole lot more to Hilary Swank. Even in a town like Hollywood, she's unique. She's intelligent, articulate, and worldly, yet she's a high-school dropout. She's arguably the best American actress of her generation, yet she wasn't good enough for 'Beverly Hills 90210.' Now, thanks to Clint Eastwood's hit *Million Dollar Baby*, the failed soapy star has just won her second Academy Award and Hilary Who is Hilary Superstar" (6 March 2005). In the story that followed, Mike Wallace emphasized Swank's humble roots, approachability, and committed involvement in various charitable causes, all of which continued to figure in accounts of the star for years to come; even after achieving superstar status, Swank has remained a kind of Hollywood outsider, reputably removed from the excess and nepotism for which the movie colony is infamous. In short, "60 Minutes" perfectly summed up a star image that circulates far and wide, one that is downright democratic in sensibility and earns Swank the title of "regular-girl movie star" (Allison Glock, "Hilary Swank: To Hil and Back," *Marie Claire*, March 2006).

In addition to typifying the way Swank's life is regularly encapsulated—in terms of sudden and severe reversals of fortune—the introductory spiel quoted above also employs a familiar strategy in the process of doing so. Specifically, it telescopes Swank's career, suggesting that prior to Eastwood's intervention, she was Hilary Who, when in fact she came to *Million Dollar Baby* with not only a well-established career but also a previous Academy Award (for *Boys Don't Cry*, 1999) under her belt. In this way, "60 Minutes" repeats a gesture familiar from both previous and subsequent profiles of the star, downplaying a certain portion of Swank's career in order to imbue her award-winning performance with the affective currency of a sudden windfall. Usually that portion is the full decade she spent working in television and film prior to *Boys Don't Cry*. Catherine Hong's account is exemplary in this regard: "At age 15 the aspiring actress persuaded her mom to move to L.A., where they lived out of their Oldsmobile for a time. She had a role on 'Beverly Hills 90210,' but when she was fired after 16 episodes, she nearly quit the business. The next year she filmed *Boys Don't Cry*" ("Hilary Swank," *W Magazine*, January 2008). Yet, as "60 Minutes" demonstrates, other portions can be subjected to revision as well when what is at stake is a fairy-tale version of the American Dream, which stresses success and the determined pursuit of its continuation over the work and calculation required to achieve that success in the first place.

In light of her own well-publicized trajectory, it is not surprising that Swank has consistently chosen, and been chosen, to play characters who display tenacity and integrity in a single-minded pursuit of some goal and, in so doing, inspire others to follow suit. In some cases, such as the science fiction catastrophe film *The Core* (2003) and the horror film *The Reaping* (2007), such characters serve the needs of a generic formula by propelling the plot into increasingly more fantastic situations, be they ones that take place in subterranean depths or during a biblical plague. In other cases, they are figures whose heroic actions constitute an inspired response to the charged history that serves as their backdrop: in *Red Dust* (2004), she plays Sarah Barcant, a lawyer from New York City who returns to her native South Africa in order to represent an apartheid-era political activist during his torturer's bid for amnesty, while in *Freedom Writers* (2007) she plays Erin Gruwell, a high school English teacher in Los Angeles who transforms her students' lives in the wake of the 1992 Rodney King uprising and L.A. riots. Finally, in still other cases they are the focal point in an act of feminist historiography, as in the HBO production *Iron Jawed Angels*, where she plays suffragist Alice Paul, and the biopic *Amelia* (2009), which is dedicated to the life of aviatrix Amelia Earhart.

These last two features are of particular interest since they necessarily confront the question of how to make a history of women's achievement, their rise from obscurity to fame, accessible, relevant, and engaging to a postfeminist audience. To a large extent, *Amelia* answers this question by resorting to the generic conventions associated with the classical biopic so as to lend Earhart's life the dramatic arc of any Great (Wo)man, including Swank herself (see Bingham). That is, it distills that life down to a series of important moments, including both public achievements and intimate encounters, and, in the process, constructs her as a singular hero capable of transcending her social circumstances. Additionally, however, in a postfeminist twist on a familiar formula, *Amelia* fails to explain how Earhart developed that which distinguished her professionally—the will and capacity to defy social mores by pursuing her passion for flying without apology—while allowing her private life with husband George Putnam and lover Gene Vidal to dominate the narrative. The result was deemed dull by most; in the words of two reviewers, *Amelia* is a "tame and conventional" film with "no stakes in [its] portrayal of women, society, pilots, marriage" (Michael Phillips, *Baltimore Sun*, 23 October 2009; Geoff Berkshire, *Metromix*, 22 October 2009).

In contrast to *Amelia*, *Iron Jawed Angels* has the distinction of being "the only feature film that takes feminist organizing as its subject" (Maddux 74). As such, it necessarily regards its protagonist, Alice Paul, as a part of something larger than herself: not only a social movement but also the historical circumstances that catalyzed that movement. Yet it also produces a vision of feminist history that resonates with postfeminism, in this case by employing what Maddux calls "retrospective framing," a process that entails "selecting and deflecting the elements [of the past that are] most and least intelligible in contemporary terms" (75). For example, it replicates the gesture of "disidentification" (as McRobbie calls it) by which both post- and "third-wave" feminists distinguish themselves from their "second-wave" predecessors when it constructs Paul and her cohort of activists as the more spirited and effective counterparts to their older colleagues; it emphasizes women's freedom of choice by showcasing a plurality of ways to achieve a balance between work and family; and, finally, it strategically limits its focus: to one particular moment in early feminism, the pursuit of women's suffrage at the federal level; to the most spectacular methods of protest employed, including parades and picketing; and to a liberal-citizenship argument for expanding the franchise, which emphasizes individual rather than class rights.

Describing the net effect of all these creative decisions, Maddux sings a tune familiar from the above discussion of Zellweger: "Investing faith in individual agency, *Iron Jawed Angels* . . . closes down the possibilities for collective action" (90); indeed, given that the mythos of the American Dream informs Swank's persona so acutely, such an observation could be generalized to most of the parts she plays. The acuity of this conclusion notwithstanding, however, there are substantial differences between Swank's and Zellweger's bodies of work. First, Swank's characters, especially Alice Paul but also Amelia Earhart, Erin Gruwell, and many others, actively engage with the world around them, often in order to resist injustice and to produce social change. Moreover, what both qualifies Swank for such tasks and enables her to pull them off convincingly is her distinct bearing, which differs substantially from that of not only Zellweger but almost every American actress of her generation.

Tough and vulnerable, athletic and graceful, square-jawed and doe-eyed, Swank evokes the kind of ideal that Virginia Woolf posited when she coined the terms "man-womanly" and "woman-manly" in *A Room of One's Own* (1929): one that reflects androgeny, a state wherein feminine and masculine aspects of the self are not locked in battle but harmoniously synthesized to generative ends. While this quality is central to her gender-bending performance as transgendered teenager Brandon Teena in *Boys Don't Cry*, it also allows her to model a variety of feminine identity that is in short supply in a postfeminist culture that insistently reclaims all things feminine while encouraging women, no matter how old, to be "girls." In other words, like Jodie Foster, the contemporary actress whom she most resembles in her androgyny, Swank's unique gender identity enables her to bring tremendous dimension to characters who figure relatively rarely in contemporary American cinema: young women who hail from a working- or squarely middle-class background and mature either in the context of a largely male milieu or under the guidance of a father figure. *Million Dollar Baby* offers the most obvious evidence of this, especially since Swank identified Eastwood as her offscreen mentor as well as her onscreen one during her Oscar speech, but the police thriller *Insomnia* (2002), wherein her role model is a beleaguered Al Pacino, and the aforementioned *The Core*, *Red Dust*, and *Freedom Writers* do so as well. While one consequence of Swank's association with masculinity throughout the 2000s was a repeated effort on the part of the star herself and journalists to testify to her femininity, another one proved less normalizing: to a certain extent, she was exempted from the hyper-vigilance with which women's bodies are surveyed. When Zellweger put on approximately twenty pounds to play Bridget Jones, it was the subject of extensive extratextual discussion; Swank's equivalent weight gain for *Million Dollar Baby* was noted far less frequently.

While Swank's performances in the above films have been generally well received, earning her respect if not raves, she tends to fall flat when

Maggie (Hilary Swank) receives support from her mentor in *Million Dollar Baby* (Clint Eastwood, Warner Bros., 2004). Courtesy Photofest New York.

playing more stereotypically feminine women, be they ones from past eras who craftily trade on their feminine wiles (as in *The Affair of the Necklace* [2001] and *The Black Dahlia* [2006]) or ones who, like Bridget Jones, derive from the world of contemporary "chick lit" (as in *P.S. I Love You* [2007]). As Ella Taylor puts it in the *Village Voice*, Swank "was not put in this world to simper"—nor, for that matter, to play the seductress—and when she is required to do so, the results are unconvincing ("*P.S. I Love You*," 11 December 2007). This fact helps account for the uneven nature of Swank's body of work throughout the 2000s; as an actress she tends to deliver either superlative or poor performances and little in between. Yet her work also has a subversive potential, as indicated by Dargis's take on a performance (and a film) that left many critics cold: "One reason [Swank] was so good in Brian De Palma's convoluted noir *The Black Dahlia*, in which she crept around like poison ivy, is that her performance as a femme fatale is set inside quotation marks. She didn't register as a toxically dangerous woman but as an idea of that irresistible sexist cliché. She filled out her character's snug gown as a drag queen would" ("*P.S. I Love You*," *New York Times*, 21 December 2007). Employing language that evokes unmistakably both Mary Ann Doane's work on the female masquerade and Judith Butler's ideas on gender performativity, Dargis's comment suggests that even Swank's relatively unsuccessful performances have political potential insofar as they undercut the "idealized, essentialized femininity" that postfeminist culture promotes (Tasker and Negra 10). Granted, this is both a sympathetic and a resistant reading of Swank's persona, but when paired with that which qualifies her as "arguably the best American actress of her generation"—her extraordinary skill at playing characters who are at variance with a post-feminist culture of privilege, convention, and normative femininity—it suggests she is of singular significance, both artistically and politically.

☆☆☆☆☆ Maggie Gyllenhaal: The Interpersonal Is Political

In December 2009, while doing publicity for *Crazy Heart* (2009), Maggie Gyllenhaal intimated to interviewer Charlie Rose that the role of Jean Craddock, the single mother who falls for a gentle-hearted but alcoholic country singer well past his professional prime, marked a turning point in her emotional maturation. When asked what drew her to the film, she answered: "[Jean's] so much more vulnerable than anybody else I've played. And I think it's only recently, like in the past few months in my own life, that I see how important that is. . . . I used to think the idea was to just be as strong as you could be and just as . . . fierce as you could be, and, I don't know, I don't think that anymore. And that was in Jean. I think she's soft, you know?" Buttressed by sensitive direction from Scott Cooper—at least two reviewers noted that Gyllenhaal had never been lit and filmed in such a flattering manner—this performance of a newfound vulnerability marked a turning point in her career as well, since it earned her an Academy Award nomination (her first) for Best Supporting Actress. With such mainstream recognition under her belt, the 2010s promise even more attention for the actress whom *Vanity Fair* dubbed "the hipster's heroine" in March 2004.

As much as the above comment portends a potential new direction in Gyllenhaal's development, however, it also sums up her work in the 2000s aptly: strength and fierceness, along with a good measure of eccentricity, are indeed traits that have characterized her both intertextually and extra-textually. Relative to her work, this much is evident from even the most cursory description of her various film roles, from the Satan-worshipping makeup artist in *Cecil B. DeMented* (2000), with which she began the decade, to the self-righteous earth mother in *Away We Go* (2009), with which she rounded it out; in between those bookends lies a catalogue of offbeat characters distinguished by the bold strokes with which they are drawn. Yet even when playing a relatively conventional character, as in *World Trade Center* (2006), which charged her with the exclusive task of reacting to her husband's disappearance and subsequent rescue, her performance brims

with intensity: critics credited her with both transmitting "a fluttery nerv-
ousness that nonetheless has reserves of strength and resiliency at its core"
and suggesting "a complicated, prickly personality underneath the panic
and grief" (Stephanie Zacharek, *Salon*, 9 August 2006; A. O. Scott, *New York
Times*, 9 August 2006).

Along with her resume as an actress, Gyllenhaal's public engagement
with certain political issues has also contributed to a star persona predicated
on strength. Between her participation in multiple efforts to mobilize young
voters, her support of presidential candidates John Kerry in 2004 and Barack
Obama in 2008, her suggestion that the United States was "responsible in
some way" for 9/11, and her opposition to the Iraq War, she has demonstrated a consistent refusal to equivocate, even when it has threatened her
career. To wit, her comments about 9/11, which she refused to retract, faced
Gyllenhaal with the prospect of having to withdraw from *World Trade Center* (see "Gyllenhaal Nearly Quit Sept. 11 Movie," *USA Today*, 8 May 2006).
Moreover, when she talks about her films she demonstrates a keen awareness of something that does not figure explicitly in the above positions: the
politics of gender and sexuality. For example, in the midst of promoting *Secretary*, she made an appearance on "The Late Late Show with Craig Kilborn"
(22 January 2003), in which she frankly acknowledged her concerns about
playing a female submissive in an S/M relationship, noting that it was "politically . . . a complicated thing to do," and then expressed her satisfaction
with the outcome: "It could've been a reactionary movie, and it just isn't."

Years later, she made an even more pointed comment in "What Women
Wanted: 1953," a bonus add-on to the DVD of *Mona Lisa Smile* (2003), a postfeminist text par excellence set at Wellesley College in the 1950s. (Crystallizing the film's postfeminist sensibility is a scene in which a model student tells
her protofeminist professor that she must learn to respect any choice a
woman makes, including that of abandoning her professional ambitions so
she can support her fiancé as he pursues his.) While the featurette describes
the severely limited role that (white and wealthy) women were expected to
play in society at mid-century in order to underscore how different things are
now that women have achieved equality, Gyllenhaal's comment about the
division of labor that prevailed on set suggests that our current reality might
not be so different, after all. Over images of director Mike Newell working
with an all-female group of actors, Gyllenhaal says, "In 1953 and '54 women
were perceived through the eyes of men. That's just the way it was. And, so,
I think there might be something really fascinating about the fact that there's
all these actresses, who are very opinionated and specific and thinking as well
as feeling people, being manipulated by a man, who is also very powerful and

interesting and smart and feeling, you know? I think it sort of mirrors, in a way, the situation that was happening in 1953." While spoken with a seeming authentic ebullience, something Gyllenhaal brings to most discussions of her work, this comment makes a noteworthy point incisively: drawing an astute parallel between the past and present, she suggests that women have not necessarily come a long way, baby—at least not in the film industry, where men still call most of the shots.

Fueled by ferocity and fierce engagement with the social world, Gyllenhaal's career has developed along different lines than those of Zellweger and Swank. First, unlike the former, who spent much of the 2000s in some other decade, and the latter, who has played both feminist icons and feminine clichés from the past, Gyllenhaal is most at home in the present era. She has appeared in only two period films—*Mona Lisa Smile* and *Confessions of a Dangerous Mind* (2002), which locates her in the early 1960s—and both characterize her as, above all else, sexually promiscuous and therefore ahead of her time, as if she were anticipating the sexual revolution to come and the terms—outspoken, sexually frank, and politically progressive—of her own stardom. The rest of her films, even *Donnie Darko* (2001), *Stranger than Fiction* (2006), and *The Dark Knight* (2008), all of which take place in a reality that runs parallel to our own, speak in the present tense. Some, moreover, site themselves in the 2000s quite self-consciously, as evinced by those that assess the effects of 9/11: not only *World Trade Center* but also the HBO production *Strip Search* (2004), which was shelved after provoking controversy with its dramatization of interrogation methods shared by the U.S. and Chinese governments, and *The Great New Wonderful* (2005), which examines the quotidian lives of a handful of New Yorkers one year after the attacks.

Second, in keeping with the period pieces already mentioned, many of Gyllenhaal's characters are defined largely in terms of their sexuality. This point is particularly noteworthy given the central position that women's sexual subjecthood assumes in postfeminist culture, which tends not only to "[herald] sexually provocative appearance and behavior (including exhibitionist stripping) as acts of female empowerment" (Genz and Brabon 91) but also to dismiss as prudery any objections to this position, be they predicated on arguments about compulsory heterosexuality, risk, or the self-disciplining subject. With a story line that emphasizes self-actualization by way of sexual submission, *Secretary* is arguably the most provocative—and potentially postfeminist—film in her body of work. In it she plays Lee Holloway, an introverted young woman who takes a secretarial job in a law office and soon afterward, mixing business with pleasure (and pain), develops a consensual and mutually fulfilling S/M relationship with her boss, Mr. Grey. Yet

Their S/M relationship under way, Lee (Maggie Gyllenhaal) delivers a letter to Mr. Grey (James Spader) in *Secretary* (Steven Shainberg, Lions Gate Films, 2002). Courtesy Photofest New York.

as much as this premise might suggest a text that breezily promotes "[sexual] self-objectification as a way of achieving active subjectivity" (Martin), *Secretary*'s representation of sexuality is far more considered than that, since the question of power is of central and explicit concern throughout. Indeed, it is not the premise but rather the conventional ending, with Lee married to Mr. Grey and living in the suburbs, yet no longer employed, that proves troubling to the film's most politically minded critics (Weiss). Two other signature roles further attest to the fact that the sex at issue in Gyllenhaal's body of work is a complex matter: in *Happy Endings* (2005) she plays Jude, a singer who beds a young man and then his father in the course of satisfying her voracious appetites, and in *SherryBaby* (2006) she is Sherry Swanson, an ex-con and recovering addict who impulsively uses sex to get what she wants, be it her pick of jobs, attention from others, or physical satisfaction. In light of how fleeting they are, the gains these characters make by using their sexuality are an occasion for reflection more than celebration.

As important as the stories in which Gyllenhaal's sexuality figures, however, it is the way she performs that sexuality that most distinguishes her work from an exercise in empowerment through exhibitionism. Specifically, sex is not, in Gyllenhaal's career, an occasion for spectacular display, but rather continuous with a range of other activities that she performs in a thoroughly embodied fashion. In a review of *SherryBaby* in *Sight & Sound*,

Hannah Paterson writes, "There's something about her physicality, her fizzing energy, that demands attention" (August 2007, 77), and, as evinced by the reviews Gyllenhaal has elicited over the entirety of her career, this sentiment is widely shared. Critics frequently mention Gyllenhaal's body, but not in order to draw a universal conclusion about her disposition, as happens with Zellweger, or to comment on her relationship to conventional gender norms, as seen in accounts of Swank. Rather, they single out everything from her "long, loose limbs" to her "Betty Boop eyes," her small gestures to her distinctive posture, in order to account for the power of her performances. As a result, it is less her sexuality than an all-encompassing sensuality that defines her in (re)viewers' eyes, which makes perfect sense for an actress who has twice played both a baker and a makeup artist, two vocations that demand hands-on engagement with the material world.

Finally, while Zellweger and Swank are typically characterized in individualistic terms, as, respectively, the self-absorbed dreamer or ambitious achiever, Gyllenhaal is regularly presented as the member of a community. Just like her life offscreen, where she is enmeshed in a network of salient ties to the film and television industries—her father, Stephen, is a director; her mother, Naomi Foner, is a screenwriter; and her brother, Jake, is an actor—her life onscreen often locates her within a larger group of people: the ensemble of actors with whom she is working as well as the community that ensemble is portraying. Moreover, in the case of many of these films, including, for example, *The Photographer* (2000) and *The Great New Wonderful*, their very structure speaks to the connections that people make, or miss, with each other. For this reason her work contributes to the same enterprise that compels a filmmaker like John Sayles, whose *Casa de los babys* (2003) features Gyllenhaal in good company as it broaches the issue of international adoption, to think through the personal and, by extension, political dimensions of sociality. In this way, more than perhaps any other, Gyllenhaal as star serves to subvert the logic of postfeminism, especially as it dovetails with that of neoliberalism, and in the process to acknowledge what the 2000s have dramatically laid bare, the possibility that our inevitable interdependency, and the sense of vulnerability it engenders, can serve as the basis for global political community (Butler, *Precarious* xii–xiii). To be sure, this is a rather exalted function, but one for which Gyllenhaal is uniquely suited, given Dargis's contention that "there isn't an American actress in movies today who holds the screen with as much deep-seated soul" ("Happy Endings," *New York Times*, 15 July 2005). Be it through the skin's surface or an emotional core, she offers a distinctly contemporary conduit for connectivity.

8 ★★★★★★★★★★★★
Heath Ledger
I'm Not There

CLAIRE PERKINS

At the time of his death, Heath Ledger was twenty-eight years old, with the looks that Lasse Hallström once summed up as *"that physicality"* perfectly intact (Belinda Luscombe, "Heath Turns It Around," *Time*, 28 November 2005, 68). He had recently wrapped the role that sent the "rugged" and "mischievous" dimension of his star image into overdrive, but at this moment he lost the tenuous control that any actor ever has over this image. His persona was simultaneously frozen—in the performances he had already given—and abandoned—to the powerful play of memory and speculation. "Heath Ledger" was lost, but he also became what he had only ever been. On James Dean, Edgar Morin has written:

> Death fulfils the destiny of every mythological hero by fulfilling his double nature: human and divine. . . . Thus amplified in the character of James Dean are the phenomena of divinization that characterize but generally remain atrophied in the movie stars. . . . His death signifies that he is broken by the

Heath Ledger. Courtesy of Photofest New York.

hostile forces of the world, but at the same time, in this very defeat, he ultimately gains the absolute: immortality. James Dean dies; it is the beginning
of his victory over death.   (100–7)

This "victory" crystallizes the mysterious process that allows for the creation
of every star image. A star who dies is in this way a doubled or pure star,
but also a reflexive one and, in this sense, an autonomous star whose performances can never again be completely absorbed into the dramatic fiction
of which they are a part. It is the concern of this chapter to examine
Ledger's persona in terms of this particular and peculiar autonomy: his
image as filtered by his death, and as a victory *over* death.

★★★★★ Untimeliness

The case of Ledger raises the broad and interesting question as
to how a star's death affects spectatorship. The focus here is on a death perceived or constructed as "premature" or "untimely." An article titled "When
Icons Die Young" that appeared in the *New York Times* five days after Ledger
died unhesitatingly placed him alongside figures such as John Keats (died at
twenty-five), Rudolph Valentino (thirty-one), Marilyn Monroe (thirty-six),
and Kurt Cobain (twenty-seven). Other commentators made comparisons to
Elliott Smith (dead at thirty-four), River Phoenix (twenty-three), and Jeff
Buckley (thirty-one), all of whom have entered the particular iconography of
fated youth, of potential untapped (Colin Carman, "Heath Ledger and the
Idolatry of Dying Young," *Gay and Lesbian Review*, 1 May 2008, 28). The thou-
sands of tributes to Ledger stress this injustice: that "to stare at him was to
receive a sense of power, and potential. . . . That's why his death feels wrong
[because] it means youth and vitality aren't enough" (David Lipsky, "Heath
Ledger 1979–2008," *Rolling Stone*, 21 February 2008, 35), or that, in Naomi
Watts's comment in an *Interview* article, "deep down, he enjoyed that he was
being recognized for his talent—I think he was starting to own that and that's
the deepest tragedy." Many articles also comment on the instantaneous web
activity that followed his death: "The blogosphere went into overdrive. In
two days his memorial page on Facebook had over 30,000 members. . . .
Hundreds of eulogies for the 28-year-old Australian appeared on *The Sydney
Morning Herald*'s site" (see Jenny Lyn Bader, "When Icons Die Young," *New
York Times*, 28 January 2008). As Bader suggests, Ledger's "transformation"
was underway immediately, "from acclaimed actor to most-searched internet
term, from film star to cultural touchstone."

In this transformation lies a pure expression of stardom as a mythologizing process. As semiotic, intertextual, psychoanalytic, and audience-

based studies have all variously emphasized, the star is an *image*—an ideological sign, a shifting series of interactive texts, and an incomplete object of desire and/or identificatory fantasy (McDonald 81–95). While this logic is too well known, it contains the contradiction that the anchor of the deciphering refraction and desire is a real aging body that both is and is not fundamental to the star image. The knowledge that this body is "out there," existing, is the foundation of a "paradox of presence" (McConnell 168) that is only fully recognizable once the body is taken away and can no longer physically transform. At this point the star truly becomes the product of the divinization activity that founds their construction and spectatorship. This transformation is exaggerated by the way that a star's death provokes a groundswell of attention. In Ledger's case, obituaries and tributes were full of reflections on both what he meant and could have meant as an actor: his agent Steve Alexander emphasized how "he wanted to play characters that he could disappear into and not the leading man, which might have been an easier path for him" (*Interview*, April 2008), while Terry Gilliam's cinematographer Nicola Pecorini claimed he was mesmerized by Ledger, who reminded him of a young Richard Burton: "I'm sure that, if Heath would have aged, he would have aged that way, like scars, but carried with pride" (Peter Biskind, "The Last of Heath," *Vanity Fair*, August 2009, 84).

The sheer fact of his death found Ledger represented across a wide range of magazines, entertainment outlets, and websites, and connections arose that brought to light dimensions of his image that had remained mostly veiled during his life, such as his close involvement with the L.A art collective The Masses (Randall Roberts, "Port in the Storm," *L.A. Weekly*, 11 July 2008). Most obviously, Ledger became an object of critical scrutiny and audience desire. Reporters tried to quite literally "complete" his image in speculating on the "truth" of his emotional state, and fans posted memorial rituals reflecting a real sense of identification: "So, so sad, all of Perth is so sad, at the loss of a real gentleman. . . . I have so admired you as a recognized actor, you did not allow Hollywood to take away the Aussie in you. . . . Australia Day will be your day. . . . We will honor you on that day. . . . RIP Heath" (post by Lindy McQueen at facebook.com/group.php?gid=8054513475&v= wall, 23 January 2008).

★★★★★ Canonization

On the basis of eight years of work in Hollywood performing lead roles in a combination of epic historical films (*The Patriot* [2000], *A Knight's Tale* [2001], *The Four Feathers* [2002], *Casanova* [2005], *The Brothers*

Grimm [2005]) and intimate character pieces (*Monster's Ball* [2001], *The Order* [2004], *Lords of Dogtown* [2005], *Brokeback Mountain* [2005], *I'm Not There* [2007], plus the Australian films *Ned Kelly* [2003] and *Candy* [2006]), Heath Ledger was, by 2008, a star classified in the so-called "Australian Invasion" of actors who began regularly appearing in high-profile and award-winning roles throughout the 1990s and 2000s, including Mel Gibson, Russell Crowe, Nicole Kidman, Cate Blanchett, Hugh Jackman, Eric Bana, Rachel Griffiths, Toni Collette, and Geoffrey Rush. Opening an exhibition titled "Australians in Hollywood" at Canberra's National Portrait Gallery in 2003, Rush attempted some generalizations on the group: "They're a breath of fresh air, there's a different twist to their talent. Is it fearlessness? A hard-wired Hibernian love of a good yarn? Something in the Vegemite? They're rugged and unpredictable, sexy and dangerous and sweet" (Geoffrey Rush, "Australians in Hollywood" opening speech, www.portrait.gov.au/exhibit/hollywood/index.htm). Many interviews with Ledger evoke these characteristics in their summation of his star quality in terms of a character "at once laconic and focused" (Paul Cullum, "Heath Ledger," *Variety Life*, December 2005, 57) with a "calm self-assurance—[an] essential *whatever* at the core" (Jeff Giles, "Young Wonder from Down Under," *Newsweek*, 7 October 2000, 63). It is these qualities that have also been canonized after Ledger's death, a point amply proven on the tribute sites, where appreciation frequently morphs into an expansive celebration of broader characteristics of sincerity and grace: "Such a beautiful person and a huge talent. You don't find his breed anymore. Today's talent is full of fake and vain people. He showed true grace and the screen will never be the same without him. God bless you Heath" (post by "Jennifer" at heathledger.com/tribute).

As Therese Davis has pointed out in a discussion of the death of Diana, Princess of Wales, the key question in such processes of canonization is of a person not *being* saintly but being *recognized* as such (75). Death authenticates the star image *as* image—as belief and not being. The canonization is also aided by the way that death quite literally amplifies a star by exaggerating his or her visibility and stature. After Ledger's death, a high-rise billboard for the release of *The Dark Knight* located on Hollywood Boulevard stayed in place from April to December 2008. His "grimacing, sinister Joker . . . lorded over Hollywood for eight months, both a symbol of the film's box-office muscle and a reminder of the tragedy that lay at its feet" (Randall Roberts, "Movement of the Masses," *L.A. Weekly*, 1 January 2009, 35). The ad is a fitting metaphor for Ledger's presence throughout the 2009 awards season, where his star image was enlarged again by his posthumous *The Dark Knight* wins at the Critics' Choice, Screen Actors Guild, Golden Globe, and Oscar cere-

Heath Ledger is the site of *The Dark Knight*'s fantasy of anarchy and destruction (Christopher Nolan, Warner Bros., 2008). Courtesy Photofest New York.

monies, the last consolidating for him a particular place in film history as only the second person posthumously to win an acting Oscar.[1]

Contained within the explosion of memorializing and speculative images that emerged in biographies, magazines, tribute DVDs, YouTube videos, and television shows in the wake of his death, the "official" amplification of Ledger during this period took the form of the marketing and Oscar campaigns for *The Dark Knight*, released in July 2008. On the former, Ledger's family reportedly asked Warner Bros. not to take down any ads using his image (Rachel Abramowitz, "Studio Is Carefully Balancing Ledger," *Los Angeles Times*, 6 December 2008, A18), with the result that his turn as the Joker anchored the film's campaign through images that held a good deal of ominous power even without the knowledge of his death: Ledger in close-up, chin down and glowering behind blacked-out eyes and a whited-out face; towering as an immoveable roadblock, machine gun in hand; disguised in police and nurse's uniforms, and blurred behind glass smudged with the bloodied taunt, *Why so serious?* In emphasizing the distance between Jack Nicholson's pristine Joker in *Batman* (1989) and Ledger's interpretation of—in his oft-cited words—"a psychopathic, mass-murdering clown with zero empathy" (Lipsky 35), these images confirm Ledger's performance as the site of *The Dark Knight*'s ultimately repressed fantasy of anarchy and destruction. The presence of such overtones in the Oscar campaign for Ledger himself—as Best Supporting Actor—was generally regarded as being more problematic. While some reports describe the campaign as "cautious" in relying upon the "steady (and not frantic) visual presence of somebody now best known for his absence" (David Carr, "Delicately Campaigning for a Star Now Departed," *New York Times*, 6 February 2009, C14), others perceived exploitative tones in the frequent appearances in the trade press of a specific image from the film, where Ledger as the Joker laughs out the window of a stolen police car as he careens through the gleaming lights of a Gotham City night: "It is a vivid image, but you don't have to veer too far into semiotics to see that the man hanging his head out the car window is on his way to a reckless, chaotic death" (Carr). The implication is clearly that the campaign capitalizes upon Ledger's demise by using an image whose power is attributable to its apparent prescience, its blurring of diegetic and nondiegetic worlds.

The power of this coincidence and its part in amplifying Ledger's star image is compelling insofar as it rests upon the assumption that his death, and by extension Ledger himself, is *there*, visible in the image. The performance of the Joker is obscured by the performer: the knowledge of Ledger's death functions as a digression into which the character effectively disappears. The effect is explicable through the distinction that Richard Maltby draws between integrated and autonomous performance, where the balance in any individual performative act rests upon the audience's experience of the presence of both performer and character in the same body (248–49). Maltby's discussion of this phenomenon owes much to Frank McConnell's romantic concept of the existential paradox of film presence: the "warfare between personality and mechanism" that arises from the knowledge that "though no one is really there on the screen, people are also more really *there* than most of us ever manage to be in our daily lives" (168). As the site of—or the *effect* of—the human in the machine, acting is thus the primary means by which audiences understand characters psychologically (Maltby 248). The bodily presence of the performer is one of the principal means by which viewers invest in the existence of the characters as real people, but is also a distraction from this fiction.

While acknowledging that most Hollywood films are organized to juxtapose integrated and autonomous modes of performance, Maltby doesn't consider the extent to which the spectator's experience of the performance, at the levels of both investment and distraction, is necessarily a subjective and discursive one. The extent to which the performer escapes the character is significantly determined by spectator knowledge: her awareness of the performer's screen persona, her status as fan or non-fan, and extratextual information she possesses. The accounts of the female spectators surveyed by Jackie Stacey for her book *Star Gazing*, for example, overwhelmingly suggest that the characters the stars enacted were important only as a point of access to the performer "herself": "I'll never forget the first time I saw her, it was in *My Gal Sal* in 1942, and her name was Rita Hayworth. I couldn't take my eyes off her, she was the most perfect woman I had ever seen"

(Stacey 143). Stacey's accounts demonstrate a precise expression of McConnell's paradox of presence insofar as spectators simultaneously fantasize about their similarity to and distance from the star, who is at once "there" for them to admire and identify with, and "out of this world" (142), an impossibly glamorous figure in whose unreal situation the spectator can place herself for a short while (151). Here, it is the spectator's identificatory activity that is fundamental in conjuring the autonomous star as "a 'reality' which is not there" (175).

Spectator activity is similarly important in the case under discussion here, where the star onscreen is no longer alive. The situation presents a direct form of the paradox, as is demonstrated by McConnell's "ghoulish" fascination with the performance of a dying Spencer Tracy in *Guess Who's Coming to Dinner* (1967). McConnell suggests that, beyond being a memento of his decline, Tracy's performance is "a statement of life and persistence whose existential profundity goes far beyond the simple morality which the film intends to convey," and that his present interest might appear morbid only "because we have not yet invented an honest vocabulary for the art that will allow us to discuss such things" (167). The power of Tracy's performance for McConnell lies in the extratextual fact that is the knowledge of his death two weeks after production ended: the site of the human is perceived specifically as the "statement of life" expressed in the presence of a moving, living body that no longer exists. The profundity of this performance in a film that is essentially—for McConnell—"simple-minded" is something he suggests is important not just for his own spectatorship, but for film aesthetics and history. Introducing the dimension of time, Maltby also comments on how a star's death affects the ostensiveness of a performance that could otherwise appear natural: "with the passage of time and the completion of a career, a star's presence tends to overwhelm the presence of character in his or her performances: in *The Shootist* (1976) we witness not so much the death from cancer of J. B. Books, famous fictional lawman, as that of John Wayne, whose last performance this was" (Maltby 257).

Maltby's and McConnell's comments resonate with the critical interest that has been taken in the associations of death and indexicality in the photographic and cinematic image by writers including André Bazin, Siegfried Kracauer, and Roland Barthes. Returning to visit some of this work in a discussion of new technologies and changing patterns of spectatorship, Laura Mulvey focuses again on the paradox that lies in the way "the cinema combines, perhaps more perfectly than any other medium, two human fascinations: one with the boundary between life and death and the other with the mechanical animation of the inanimate, particularly the human, figure"

(11). In the dead star's "victory" over death onscreen, these two fascinations coincide. The impact on spectatorship is most precisely described by the second instance of the *punctum* that Barthes dwells upon in *Camera Lucida*, where the prick of the image of a condemned Lewis Payne comes not from a detail within its field but from external knowledge on its situation: "the photograph is handsome, as is the boy: that is the *studium*. But the *punctum* is: *he is going to die*. I read at the same time: *This will be and this has been*; I observe with horror an anterior future of which death is the stake" (96). The power of Ledger's image circulated in the trade press as part of his Oscar campaign—and, by extension, *any* image of Ledger as the Joker—derives from the effect of this *punctum*, where the spectator oscillates between the index of his death *"that-has-been"* (96) and the apparently prescient fiction of the nihilistic role.

In Mulvey's work, this affective phenomenon is discussed in relation to the "possessive spectator" who, in the delayed cinema of electronic viewing, is able to pause, extract, repeat, and possess the previously elusive image of the star (161). This spectator searches for the star's "pose" in the film, the stillness that she argues underlies every star performance as a display for the visual pleasure of the viewer. In the case of the dead star, the impact of the point of pose, already a digression from the fiction of the story, is doubled. In the iconic, posed image, the spectator encounters the index of the star's extradiegetic absence: "an acute consciousness of [her] 'then,' before [her] death, condenses with the image as death mask and the poignant presence of the index as the 'this was now'" (173). Mulvey's work here suggests a way of explaining the peculiar spectatorship experienced when watching the performances of a recently and prematurely dead star. As she describes, the reverie on fate and biography that is provoked by encountering the index does not persist in dwelling away from the image. Ultimately it gives way to return to the diegetic space of the story, where "the symbolic iconography of the star is indelibly stamped onto his or her presence both as 'character' and as index" (174). The slippage between the star's iconic and diegetic presence in the spectator's perception is, of course, a key aspect of star performance, insofar as the commercial star system relies on a star's visibility through his character (Maltby 252). But while directors will frequently leverage this transition for dramatic impact in a sequence, the situation under consideration here is entirely a function of spectatorship: it is the viewer who finds the star's pose—and death—in the diegesis and feeds this autonomous image back into the image. The dead star is, in this way, made unusually visible as his- or herself; his screen persona is *crystallized* for the possessive spectator, who finds presence in the order of Barthes's "first impulse": "There [s]he is! [S]he's really there!" (99). In the tricky field of star/performance studies, where the central challenge is *ekphrastic*—"a romantic yearning for language to convey or even recover a sense of corporeal presence" (Stern and Kouvaros 11)—this subjective location of the star's death as a "statement of life" offers a "map" of the star's persona. In the case of Ledger and my own possessive spectatorship, this map has three key points of orientation: history, modernity, and love.

★★★★★ History

Barthes acknowledges that the idea of the *punctum* is blurred in the extreme abundance of contemporary photographs. In historical photographs it is "vividly legible . . . there is always a defeat of Time in them: *that* is dead and *that* is going to die" (96). In this vein, there is a distinct poignancy in the historical persona that is constructed for Ledger as a result of several of his performances across the first half of the 2000s. As he proceeds to play a series of figures battling to prove the sweeping values of nation, family, love, and self-belief, acute associations of courage, chivalry, and self-sacrifice begin to stick to him. He is the natural soldier, the favorite son and brother, the absent and yearned-for lover, the underdog, the "swashbuckler," headstrong but principled, earnest but impish. Underpinning all his historical films—*The Patriot*, *A Knight's Tale*, *The Four Feathers*, *Ned Kelly*, and *The Brothers Grimm*—is a balance of violent action and genial sensitivity that speaks directly to a brand of "masculine ease" touted early on for Ledger, who was pegged by *Vanity Fair* as a classic screen idol distinct from other "dollish bad-boy idols" of the early 2000s. "When Heath smiles, it's Errol Flynn," claimed Brian Helgeland: "once every 50 years a guy like that comes along. For his age, Heath has an incredible manliness about him" (Kevin Sessums, "We're Havin' a Heath Wave," *Vanity Fair*, August 2000, 105). Ledger's sensitivity is principally expressed in these roles through his characters' strong attachment to family: above all he is a noble son, with all plots set up around his desire to honor and protect his parents (*The Patriot*, *Ned Kelly*), to prove his valor to them (*The Four Feathers*), or to demonstrate his transformation from his roots (*A Knight's Tale*, *The Brothers Grimm*). Ledger melds seamlessly into the melodramatic illusion of the historical film and its "scenarios of physical and spiritual struggle; of personal, familial, and group sacrifice; of patriotism; and of an intense and excessive concentration on belonging and exclusion" (Landy 17). As Marcia Landy has described, melodramatic representations of history are frequently more dependent on gesture and music than on narrative, and Ledger demonstrates a particular

Ledger fits the melodramatic illusion of the historical film in *The Four Feathers* (Shekhar Kapur, Paramount, 2002). Courtesy Photofest New York.

flair for historical action and body language. He looks effortless on a horse; with a sword, jousting post, or bow and arrow; and in period costume.

Further, he performs the actions and gestures with such props in the specifically reiterative manner that, Landy argues, the historical mode relies upon. He slips easily between different accents (American, English, Irish) as well as distinct dialects and style (from peasant to nobility, fourteenth century to nineteenth), and he is frequently the voice of heroic voiceover narration, as well as the utterer of the pithy and/or clichéd truisms that such stories rely upon: "We need to be reborn . . . like a phoenix rising from the ashes" (*A Knight's Tale*); "I am a widow's son, outlawed . . . my orders must be obeyed" (*Ned Kelly*). But he evokes pastness and its specific propriety most powerfully with his voice itself, where his deep and harmonious timbre (which more than one commentator has linked to his Brontë namesake) softly draws out vowels and his meticulous diction neatly clips words and phrases, all in a manner that makes everything he says sound like an aphorism or a private aside. The malleability of Ledger's voice is matched by an aptitude for physical transformation, which is also introduced in the early historical films: each crucial turn from peace to war is underlined by his striking transition from a clean-cut character absorbed in his daily routine to a bearded, beaten, and practically unrecognizable figure suddenly engaged in violent battle. Played in reverse, the tactic anchors the moment

of his star emergence in *A Knight's Tale*. Having won his first jousting con-
test pretending to be his dead master, the scruffy squire William Thatcher
emerges over the crest of a hill as his noble, clean-shaven alter-ego "Ulrich
von Lichtenstein." The moment is the first in a long series of plot points
throughout Ledger's career where his characters cannot be seen as themselves, and it sets in play an association with disguise that is later mobilized
to powerful effect in *I'm Not There*, *The Dark Knight*, and *The Imaginarium of
Doctor Parnassus* (2009).

It is Ledger's performance in Gregor Jordan's *Ned Kelly* that crystallizes
the historical image and in which the encounter with his index is starkest.
The role grafts Ledger's persona onto Kelly's historical figure as a romantic
outlaw fighting against the persecution of Irish Catholic immigrants by the
Protestant English establishment in Australia in the late 1870s. The legend
of Kelly—subject of several feature films before this one—rests upon a
nation's belief in the authenticity of the bushranger's courage, resolution,
and independence, and in a collective sympathy for the underdog, qualities
that resonate closely with the screen persona built up from Ledger's previous historical roles. In this bleak and elegant film, the full array of attitudes,
poses, and motifs associated with his professional "heritage" image appear:
a fierce, self-sacrificing love of family, a chivalrous drive to protect, pithy
phrases ("Such is life"), attractiveness for "noble" women, a competent reluc-
tance in warfare, resonant voiceover narration, physical disguise through
iconic, boxy armor, and the mischievous, notorious charisma—articulated
in the specific form of Australian larrikin mythology.[2]

The "authenticity" of Ledger's image here, summed up most eloquently
in his impassive stare in *Ned Kelly*'s key publicity shot, is also a tangible
upshot of his offscreen determination, from early in his career, to avoid the
"heartthrob" branding attempted upon him by Hollywood after the teen
film *10 Things I Hate About You* (1999) and *A Knight's Tale*. The *Ned Kelly*
image thus forms a key counterpoint to the rejected beefcake star image
expressed most purely in the Bruce Weber shot used for the cover of *Vanity
Fair*'s August 2000 issue, where a blond and smirking Ledger leans against
a wall in a white singlet, thumbs hooked into low-slung jeans that reveal
the band of his underwear and a few dark strands of pubic hair (later air-
brushed out for the magazine cover).[3] The image unambiguously illustrates
the "effortlessly seductive masculinity" in everything from Ledger's expertise on a horse to his taste for Gene Kelly. This hyperbolic image amounted
to what was for Ledger a manufactured career that he wanted to "scrub
away" (Luscombe 68). Practically all interviews and profiles on Ledger
stress this attitude and its perceived ruthlessness. Frequently linked to an

independent antipodean streak mythologized in *Ned Kelly*'s larrikin persona and the rhetoric of the "Australian Invasion" actors described above, Ledger's determination to "destroy [his] career a bit . . . to take the shine off it a little" (Cullum 57) is applauded as evidence of a drive to engage only in projects he believed in. Jordan, who also directed Ledger in *Two Hands* (1999), has put it most succinctly: "They wanted him to be Harrison Ford. He want[ed] to be Sean Penn" (Luscombe 70).

The extent to which Ledger's persona is submerged in the Ned Kelly myth is exaggerated by his death, for Kelly was also a "star" who died young: he was hanged in Melbourne at the age of twenty-five, despite a petition for clemency containing 30,000 signatures. However, aside from the coincidence of this fictional death and of those whereby Ledger dies as Gabriel Martin in *The Patriot* and comes close as Harry Feversham in *The Four Feathers*, the encounter with Ledger's index in the historical narratives is largely an effect of the emphasis on transformation and disguise. For the power of his performances lies not in his embodiment of a "true" character who emerges at the narrative's end but in the ambiguity that precedes this: Ledger's skill is in conveying the uncertainty of characters who are not yet themselves, who are "learning how to be" (Lipsky 35), often in the shadow of troubled family relationships. In the historical films this speaks simultaneously to a coming-of-age mythology and to the mode's narration of particular "types" in place of rounded, human figures: the son who makes his father proud, the peasant who "changes his stars," the coward who redeems himself. *Monster's Ball* and *The Order* are not period films, but Ledger performs similarly unfixed characters upon which the burdens of a patriarchal figure trigger realization of some kind. In the former film the hatred and dissatisfaction of his prison guard father (Billy Bob Thornton) leads Ledger's Sonny Grotowski to a shocking suicide; in the latter, the death and "sin eating" involvements of his Catholic mentor engage the young priest Alex Bernier in an investigation that rocks his understanding of the nature of evil. In these roles, Ledger is *in process* and thus ungraspable, uncentered, provoking a sensation that cannot help but resonate with the iconography of the prematurely dead that has canonized Ledger as a "doomed beauty . . . a face frozen in time, a youth who never grew up" (Carman 28).

★★★★★ Modernity

A profound consequence of Ledger's "authentic" historical persona is that it throws his contemporary performances into relief. He never seems quite at home in the modern world. The effect is the exact opposite to that which Adrian Martin has identified in Dennis Hopper: "It is as if (like [Jean-Pierre] Léaud) Hopper is too much, too extravagantly 'himself'—and also too much an emblem or mirror of present-day associations and idioms—to be accepted within the dramatic illusion of the historical film" (Martin 9). Ledger's persona is based on never embodying an image that could be perceived as a present-day "self" in this way. The majority of his performances present emphatically *posed* characters constrained by period or fantasy frameworks: California's 1975 skate scene, a millennial Rome plagued by demons, the culturally conservative American West of the 1960s to the 1980s, lush eighteenth-century Venice, Bob Dylan's early 1960s bubble of stardom, the eternally futuristic fantasy of Gotham City. In *The Imaginarium of Doctor Parnassus*, the build-up of this effect is felt most fully, with Ledger the central figure in the surreal, archaic world of the Imaginarium as transplanted into modern locations. Ledger's disjunctive effect is expressed directly in the early sequence where, clad in his nineteenth-century outfit, he chats with women in a "Homebase" superstore among computers and Coke machines. He is the perfect motif for Gilliam's signature fantasy/reality threshold.

The jolt of the contemporary is felt most acutely as a sensation of life breaking through Ledger's impassive, heritage façade. As a force clearly repressed in the traumatized Sonny Grotowski and the principled Alex Bernier, Ledger's liveliness is first felt in the kinetic, spirited context of *Lords of Dogtown*, where his "Pied-Piper"–like Skip Engblom is first seen surfing around a pier at Venice Beach. The hedonistic joy of the experience, completely at odds with the righteous persona of his previous roles, signals how Ledger will be wonderfully loose, free, and lazy in this film. His sonorous historical intonation curls up into a sneering, nasal California drawl, and his face is transformed by the appearance of his teeth beneath his drawn-up top lip. His vowels become longer again, their purposeful softness translated into a whining, sustained inflection: "You guys *lawst* or *whaaat*?" he demands of a pair of itinerant surfers crashing his territory. Within the context of the film, Skip's persona is directly linked to the drug culture of his environment. As the film's director, Catherine Hardwicke, notes: "In most of *Dogtown*, Heath's character is drinking or high, so that's a state he had to get to every day" (Josh Rottenberg and Christine Spines, "He Knew He'd Done Something Special," *Entertainment Weekly*, 23 January 2009, 22). Here the self-sacrificing drive of the earlier roles is replaced with a self-destructive impulse, as the oddly patriarchal Skip embraces the lifestyle of this 1970s counterculture in an effort to cover his own loneliness and insecurity. For the first time, there is no foundational family connection to anchor and direct Ledger's character, only the talented teenagers who one by one abandon his local skate team.

In the film's key sequence, a party at Skip's Zephyr shop, Ledger performs the antithesis of the impassive, historical image. He ducks and weaves through the crowd as though on a surfboard, his face contorting in delirious satisfaction and his tongue emerging to gesture emphatically. The sequence hinges on the last scene, where Skip throws surfboards from the roof of the shop in a drunken rage. Hardwicke admits she was "semi-terrified" during the filming of this scene, as she had noticed "when [Ledger] was drinking a beer in a scene, he'd ask the prop people for a real beer, not a fake beer. [When] he got up on the roof . . . we didn't know if he was going to fall off and kill himself. . . . You just didn't know where his chemistry was. . . . You feel that in the film. You don't know how far this guy is going to go. That's how we felt in some ways about Heath" (Rottenberg and Spines 22). It seems no accident that the other role in which Ledger seems emphatically "alive" in this way is also a drug film, but in *Candy* the brashness and energy of his performance as Skip has morphed into vulnerable underachievement. As the junkie Dan, Ledger is animated not just by heroin but by his obsessive love for his girlfriend (Abbie Cornish).

Both *Lords of Dogtown* and *Candy* frame Ledger in the type of "altered state" that Anna Powell has identified in films featuring drug trips. She focuses on cinematic images of drug use as an "intoxicant cluster of images, music, editing and other stylistic techniques" (Powell 54). Where Hardwicke's film expresses this intoxication through the restless, hand-held camera movement, the "counterculture" music, and the stylized abandon of the actor's bodies, *Candy* mobilizes the realism of drug addiction through the three acts: "Heaven," "Earth," and "Hell." The experiences of intoxication and deprivation rest entirely upon the lead performances, where paradoxically it is Ledger's naturalism that gives rise to the "alterity" that Powell describes. The transcendence of the initial "Heaven" sequence is depicted in the low-key trips of a theme park ride, a car wash, and the girlfriend's parents' bathroom where, for the first time, Ledger is a character entirely (if artificially) content with the world. His individual animation manifests as a loose ease in his body and environment, a physical state that mimics the dumb bliss of heroin. While Ledger's own vigor here stems again from a hedonistic lack of purpose, the overarching moral logic of *Candy* is unmistakable. As with many drug and addiction films, the emphasis is on degradation as punishment. The narrative trajectory is classic in its spiraling downward and slow movement up again, as both Dan and Candy are scared straight by her mental breakdown but lose each other in the process.

Interestingly, one review finds in this trajectory "a palpable sense that the filmmakers are relishing the chance to fuck up their bright young leads" (Dave Hoskin, "Candy: Wasted Youth," *Metro*, June 2006, 25).

For Ledger, this impression manifests most directly in the grueling detox scene where he cries out and punches himself in the shower. The scene is a mirror to the drunken scene in *Lords of Dogtown* in that it also amplifies the openness and intimacy of his performance in a highly cathartic and improvised moment. Director Neil Armfield describes how "it was written that he just sits in the shower whimpering. . . . It was his idea, and he did give himself a black eye in the process. . . . It was scary, for a while I thought, 'oh, I think it's gone too far'" (Dave Hoskin, "Rebelling Against Heroin Chic," *Metro*, June 2006, 30). In the context of Ledger's career, though, the "fucking up" impact of the *Candy* role extends to a lack of direction and control that is broader than this moment. Complementing the sense of his indeterminate screen persona, Ledger is often ascribed a man-boy status. Steve Alexander claims he had "all the characteristics of a man, yet he was a boy" (*Interview*, April 2008); Brian Helgeland describes him as an "old soul" (Fred Schruers, "On the Ledge," *W*, May 2001, 213), although here this is cast in an especially hopeless light, as Dan is repeatedly reminded that he's "not a teenager anymore." Ledger's boyish, unabashed stance is contained in his grin, which emerges naturally for the first time in a summation of his claim that "the world is very bewildering to a junkie." Ledger's grin etches the deep creases at the edge of his mouth that will be exaggerated in the crazed motif of the Joker's own dynamism, where it evolves to express a hyperbolic version of this chaos, a pure statement of life as a utopian force: "Introduce a little anarchy, you upset the established order, and everything becomes chaos . . . and you know the thing about chaos? *It's fair.*"

⭐⭐⭐⭐⭐ **Love**

Brokeback Mountain unquestionably marks a turning point in Ledger's career, and for many critics constitutes a specifically "redemptive" turn. It is with Ang Lee's film that Ledger is generally understood to emerge from the period of invisibility effected by his rejection of the glossy star image, the period in which, as *Time* had it, he "virtually disappeared from the kind of movies . . . everyone enjoys" (Luscombe 68). With *Brokeback*, Ledger gains from his association with a film event, the kind of cultural phenomenon that is "transformed . . . from a marketplace product into a signifier of personal worth, political position, and cultural values, accelerating the process by which, more commonly, classic films organically acquire

Ledger as western archetype in *Brokeback Mountain* (Ang Lee, Alberta Film Entertainment, 2005). Courtesy Photofest New York.

meanings and communities years after their initial release" (Rich 44). In the positive appraisal of this phenomenon, Ledger is fundamental for two reasons. First, his star status, variously interpreted as "A-list heart-throb" (Ara Osterweil, "Ang Lee's Lonesome Cowboys," *Film Quarterly*, Spring 2007, 38) and "up-and-coming [actor] with major sex appeal" (Rich 44), is a central factor in the perception of the film as a breakthrough in commercial cinema: "Of all the popular renditions of gay relationships in mainstream American films, it's hard to think of even one that presents an outright, unabashed love story, much less between movie stars" (Cullum 58). While Ledger and his co-star Jake Gyllenhaal are given equal credit on this score, it is Ledger's performance that is typically understood as the site of the film's dramatic force, a fact directly signaled by his Oscar nomination for Best Actor. As Todd Haynes has said, in an evaluation that obviously led to his choice of Ledger for *I'm Not There*: "The entire emotional power of that film, which is enormous, resides in that performance, and how much Heath holds in. That restraint is what makes us yield emotionally and fill in all of the pieces ourselves. So he sort of unleashes the audience's emotions by controlling his own" (*Interview*, April 2008).

Haynes's point demonstrates the second way in which Ledger is fundamental to the film's effect. He is read as the site of its western/melodrama hybridity. This generic status is another aspect that is typically regarded as central to its "breakthrough" capacity, insofar as the tragedy of Ennis and Jack's love story is linked directly to their apparently traditional masculinity in a way that is seen as accurate to some gay men's experience (Joshua Clover and Christopher Nealon, "Don't Ask, Don't Tell Me," *Film Quarterly*, Spring 2007, 62). Where Gyllenhaal's "pretty" looks and associations, his "soulful eyes and gleaming teeth" (Polly Vernon, "The Heath Factor," *Madison*, February 2010, 46), are ideal for the more active and optimistic Jack, it is Ledger's historical persona that is ultimately mobilized as the site of the repressive experience they share. It is the impassive, principled demeanor of *The Patriot*, *Ned Kelly*, and *The Four Feathers* that conveys this masculinity, albeit with none of the confidence that Ledger exhibits in any of those roles. Interviewed about his performance, Ledger claimed that "Ennis Del Mar is probably the most masculine character I've played to date. . . . For me, I think the violence in Ennis is from the battle against his genetic structure. The beliefs that have been handed to him from his father and his father's father" (Cullum 56–57). As imagined by Ledger, Ennis's masculinity is nothing more than these beliefs, which form an empty shell, a moral purpose without purpose. The strength of his performance again comes from his impression of threshold status, of not yet being himself. The melodramatic force of the film, of course, lies in the recognition that he is frozen to the point that he will never become this, a tragedy underlined by Ledger's most impressive physical transformation, where, over twenty years of story time, the sheer weight of his paralysis registers in his body and voice.

The perceived realism of Ledger's performance as Ennis owes a great deal to his historical persona. In a *Brokeback Mountain* featurette, screenwriter Diana Ossana describes how Ledger rode a horse "like he was born on one," but Ennis's laconic attitude also mobilized much of the measured way that Ledger spoke, moved, and engaged with other characters as Gabriel Martin, Harry Feversham, and Ned Kelly. The force of this persona is expressed in a single image in *Brokeback Mountain*, where Ennis, clad in denim and cowboy hat at a Fourth of July picnic, is framed in a low-angle profile shot against a sky full of fireworks, his right fist loosely clenched at his side. Framing him as western archetype, the moment is a highly stylized one in the context of the film. In his first expression of real anger, Ennis has just physically threatened two bikers who asked, "Where's the pussy?" in front of his two infant daughters. As Ennis kicks them both to the ground the camera looks up at him from the bikers' perspective, then back at them both cowering away from him. It then moves back to a medium shot of Ennis before crossing the 180-degree line to frame him in the stance against the fireworks. The sudden shift in perspective makes the shot jump out from the screen. After the energy of his violent movement Ennis appears unnaturally still, the bright sky surrounding him like an aura.

As a display of protective masculine strength, this image is a precise expression of Ledger's star *pose*. It is a moment of "almost invisible stillness" (Mulvey 162) that derails the realism of the film for an instant to dwell on the messages of control and principle contained in his body. What the narrative of *Brokeback Mountain* adds to this pose, of course, is the dimension of repression, which is expressed here as Ennis's containment of the anger that the bikers' heterosexual dirty talk has sparked in him. The role thus marks another significant shift in Ledger's persona, for the repression that has been a generic aspect of his image in the controlled historical roles becomes the *subject* of his performance, and of *Brokeback Mountain* itself. The melodrama of action and gesture becomes melodrama as pathos, as Ennis's learned beliefs are undermined and emptied out by his hunger for Jack. The signs that have formerly conveyed impassive strength—the pursed lips, the evasive eyes, the mannered enunciation—come to life in the expression of real feeling. As in the drug roles, the animation that this produces in Ledger is a function of addiction: the young men's attachment, as Jack describes, is a situation of being unable to "quit" one another. As D. A. Miller has suggested, though, Ledger's performance of repressing *this* addiction can be read into his very person: "Just how thoroughly Ledger threw himself into this repression is suggested in the fact that, on the same set where he was playing at falling in love with Jake Gyllenhaal, he really did fall in love with Michelle Williams, reversing Ennis's swing from Alma to Jack with fastidious precision" (D. A. Miller, "On the Universality of *Brokeback Mountain*," *Film Quarterly*, Spring 2007, 54).

The consideration of an untimely star end connects in compelling ways to the history of ideas on death, memory, and photography. The Heideggerian notions of "angst" and "being-toward-death" suggest that an awareness of one's human temporality and mortality is fundamental for an authentic, attuned existence. In a similar vein, the existential psychotherapist Irvin Yalom describes how the confrontation with one's own death or that of someone close functions as an "awakening experience" that can impel a transformation to a life of engagement, connectivity, and self-fulfillment (34). A star's death prompts a reverie that mobilizes these sensations of awakening and attunement in the experience of spectatorship, simultaneously highlighting the mythologizing process of stardom as audience investment, and isolating the index of the star's persona. In the case of Heath Ledger, this index emerges in direct coincidence with his demise and canonization. His performances collectively construct an image of a character always in the process of becoming something else, indeed, stunningly, always marching toward death. This ungraspable nature is the performative foundation of Ledger's repeat embodiments of mythical and mythologized figures. In his most iconic roles it is sent, respectively, into atrophy and hyperbole. As Ennis Del Mar Ledger froze in an inherited persona he could not overcome. As the Joker he evaded the very notion of identity in a mission of constant transformation.

NOTES

1. The first posthumous winner was Peter Finch for his role as Howard Beale in *Network* (Sidney Lumet, 1976). Other actors who have been nominated for Oscars after their death include Spencer Tracy, Ralph Richardson, James Dean, and Massimo Troisi.

2. The Australian National Dictionary traces the genealogy of "larrikin" from a historically negative term to one that has come to be used affectionately to mean "a person who [does] not always adhere strictly to polite social conventions; a bit of a stirrer." See www.anu.edu.au/andc/pubs/ozwords/June_98/5._larrikin. htm.

3. This image and others from the photo shoot can be viewed at www.vanityfair.com/culture/features/2009/08/heath-ledger-portfolio200908#slide=14.

9 ★★★★★★★★★★★

Leonardo DiCaprio and Sean Penn
Acting Authentic

MICHAEL K. HAMMOND

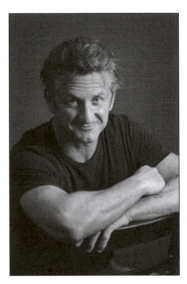

The star personae of Sean Penn and Leonardo DiCaprio are built around a publicly celebrated ability to act. Each established early in his career performances that were remarked upon as revealing a character while concealing the actor. They are consistently described in the press as disappearing into their roles. Both are also connected, although in different ways, to American traditions of film acting, whether linked to the Actors Studio "Method" as with Penn or through endorsements by Robert De Niro and Martin Scorsese as in the case of DiCaprio. In this decade they both chose to redirect the presentation of their private selves through the support of political causes. The comparison of these performers demonstrates two instances in which the overlap between stars' public and private lives is utilized to publicize film projects, build audience expectations, and reveal themes of historical and social change against which the life of a recognizable and "real" individual plays out.

Leonardo DiCaprio. Courtesy of Photofest New York. Sean Penn.

In 2004, Sean Penn recorded the narration for the audio book of Bob Dylan's autobiography *Chronicles Vol. One*. "I see Sean with Kerouac or the young Bob Dylan," Angelica Huston once remarked. Here, his voice is immediately recognizable by its low register, thin texture, and slightly blurred articulation. As each sentence drifts by, the voice imperceptibly shape-shifts so that soon, Sean Penn has disappeared: into a prose that recites the names of American icons such as Dempsey, Gorgeous George, Judy Garland, Charlie Parker, and Billie Holiday. Penn, the born-too-late icon of the past that Anjelica Huston conjures up, appears here in the guise of Dylan with his distinctively American voice, but also speaks in his own voice. This bestows upon Penn the mantle and scepter of authenticity that is validated by attendant associations with the image of the political, social, and artistic rebels and colorful characters who passed through Dylan's early life. This is the voice that positions Penn within what Greil Marcus has termed an "invisible republic." Placing Penn next to Dylan, Penn as Penn as Dylan in this way offers an example of the trajectory of Penn's star persona during the 2000s. The upheaval of the 1960s that frames Dylan rhymes with Penn's political activism that emerged forcefully in the first decade of the twenty-first century via his visits to Iraq and Iran, and his public outrage at the illegal Iraq war and the disaster of Hurricane Katrina.

Penn is consistently described in press books as "a unique American icon." The connection with iconic American revenants, rebels who do not fit with "corporate America," remains consistent throughout the decade, from his portrayal of historical iconoclasts such as Huey Long and Harvey Milk to his impersonations of dispossessed and traumatized outcasts such as Paul Rivers in Alejandro Gonzáles Iñárritu's *21 Grams* (2003) or Samuel Bicke in Niels Mueller's *The Assassination of Richard Nixon* (2004).

A younger version of this figure is Leonardo DiCaprio. Like Penn, DiCaprio is identified as being in touch with American traditions of acting. His various biographical sources list his favorite actors as Robert De Niro, Meryl Streep, Jack Nicholson, and James Dean, choices that mirror, or even mimic, Penn's connection with the male tradition of Nicholson and De Niro, although in adding Streep he appears to suggest a kind of masculinity more attuned with the "kinder, gentler" decade of the 1990s. His private life, while offering a whiff of violence (he was unsuccessfully sued for allegedly instigating a street fight, and in 2005 he was attacked by a woman with a glass), has not shown the kind of aggression toward the media that Penn has displayed. However, like Penn, DiCaprio has been involved in political causes but primarily those that overlap with the broader themes of his films. His commitment to ecological responsibility inspired his interview of

President Bill Clinton in March 2000 for the ABC news documentary "Planet Earth 2000" (see "Actor Interviews Clinton," *New York Times*, 1 April 2000). The publicity accorded to the interview can also be seen as a prelude to the February 2000 release of *The Beach*, if not simply a recasting of image from teen heartthrob to serious actor interested in serious causes. Such a move was noted by Michele Willens in a *New York Times* piece two weeks later:

> The suddenness of Mr. DiCaprio's emergence as an environmental champion—he had not publicly flexed his social consciousness before—suggests some intriguing questions about the relationship between celebrities and the causes they espouse. To what degree are a star's motives altruistic, and to what degree self-promotional? When is an actor using a high profile to draw the spotlight to a worthy cause, and when is he or she hoping for a more flattering form of personal media coverage?
>
> ("When Celebrity Hearts Bleed," 16 April 2000)

There is an obvious tension here. Stardom has been variously described as a phenomenon whereby the actor's private life merges with his onscreen characterizations, as an asset in bringing audiences to films, as a power brokerage in the inception and production of films, as an individual instance, or as performance—the intersection of sociocultural and political discourse. DiCaprio's move to distance himself from his pretty-boy phenomenon of the 1990s has been successful and consistent throughout the 2000s, in his choice of films and his work with two icons of American cinema, Steven Spielberg and Martin Scorsese. In a different way, Penn's countercultural rebel tag demonstrates Barry King's observation that the star sits between "capital and labor" (King "Stardom"). Penn is not only spiritually and temperamentally connected to a mythical past but also describes, with his commitment and in his performance, a community of concerned citizen/artists, who are spokespersons for addressing the ravages and transgressions of that commercial, capitalist enterprise, that imago-corporate America, Hollywood. As Sean Penn, playing himself in Barry Levinson's *What Just Happened* (2008), says to the fictitious out-of-control British director Jeremy Brunell (Michael Wincott), changes are okay in the film he has made with him, "as long as we kept our edge."

★★★★★ Rebels with a Cause

Penn entered the 2000s with this rebel image more or less ascendant. He was discussed in the media mainly as a tempestuous if intense actor whose personal life had in the past included a much-publicized marriage to and then divorce from Madonna amid accusations of spousal abuse, and a jail term for assaulting a photographer. Now he developed from bad boy to "American icon" in three areas of his persona: actor, writer/director, and activist. Arguably, the angry young man of his personal life morphed into a more focused adulthood as political activist. In this role he began using his star clout to support Democratic candidates in both the 2004 and 2008 elections and became a decade-long outspoken critic of the policies of the presidency of George W. Bush, most intensively following the invasion of Iraq. He also came into conflict with right-wing commentators in the media, particularly Fox News opinionators Bill O'Reilly and Sean Hannity, for his outspoken views on the Bush administration and for his 2009 Oscar acceptance speech that condemned California's Proposition 8 (banning gay marriage). Penn was awarded two Academy Awards as Best Actor, for *Mystic River* (2004) and *Milk* (2008). He directed two films, *The Pledge* (2001) and *Into the Wild* (2007), both of which received critical acclaim, as well as an eleven-minute-nine-second-and-one-frame segment of *11'09"01—September 11* (2002). His status as virtuoso actor and maturing director frequently overlapped with his personal and political life through his choice of material, whether as narrator of documentaries such as Loretta Laper and Jeremy Earp's *War Made Easy: How Presidents and Pundits Keep Spinning Us to Death* (2007) or in playing historical figures such as San Francisco city supervisor Harvey Milk. His projects and appearances on television talk shows (such as those of Bill Maher and Charlie Rose) consistently addressed the politics of the period to the point that Penn's star presence in film and in the media generated expectations of a political "message" and prompted commentary from political media commentators as well as entertainment journalists.

Penn's stardom predates, then coincides with, the arrival of the Internet and the advent of a shifting mediascape where the star's virtuosity is but one part of his persona, and where there is a demand for an increasing emphasis on presenting a "real self" as opposed to characters or types. Such a shift is characterized by Barry King in this way: "As the primary source of personal accumulation has ceased to be a set of 'organic' performance skills . . . the concept of performance has shifted from representation to presentation" ("Stardom" 9). The presentation of the self has an economic expediency which, as King suggests, allows the star to literally own his image, and therefore control it. "Their original sphere of endeavour (in Penn's case consummate actor) shrinks before the drive to maximize the media visibility of their names and the branding opportunities that come from the intensive marketing of their personae" (9). This is a significant shift away from stardom of earlier eras. Penn's presentation of "self" brings his virtuosity into line with his political views and beliefs, themselves delivered with a similar "Method-acting" intensity. In Penn's case the realms of performance as actor and director coexist and inform the star persona, because he exists as a celebrity in ways that endorse politicians, react to historical events, and solicit causes rather than sell products. The 2000s see Penn's persona take full flight in this direction.

By comparing Leonardo DiCaprio's image readjustment during the decade it is possible to see how certain tropes are present in both personae. DiCaprio shares with Penn the "original sphere of endeavor" of virtuoso acting. At the end of the 1990s, he reflected to Cal Fussman of *Esquire*, "I set up everything in my personal life to rebel against [my earlier] image in order to strip it down. I had a lot of fun stripping it down. But ultimately, that knocked me a few rungs down the ladder" ("10 Essential Lessons from Leonardo DiCaprio," 11 February 2010). DiCaprio reworked that matinee-idol image through choosing projects that simultaneously connected him with independent production, with mainstream filmmaking, and with his prowess as an actor. In 2001, *Don's Plum*, a film he had shot as an improv, was released in Europe without his approval. The films that followed—Steven Spielberg's *Catch Me If You Can* (2002) and Martin Scorsese's *Gangs of New York* (2002), *The Aviator* (2004), and *The Departed* (2006)—not only attached him to two auteurs of American cinema but also centered him within both the commercial Hollywood that Spielberg connotes and the wellspring of American art cinema associated with Scorsese. Where his persona departs from Penn's combination of acting virtuosity and personal commitment lies in this ability to attenuate both indie and studio connotations. Looking at his career trajectory, Caryn James of the *New York Times* noted:

> Mr. DiCaprio has smartly parlayed that success into the kind of career few actors can get away with in the age of relentless gossip: a new form of old-fashioned Hollywood stardom that uses celebrity to advance social causes yet rarely lets the public beyond the glittering veil of the photo op. . . . How many times can one almost-32-year-old movie star be told he's finally outgrown his baby face?
> ("The Baby-Faced Kid Has Developed Quite a Stare," 29 October 2006)

This coming of age trajectory from boy in the 1990s to mature—and controlling—actor and activist reworks the time-honored trope of the youthful star finding salvation from the temptations of celebrity in his craft. His description as "a new form of old-fashioned Hollywood" (James) suggests a connection with the American film and acting tradition different than Penn's, although they share some of the same touchstones. The focus on the combination of acting and activism across the public/private dynamic is worked through in a quite different way with Penn.

⭐⭐⭐⭐⭐ **A Method Man**

In the year 2000, Penn acted in three films: Philip Haas's *Up at the Villa*, Julian Schnabel's *Before Night Falls*, and Kathryn Bigelow's *The Weight of Water*. None of these provide an overt example of the earlier bad-boy image, but instead they delineate a committed actor and filmmaker. *Up at the Villa*, a period piece from a Somerset Maugham story, received lukewarm reviews, yet Penn was associated with the exclusive club of American Method actors, in this case Anne Bancroft. "It's tempting to say that she . . . and Mr. Penn are miscast, but the movie is such a slapdash affair that one is grateful for the odd, inventive Actors Studio inflections they bring to it, like a jolt of bourbon in a cup of weak tea" (A. O. Scott, "By Jove, This Tuscan Sun, It's a Bit Dicey, Eh What?" *New York Times*, 5 May 2000). The review uses a theme of effete Britishness to cast the two American actors in high relief, hitting two notes that resonate with Penn's persona, Americanness and virtuosity, while also implying an anti-Hollywood angle that connotes authenticity and intensity. This theme remains somewhat consistent in the reviews for Penn's other two films of that year. In *The Weight of Water*, an eagerly awaited opus seen by reviewers as admirable but flawed, Penn's role as a poet is a counter to the usual type of masculinity that Bigelow explores. Stephen Holden of the *New York Times* felt the film missed a chance with the actor: "Although Penn gets to quote from Dylan Thomas his talents are wasted in a role that remains largely underwritten" ("Women at the Edge a Century Apart," 1 November 2002). *Before Night Falls* offers an example of Penn's political commitment and his ability to bring offbeat projects to the screen through his involvement, highlighting his continued association with the independent filmmaking community. This was a cameo appearance for him, which he did in order to help get the film made. "I wanted to help Julian out because I know what it's like to have to hustle to finance a film" (Kelly 368).

Penn appeared next in *I Am Sam* (2001), playing a mentally handicapped father fighting for the custody of his child. This film was for all intents and purposes a mainstream Hollywood release. The reviews were mixed, although most found fault less with Penn's performance than with the film itself. Robert Kohler's review in *Variety* was couched in terms of the conflict between Penn the committed actor and the cop-out sentimentality of the film, by this time an established trope in Penn's star discourse. Kohler casts Penn's performance as "fenced-in" by the demands of mainstream Hollywood: "Here, Penn the actor is constrained to a purely technical, behavioral perf as Sam, with helmer Jessie Nelson making the most elementary possible movie from a complex welter of emotions, human demands and societal responsibilities." The writer strikes an equivalence between the character fighting a system and the actor up against a commercial aesthetic. Kohler also wonders "what a meatier—and doubtless more despairing—film Penn the director would have culled from the same dramatic situation" ("I Am Sam," 24 December 2001, 22). Penn's virtuosity as an actor draws attention to the absence of his darker directorial vision.

But the stage was being set for the emergence of Penn the activist by George W. Bush's arrival in the White House in January 2001 and the terrorist attacks of September 11. Of the latter, Penn told Alex Simon in an interview with *Venice* magazine in 2002 that he hoped that now "instead of avoiding thoughtful things . . . (in movies) . . . perhaps [film audiences] would seek them out" ("I Am Sean," February 2002, 50). Penn's statement characterizes mass audience taste as the driving force behind the aesthetic constraints of the industry but it also positions him as representative of just such thoughtful filmmaking. Penn's anti-Hollywood reputation, partly generated through this combination of acting virtuosity, his directorial efforts, and his publicly stated politics—all significant aspects of his star persona— was well established by 2001. In an article in *Variety* on the merger between French production house StudioCanal US and Universal, Pierre Lescure, head of the resulting Vivendi-Universal, explained his own role as a translator between European talent and Universal studio executives. He recounted that "Universal's first reaction was, 'Give us the money and we'll make those little films for you.' . . . But we had relationships with directors like [Jim] Jarmusch, [David] Lynch and Sean Penn who wanted to work with Europeans" ("Synergy—That Lescure Object of Desire," 12 November 2001, 46). Penn's business reputation is consonant with the integrity/ authenticity discourse that forms a considerable aspect of his public persona, and one that an association with European cinema enhances. This seems to be at play in the decision by Alain Brigand when he asked Penn to make the U.S. contribution to his portmanteau of eleven short films, *11'09"01—September 11*. Penn's contribution to this project was a one-man performance by veteran actor Ernest Borgnine, who plays a widower unable to come to terms with the death of his wife. His grief has become an obsession as he talks to her and lays her clothes out each day. The shadows of skyscrapers collapsing and letting sunlight into his small apartment has a cathartic effect on him. The choice of using Borgnine was one that signaled Penn's connection not simply to the classical studio period in Hollywood but also to Borgnine's history of working in 1950s live television and his near legendary status as consummate character actor.

★★★★★ Acting Out Trauma

Arguably the issue of trauma has been a feature of both Penn's and DiCaprio's output in the 2000s. In fact, describing his "trademark," IMDb notes that DiCaprio "plays conflicted, tortured-by-their-own-demons characters, who need to deal with their past." Examples can be found in DiCaprio's work with Scorsese, a director who specializes in cinematic studies of trauma. Also in this category is his work with Spielberg, another director often concerned with the traumas visited on children and the family. In *Gangs of New York*, DiCaprio's Amsterdam Vallon witnesses the killing of his father as a small boy. The narrative engine of the film is primarily driven by Vallon's desire for vengeance complicated by feelings of doubt. In *The Aviator*, his portrayal of the obsessive-compulsive billionaire Howard Hughes earned DiCaprio an Oscar nomination. The film opens with a primal scene of his mother bathing him that insinuates the cause of the character's disorder and obsession with cleanliness. The performance was informed by the preparation DiCaprio did with a psychiatrist, and he had on-set advice from a patient with obsessive-compulsive disorder, prompting a report in the *New York Times* that outlined the veracity of DiCaprio's performance. The article quoted Dr. Peter C. Whybrow praising DiCaprio: "You didn't feel that he was acting the pathology. . . . You felt the pathology was part of him. You could look at him and think he was really suffering" (Irene Lacher, "Method and Madness: Making Crazy Look Real," 12 March 2005). His Billy Costigan in *The Departed* was also a character who, if not quite traumatized, was certainly under enormous stress as an undercover agent infiltrating a murderous gang; he visits a psychiatrist and self-medicates. In this role his actorly qualities were again praised; according to Caryn James, Costigan was "his grittiest mature role":

> His cropped hair minimizes Mr. DiCaprio's movie-star glamor. But the performance goes deeper than those external clues. He shows in his eyes the undercover agent's fear and revulsion, a fear he has to reveal to the camera yet conceal from the mobsters in the room. We see the difference between that fear and the confusion he sometimes displays in his role as the mob's newest member, full of braggadocio. And we see how he is torn by stress almost, but not quite, to the breaking point.   (James)

James points out that the complexity required from an actor to convincingly play such a character is evidence of maturity.

In *Catch Me If You Can*, DiCaprio embodies a boy who is trying to overcome the disruption of the breakup of his parents' marriage through pretending to be various socially valid versions of manhood, an airline pilot, a doctor, and a lawyer. In *Blood Diamond* (2008) he plays a mercenary who recalls the primal scene of his parents' murder at the hands of rebels in Rhodesia.

DiCaprio rounds out the decade with two other films, again playing characters who are in one way or another living through or working out traumatic events. *Body of Lies* and *Revolutionary Road* (both 2008) exhibit what Stuart Levine of *Variety* proclaimed the "dark view." Exploring the noirish vision of America that some European directors were demonstrating, Levine noted that this theme had been consistently worked into both films. In *Body of Lies* Roger Ferris (DiCaprio) is a CIA operative who is chasing a terrorist ring but is subject to the incomplete information given to him by his superior in Washington (Russell Crowe). DiCaprio's character reacts against the organization's mis-information and blasé stance, often explosively. Crucially for DiCaprio's overarching persona, the role places him as the American hero caught between the virtually unreadable terrorist network and the kind of government agency that only shares knowledge and agendas on a need-to-know basis. He is persistently angry and in danger in this political thriller and has a number of set-piece scenes of violent reaction against the CIA. In *Revolutionary Road*, he is a young husband and veteran of World War II who is in a humdrum office job and a failing marriage. Here the issue is the darkness at home. The ability of DiCaprio to play damaged characters both highlights an acting style centered on the display of trauma and recalls the venerable tradition of traumatized characters in American cinema. Todd McCarthy's review of *Road* points to DiCaprio's ability to indicate a man's thought process "in the split second before he decides what to say. At certain moments, the conjoined cerebral and emotional aspects of his characterization summon the spirit of Jack Nicholson's breakthrough performances around the time of 'Five Easy Pieces'" ("Actors Conjure 'Road' Rage," *Variety*, 24 November 2008).

This theme of trauma and obsession carries through specifically in the three films Penn made in the middle of the decade, *The Assassination of Richard Nixon*, *Mystic River*, and *21 Grams*. Penn's star persona has always carried with it an emphasis on his body as an actor. He has been called a "hair actor"; his acting style has been referred to in terms of his remarkable control of his body; his biceps are often commented on; he has had temporary tattoos; and one of his strategies for characterization is to develop a walk. His physicality has also been a focus as a manifestation of his tempestuous nature, intensity as an artist, and anger, and has been referenced to alleged violence in his personal life. In two of the three films, *Mystic River* and *21 Grams*, this attention to the body was manifest in the critical reception of the film. *Mystic River* pro-

Sean Penn as Jimmy Markum, grieving for his murdered daughter in a swarm of policemen in *Mystic River* (Clint Eastwood, Warner Bros./Village Roadshow, 2003). Digital frame enlargement.

vided what may be the emblematic image of Penn for the decade. This is the shot from above of his character Jimmy Markum being held down upon learning that his daughter has been murdered. The *Times* description of this scene by Demetrious Matheou emphasized Penn's body:

> The moment when Jimmy steamrolls into the crime scene, knowing that the victim is his child, is when we know we are in for a meaty ride. Held back by a dozen policemen Penn seems less a man than a wounded bear, roaring out in pain, magnificent and terrible. . . . This is tension-in-the shoulders performance, edgy, dangerous, alert and full of guile. It's time for an Oscar. . . . This is mainstream entertainment with brains and balls.
>
> (16 October 2003, T2, 2)

In using the terms "steamrolls" combined with "meaty ride," "wounded bear," and "roaring out in pain"; in pointing to a "tension-in-the shoulders" performance that is "edgy," "alert and full of guile," and that demonstrates "balls and brains," Matheou points to Penn, not his character Jimmy. Thus he is able to bring together his reader's, or perhaps his own, associations with Penn's personality outside the film, layering the real Sean Penn— intense actor with integrity—both onto the figure who has lost his daughter and back onto the actor who publicly stated his devotion to his children as the reason for turning away from his bad-boy behavior of the late 1980s and 1990s. This visceral confection of language is primarily derived from the film itself: Jimmy's daughter is found in an abandoned bear cage; utilizing his street knowledge and power to try to find his daughter's killer and pitting himself against his friend Sean the detective (Kevin Bacon), he is "alert and edgy." The tension-in-the-shoulders effect is mentioned by

Sean's assistant Whitey (Laurence Fishburne) as something Jimmy gained in prison. While all these phrases are descriptive of Penn's performance, they also apply to Penn's private life (he did actually spend a short time in jail in 1987 for assaulting a photographer).

At the level of acting, Penn and his two principal co-stars, Tim Robbins (as a friend of Jimmy's and Sean's who was molested in childhood) and Bacon, offer physical interpretations of traumatic scenes. In this sense it is useful to refer to the historical concept of trauma, which, as Ruth Leys has argued, has swung between two theories, the mimetic and the antimimetic. The mimetic, which closely resembles the acting process, sees the traumatized subject as being unable to recall the traumatic event; he thus "acts it out or in other ways imitates it." The antimimetic theory suggests that the traumatized subject removes herself from the causative event and "remains a spectator of the traumatic scene, which she can therefore see and represent to others" (Leys 289). Following the antimimetic response, Robbins's Dave takes himself out of his past (through flashbacks). Conversely, Penn's character adheres to the mimetic model, as perhaps one would expect. The scene of Jimmy's anguish suggests such an overload of the senses that he has not fully taken in the murder and can only seek to reenact it through revenge. The scene is shot in that way, engaging the audience through the physicality of the response of the actor in sound and image. The anguished cries of Penn are punctuated by crosscutting between Sean, who has seen Jimmy's daughter's body in the abandoned bear cage, and Jimmy, who is demanding to know. The scene joins these two in the same experience but because it is his daughter, the impact on Jimmy is profound. That connection between the two is held intently in these connecting shots and only released with the over-the-head shot of Jimmy screaming and pinned down by policemen, firmly planting the seed of potential violence to be realized and repeated.

In an interview on the DVD, the film's director, Clint Eastwood, remarked, "It's a really fine piece of material for actors [because] it's not about special effects, everything is real." The link between the actor Penn, whom Eastwood wanted for the role, and Jimmy's motivations is the actor's process. This "realism," often nowadays associated with the Method, was not only an aesthetic goal of Stanislavski, Strasberg, and Meisner but had also motivated D. W. Griffith (Naremore 197–98).

The "real" Sean Penn, celebrity, has a narrative trajectory that resonates with Jimmy. Like Jimmy, who gave up his crew once his daughter was born, Penn has modified his behavior from bad boy toward politics and aid efforts, although his stormy relationship with Robin Wright Penn has been background noise to these. The slow-burning rage that Penn so effectively portrays in Jimmy seeps out into the mediascape as "authentic" in relation to his private "real" self. He has retained his "intensity" and "edge" as unpredictable and fiery. The discourses surrounding Penn's career in the middle of the decade take on an implicit pathology, aligned along an in-control/out-of control axis. The portrayal of characters living through traumatic psychoses continued through *21 Grams*, *The Assassination of Richard Nixon*, and *The Interpreter* (Sydney Pollack, 2005).

The structure of *21 Grams* incorporates flashbacks and flash forwards, privileging a witnessing from a distance rather than the mimetic form of displacing trauma. Will Self, in the *Evening Standard*, praises the impact of this nonlinear structure, writing that the film "is built up out of a complex pattern of flashbacks and flash forwards to make the viewer feel a greater emotional complicity in the destinies of the characters" ("Well Worth Suffering," 4 March 2004, 47). Self unknowingly describes a mechanism or dynamic between audience and characters that is strikingly similar to the antimimetic trauma model. The praise for that "greater emotional complicity" describes this model's coping mechanism utilized by trauma victims and places that distanced engagement at the heart of the film's pleasure. More succinctly, Todd McCarthy suggested of *Mystic River* and *21 Grams* (and two other films without Penn) that their "unrelieved rawness and agony" are "so pronounced that their collective arrival suggests that only now, perhaps, are we seeing the first true post-9/11 films out of Hollywood" (*Variety*, 12 January 2004, A13).

The realism trope in the publicity and critical reception that surrounds Penn continued to the end of the decade, but as throughout his career, it collects and discards contemporary concerns and associations like dust on a windscreen. In his next two films, both of which involve trauma narratives, his performances are praised as convincing and remarkable characterizations. As Samuel J. Bicke in *The Assassination of Richard Nixon*, Penn lost himself in the character. "I'd talk to Sean off the set," director Niels Mueller told Nick Roddick of the *Evening Standard*, "watch him walk across the street and by the time you start rolling the camera you just don't see Sean anymore" ("The Secret of Nixon's Suicide Bomber," 21 March 2005, 27). Derek Malcolm writes, "Penn has displayed angry frustration before—but never paired with such squirming vulnerability" ("Sean at His Peak," *Evening Standard*, 7 April 2005, 29). Although the film's reviews were not particularly favorable, Penn's performance was lauded. "Penn's magnetism and hesitant line delivery create what interest there is" (Todd McCarthy, *Variety*, 24 May 2004, 40). The film's topicality lay in its subject matter, with its frustrated and angry furniture salesman trying to hijack a plane. With *The Interpreter*, the theme of a character living through the trauma of grief was revisited, with Penn's performance seeming to attract the only critical praise. Referring to the unfulfilled love interest of Nicole Kidman and Penn, *Times* critic James Christopher wrote: "Both ache with intimacy—at least Penn does— but they dare not touch" (14 April 2005, 8).

★★★★★ Politics and Mimicry

During the decade both DiCaprio and Penn enhanced their actor credentials by portraying historical figures. For DiCaprio, playing Howard Hughes provided a means by which to develop his star persona toward more mature roles that could demonstrate actorly virtuosity. It also offered a setting for his persona as, in James's words, a "new form of old-fashioned" star. While interviews emphasized his clinically accurate portrayal of Hughes's obsessive-compulsive disorder, critical reception also centered on Scorsese's recreation of the era, marked by his attention to period detail and detailed knowledge of Hollywood film style at the time. DiCaprio's performance was praised for its intensity in spite of his lack of physical resemblance to Hughes. *Variety*'s McCarthy praised him for being "in terrific movie star mode" ("Aviator Takes Flight," 29 November 2004, 42). The role had a number of set pieces with DiCaprio pitted against corrupt senators and the villains of devious corporations. If he is compromised by his debility, DiCaprio's Hughes is also a voice for masculine individualism in the tradition of the heroes of Howard Hawks and John Ford. DiCaprio's political activism on environmental issues remained separate from his performance.

Sean Penn's choice of playing historical figures was more overtly attached to his personal politics. Penn was vociferous in his public opposition to the war in Iraq, visited both Iraq before the invasion and Iran, made a publicized visit to New Orleans to help the victims of Hurricane Katrina, and made a trip to Caracas to talk to Hugo Chavez, president of Venezuela. Each action generated a lot of chatter among the right-wing media, as might have been expected. The industry response is echoed by Elizabeth Guider in *Variety*: "Now Penn, who has been tubthumping for 'All the King's Men,' is spending most of his time talking politics—not those connected with the movie but rather those connected with George W. Bush. " And Guider might have had DiCaprio in mind when she suggested, "This is not about agreeing or disagreeing with their politics—it's simply that it would be refreshing to hear these folks discuss their craft with a bit more relish" ("Thesps' Message

After crashing in a farmer's field, Howard Hughes beams with success. Leonardo DiCaprio in *The Aviator* (Martin Scorsese, Forward Pass/Appian Way, 2004). Digital frame enlargement.

Is Garbled," 2 October 2006, 6). Guider might also have pointed to DiCaprio, with his insistence on keeping his private life away from the media glare and only "exploit[ing] his fame when he wants to."

Also offering a convergence between Penn's politics and the portrayal of a historical character was his final film of the decade, *Milk*. This film received favorable notices and was nominated for eight Academy Awards. Penn won Best Actor. The choice of this role was unsurprising, yet it nevertheless offered a departure for Penn. Charlotte O'Sullivan of the *Evening Standard* noted, "If nothing else, Penn is famously macho. Thanks to his pugnacious mane of hair and huge biceps we often fail to notice his small frame and beaky nose" (22 January 2009). The hitherto unquestioned heterosexuality of Penn's persona as detailed in his most prominent roles gave reviewers an issue to work with. *The Guardian*'s Peter Bradshaw provided a detailed outline that incorporates the usual Penn intensity with the in-control actor on film. In Harvey Milk he saw "the kind of ferocious virility and detailed concentration that only Penn can bring to a role. You can almost feel the energy with which the actor reproduces learned camp mannerisms—yet miniaturizes them, clamps them down, brings them just below the stereotype" ("From the Closet to the Grave," 23 January 2009, 7). Here we find Penn's process at work, explained by the critic. Perhaps the most poignant review came from B. Ruby Rich in *The Guardian*. Reflecting on Penn's agreement to do the role only if the film were shot in the Castro District of San Francisco, Rich says, "It was thanks to Penn, then, that I could stroll down Castro Street last February and find myself mesmerized by a 1970s version of my own city." Rich uses the film to revisit old haunts and to draw parallels between Milk's time and the present, and to highlight

Sean Penn as Harvey Milk in *Milk* (Gus Van Sant, Focus Features, 2008). Digital frame enlargement.

Proposition 8, the initiative to ban gay marriage that passed a week later. Praising the film's overall accuracy to recreate the place and the time, she provides an account of the premiere at the Castro Cinema. "When the film started and silence descended . . . the audience began to realize what a house of mirrors we had entered. As Sean Penn brilliantly disappeared into the body, voice and mannerisms of Harvey Milk, it got harder and harder to separate the world on the screen from the one we lived in." Rich recounts that when the film was over they walked back onto the streets they had just seen on film and joined a march back to the steps of city hall to protest Proposition 8. Rich concludes with the melancholic observation that with the passage of Proposition 8 came the reminder that "not all of this is over" ("Ghosts of a Vanished World," 16 January 2009, 8).

Penn's well-known Oscar acceptance speech—"You commie, homo-lovin' sons of guns"—simultaneously brought together the "in-control" and "out-of-control" aspects of the discourse that surrounds his star persona. His remark—"I think that it is a good time for those who voted for the ban against gay marriage to sit and reflect and anticipate their great shame and the shame in their grandchildren's eyes if they continue that way of sup-port"—was delivered with an actor's control and clarity. But it was to another part of his persona that he addressed his final remarks: "I'm very, very proud to live in a country that is willing to elect an elegant man pres-ident and a country who, for all its toughness, creates courageous artists." The anti-Hollywood, anti-corporate rebel had found, as B. Ruby Rich put it, that it's not over yet.

Both DiCaprio and Penn worked to build on their star image of acting virtuosity during the 2000s through their choices of roles and, in Penn's case, in his directorial efforts. Presenting ultimately divergent manifestations of American masculinity, they offer different examples of how star personae are products of information that is both within a performer's control and outside of it. While acting ability was their primary skill, both men arguably managed the portrayal of their private lives in ways that informed their onscreen personae. DiCaprio's persona in both realms operated on a trajectory of movement from boyhood to manhood, from raw talent to developed artist working with established auteurs. His move into activism on environmental issues was more or less bipartisan and his control over his private life fed into this move to maturity across the decade. Penn's trajectory differed in that his emotional and physical outbursts in his private life were channeled into partisan politics and a broader left-leaning activism. This was informed by clear links to American acting traditions associated not only with the Actors Studio but with those iconic figures such as James Dean and Marlon Brando who embodied a political rebelliousness as well as an aesthetic one. While DiCaprio exited the decade as a new type of old Hollywood star, Penn's contrasting aspects of his in-control acting and out-of-control celebrity offered another iconic image of American masculinity, restlessness turned into dissent.

10 ☆☆☆☆☆☆☆☆☆★★★

Kate Winslet and Cate Blanchett
The Performance Is the Star

CHARLIE KEIL

In a decade that saw the potency of stars challenged, as franchises and action films seemed to monopolize the attentions of both studio executives and audiences, who would believe that the career of a female star who concentrates on serious drama could thrive throughout a ten-year stretch? Yet the examples of Cate Blanchett and Kate Winslet proved that actresses who staked out a claim to stardom predicated explicitly on acting talent over celebrity could persevere, generating industry respect and a stream of challenging roles in the process, even if the box-office results were mixed at best. In the 2000s, as the market for properties featuring actress-stars progressively narrowed, the careers of these two stars flourished: both imports, one from Australia and the other from England, they dominated the field and conferred immediate prestige upon any project to which their names became attached. Why did these two actresses achieve the level of fame and success that they attained during this period when the fortunes of

Kate Winslet and Cate Blanchett.

so many of their peers faltered? One could argue that it derived from a combination of wise choices and blind luck, of refined technique and dogged determination. But beyond all else, both Blanchett and Winslet retained their images as actresses first and stars second: the pursuit of acting challenges seemingly guided their selection of roles and informed the media's coverage of each. Studying their careers and their performances over the course of the pivotal ten years from 2000 to 2009 can help us understand how one maintains a reputation as a skilled and respected actress. Ultimately, what links the two is their shared ownership of a legacy some would trace to Meryl Streep, as actresses drawn to emotionally demanding roles, deploying the tools of training, employing a wide variety of accents, and eschewing glamour and— especially in Winslet's case—clothing, when required. Their devotion to theatrical roots (Blanchett even returned to Australia to run the Sydney Theatre Co. with her husband at the end of the decade; many of Winslet's relatives have ties to the stage) and family (Winslet was for most of the decade married to director Sam Mendes, while Blanchett has enjoyed a longstanding union with writer-director Andrew Upton) lends them a sheen of hardworking normalcy, as does their decision to live outside the rarified confines of Hollywood. Defining themselves as dedicated actresses who have somehow become stars, Winslet and Blanchett stand in marked contrast to a figure like Angelina Jolie, whose acting prowess is dwarfed by her celebrity. The two actresses' ability to deflect controversy and concentrate attention on their work has led to rapturous reviews and elevation to the status of "icon[s] of the Era of New Seriousness" (Mark Harris, "Best Actress: Kate Winslet's Moment," *Time*, 19 February 2009).

★★★★★ A Luxury Liner and a Monarch: Aspiring to Stardom in the 1990s

Both actresses were within arm's reach of stardom by the turn of the previous decade, courtesy of career-defining roles that each undertook in the late 1990s. Winslet, though the younger by six years, appeared in films three years prior to Blanchett, gaining prominence with her first role, in Peter Jackson's *Heavenly Creatures* (1994), as a teenage girl who conspires with her friend to kill the latter's mother. Her participation in Ang Lee's *Sense and Sensibility* (1995) was a harbinger for numerous reasons: first, it was a period piece, as were all of Winslet's films until *Hideous Kinky* in 1998; second, it was an adaptation of a prestigious literary property, and her next two films, *Jude* and *Hamlet*, would be as well; third, it garnered her extensive critical praise and a BAFTA award, signaling that she was an acting talent to watch. Her next project after *Hamlet*, and her first American film, changed everything: James Cameron's *Titanic* (1997), despite extensive negative advance publicity, emerged as a blockbuster, setting box office records that would not be matched for over a decade. Almost overnight, Winslet became a sensation, her onscreen romantic relationship with heartthrob Leonardo DiCaprio helping to solidify the film's popularity with young female viewers in particular. Her performance led to a second Academy Award nod (the first was for *Sense*) and the press made much of the fact that, at twenty-two, she was the youngest recipient of two Oscar nominations. (Versions of this type of age-related Oscar nomination tallying would follow her throughout the subsequent decade until her win in 2009, when she emerged, at thirty-four, as the youngest actor to score six nominations.)

Even more intense was the media scrutiny of Winslet's weight. Unlike most ingénues, she was fairly curvaceous, and her body (and its significance for the host of female spectators fixing on her as a possible screen image to adulate) became an object of fascination for commentators. Debates raged: Was Winslet sufficiently svelte to become a bona fide star? Did popular acceptance of her shape mean that norms of female beauty were shifting to accommodate more amply proportioned women? Would she be forced to diet if her weight continued to climb? Amplifying the interest in Winslet's body image was her propensity for appearing unclothed in films: she had already appeared naked in *Jude*, and her nudity was key to one of the central tropes of *Titanic*. (She would continue to do nude scenes in many of the films that she made through the 2000s; four of her six Oscar-nominated performances featured nudity.) The massive popularity of *Titanic* and the type of coverage that its success spawned threatened to undercut critical appreciation of Winslet's performance, focusing attention on her physical attributes more than on her acting abilities.

Cate Blanchett's arrival as a star was more clearly attributable to her triumphing in a role designed to showcase her strengths as an actor. After appearing in only three films, the last of which, Gillian Armstrong's *Oscar and Lucinda* (1997), was the first to foster confidence that Blanchett could hold the screen as a lead, the actress assumed the hefty responsibility of carrying the title role of *Elizabeth* (1998), playing the queen of England in her early days as monarch. Reviews were rapturous and a sense of discovery accompanied the response to her commanding performance in a role previously connected to such acting powerhouses as Bette Davis and Glenda Jackson. As David Fincher was later reported to have reacted: "I remember coming out of *Elizabeth* and thinking, Who is this?! . . . I didn't know who she was, but that power from someone in relative obscurity was like seeing her leaping fully realized from the head of Zeus" (qtd. in Leslie Bennetts, "A Hollywood Elusive," *Vanity Fair*, February 2009). As with Winslet, the majority of Blanchett's films up to the point of the career-making *Elizabeth* had been period pieces, and her reputation was established in part as a purveyor of "quality" filmmaking, an impression solidified by the follow-up film she made, an adaptation of Oscar Wilde's *An Ideal Husband*. If Winslet's dilemma after *Titanic* was to demonstrate that she could negotiate the demands that stardom placed on an actress with serious dramatic aspirations, Blanchett's was almost the inverse: she had yet to establish that her estimable gifts as an actress would translate into the creation of roles that could draw audiences to her films. Both used the remaining few years of the 1990s to establish a template of role choice and performance that would serve them well into the next decade.

★★★★★ A Mind of Her Own

Winslet's decision to pursue noncommercial projects in the wake of her success in *Titanic* led to her starring roles in *Hideous Kinky* and *Holy Smoke* (1999) in the final two years of the 1990s. Defiantly contemporary and unconventional, these choices helped blunt her previous reputation as an actress most comfortable in quality period films, while also demonstrating that she had little interest in cashing in on the popularity that *Titanic*'s success had conferred on her. By the time she returned to higher budgeted and higher profile material with *Quills* in 2000, she also slipped back into a wig and a corset. Interestingly, it is one of Winslet's few victim roles, and if her character's death at the hands of a sanitarium inmate emerges as a case of innocence unprotected, the script provides Winslet ample opportunity to demonstrate that the pleasures of the flesh entrance her virginal laundress even while she remains chaste to the end. In fact, Winslet seems most engaged when reading the lascivious prose of the imprisoned Marquis de Sade (Geoffrey Rush, the indisputable star of the film), clearly energized by the pleasure that her saucy readings engender in her diegetic audience of illiterate listeners. *Quills* puts forward the idea that the threat of carnal liberty realizes itself most palpably in a woman's ability to exercise her own sexual desires, and Winslet's obvious delight in functioning as Sade's emissary further demonstrates that disseminating fantasy carries its own sexual charge.

The appeal of the text defines another supporting role, that of the young Iris Murdoch in *Iris* (2001). Winslet's Murdoch revels in defying convention, not so much for the purposes of shocking the bourgeoisie, but more because

Kate Winslet, a well-established fixture of period pieces by the early 2000s, dons another corset for *Quills* (Philip Kaufman, Fox Searchlight, 2000). Collection Charlie Keil.

it is the only way she knows how to live. Devoted to exploring the nature of goodness and moral choice, fascinated by the capacity of language, and open to the sensual experiences of sex, Murdoch finds herself drawn to the much less worldly John Bayley, even if he is often flummoxed by her attitudes. *Iris* is that rare film, one that embraces its female subject's complexities without trying to contain or rationalize them. Because the script is refreshingly non-judgmental about its heroine's behavior, it provides the fertile ground for the emergence of the first unqualified example of a trademark Winslet perform-ance, fearless in its embracing of the character's various qualities, even if some do not immediately invite sympathy or understanding. Her young Iris Murdoch is attuned to the possibilities of the world and less concerned about the perception of herself that might emerge. Likewise, she does not try to make herself overly attractive, maintaining a rather lumpy hairdo and bushy eyebrows, but neither is she characterized as homely or sexually unappeal-ing at any juncture. The film unapologetically offers a woman who is both intellectually challenging and sexually adventurous. And while she is framed by the admiring (and often bewildered) perspective of her future husband Bayley, *Iris* does not exist as a function of male fantasy but rather as a woman of accomplishment. Winslet excels in particular at capturing the sense of potential in the young Iris, her enthusiasm for ideas and action fused in an authoritative but youthful demeanor. (In reality, Winslet was far too young to play Murdoch at this stage in her life, as the writer was close to forty when she met Bayley. But Winslet embodies an admixture of freshness and maturity that seems ideal for the character.) In our introduction to her, presented as Bayley's first sighting of her as well, she holds forth on the difficulty of ascertaining the meaning behind words. In her eager articulation of challenging concepts, Winslet conveys the pleasure that discussing ideas holds for Iris herself, regardless of their effect on others. The degree of self-possession that Winslet as Murdoch possesses will inform many of her subsequent characterizations.

The Life of David Gale (2003) should have provided Winslet with another opportunity to flesh out the role of an intelligent woman who lives through language. But everything about her character, journalist Bitsey Bloom, from her improbable name to her reputation as a ballsy features writer who puts ethics ahead of convenience, seems preconceived for the purposes of the narrative and leaves Winslet little to realize through performative detailing. The main attitude conveyed by the actress throughout the film is one of irritation, as a substitute for the conflicted emotions that might well attend a journalist who realizes she is a pawn in a complicated game of revisited and revised past events.

The chief appeal of *David Gale* was probably that it allowed Winslet the chance to play a contemporary American woman close to her own age; her next film, *Eternal Sunshine of the Spotless Mind* (2004), provided a similar opportunity, but in a comic vein. It also showed us a Winslet we had never really seen before: loose, playful, and brash. *Sunshine* managed to rescue Winslet from being perceived as a performer unable to have fun. Its quirky, time-shifting narrative was also aesthetically far removed from most of the material she had attached herself to for the greater part of her career. In interviews, she has consistently claimed that Clementine Kruczynski is her favorite character, perhaps because the role's sensibility most closely approximates her own. Whatever is the case, Winslet seemed to recognize the demands of the role and thereby rendered Clementine as more than just the ingratiating kook that she might have been in the hands of a lesser actress. As Lynn Hirschberg wrote in the *New York Times*, "Unlike every other madcap but lovable heroine in films today, her Clementine is charismatic and maddening, fascinating and completely irritating." Hirschberg then quotes Winslet, who says, "Clementine is such a complex mixture of positives and negatives. I did not want her to be obvious. I didn't want her to be a nail-biting neurotic with a twitch, but at the same time, I didn't want her to be all hearts and chocolates" ("The Unsinkable Kate Winslet," *New York Times*, 29 August 2004, 236). From the moment Winslet's Clementine approaches Jim Carrey's Joel Barish on a commuter train, her energy is palpable: her motor runs too fast, she seems easily exasperated, and she manages to alienate as much as to attract. But Winslet also conveys the earnest soul of Clementine, lurking beneath the dyed, faux-boho pigtails. Her openness and eagerness to try to build a relationship with the retiring Joel give their romance its gravitas. When Joel is faced with its elimination through memory erasure, we understand what is at stake: Winslet's Clementine is a woman not easily forgotten, which is the point of this film about loss and reconstruction of the past.

☆☆☆☆★ The Woman Who Would Be Anyone

Having played the most famous of female monarchs so early in her career, Cate Blanchett worked to dispel assumptions that she could only enact larger-than-life personages by essaying so many roles in the next five years that viewers would be hard pressed to associate her with any single performance. Looking over her filmography from 1999 to 2003, one wonders how anyone could sustain the punishing rate of production that she managed over that four-year period, averaging four films a year. Part of her secret is that Blanchett was more than willing to take on small roles along with starring parts. In almost half of her films during this period, she contributed the equivalent of cameos (*The Shipping News* [2001], the *Lord of the Rings* trilogy [2001–2003]) or, in the case of *Coffee and Cigarettes* (2003), appeared in only one episode of a collection of related short pieces. The films that she selected allowed her to adopt a variety of accents, ranging from Russian to regional American to Irish; only rarely would she appear as an Australian. (Of course, this is as much a function of the limited options available to Australian actors within their own nation as it is a demonstration of the actress's fluency with dialects; virtually every Australian actor who has come to work in Hollywood has had to learn to master an American accent. Blanchett has merely broadened the range of accents that she adopts to the point where the skill is an obvious part of her performative repertoire.) And she did not adhere to any one genre, though drama remained her preferred canvas. Nevertheless, over the period she also tried on comedy (*Bandits*, 2001), fantasy (the *Lord of the Rings* films) and even a western (*The Missing*, 2003). And while the sheer volume of Blanchett's work during this period would seem to indicate that she was willing to try anything, one finds evidence that she was being selective, so often did she work with acknowledged auteurs (Sally Potter, Sam Raimi, Gillian Armstrong, Peter Jackson, Tom Tykwer, and Jim Jarmusch among them), a tendency that would become even more pronounced in the second half of the decade when she appeared in films directed by Wes Anderson, Martin Scorsese, Alejandro González Iñárritu, Steven Soderbergh, Todd Haynes, Steven Spielberg, and David Fincher, among others. She conceded in a *Vogue* profile from 2006 that she "selects projects based on the director more than on any other criteria" (Michael Specter, "Head First," *Vogue*, November 2006, 316), and as her stock rose during the decade, the directors interested in working with her apparently increased in number.

Given how many films she made up until 2003, one could expect there to be a few uninspired performances as part of the mix. What impresses one most about the body of work is the sustained level of commitment Blanchett exhibits, even as she must have raced from one film set to another. And the contrast set up by the release order of the films all but invites dedicated viewers to marvel at the range she demonstrates, as a few selected juxtapositions will reveal. In *The Gift* (2000), playing Annie Wilson, a gentle psychic who finds herself embroiled in a grisly murder, Blanchett deliberately underplays the role, with steady and measured reactions to even the most volatile of her clients. It is a thoughtful performance, with Blanchett registering how someone gifted with psychic abilities would likely develop a watchful, ruminative response to life. Her tremulous fury when her children are threatened by a wife-beating lout emerges as all the more striking for its contrast to her subdued demeanor throughout. And a scene on the witness stand during the murder trial, when she is humiliated by the defense, registers particularly strongly because of how Blanchett conveys Annie's gradual loss of composure as her pride in her gift is eroded. *Bandits* features Blanchett in a completely different mode, giving an outsized performance reminiscent of screwball comedy, using her long limbs and pliable body to considerable comic effect. Her Kate Wheeler is a breathy ball of neuroses, mercurial and intelligent, but also malleable and impetuous. Her rapport with her two co-stars, Bruce Willis and Billy Bob Thornton, is infectious: *Bandits* indicates that Blanchett's talent for comedy, *The Life Aquatic* (2004) notwithstanding, has never been properly realized.

Blanchett's enactment of *Veronica Guerin* (2003) finds her in full heroic mode, as the dedicated journalist who exposed the criminal networks responsible for Dublin's drug trade at the eventual cost of her life. The performance conveys the steely side of Guerin but balances that with her sense of fear when particular criminals strike back. One scene shows Guerin trying to confront mobster John Gilligan on his own property. She is beaten mercilessly while he berates her for trespassing, this especially effective because Blanchett is not afraid to show how unexpected blows can immediately break down the carefully erected defense mechanisms of a female journalist. Her panicked response registers the threat represented by explosive male violence as much as does the ferocity of her menacing attacker (Gerard McSorley). Throwing out her arms in self-defense, whimpering in recognition of her own vulnerability, Blanchett as Guerin abandons any pretence of stoicism and utterly distills the human dimension of being caught off-guard and not knowing what to do next. Her palpable fear in this scene recalls the distress and shock she had conveyed earlier in the narrative when an arranged hit resulted in her being shot in her home: Blanchett's full-bodied wails when under siege prevent the portrait of Guerin mounted by the film from veering too close to hagiography.

In direct contrast to *Veronica Guerin* is her vignette in *Coffee and Cigarettes*, wherein Blanchett plays both a (softly parodic) version of herself and her disgruntled and entitled cousin. This segment works on more than one level: it functions as a send-up of Blanchett's own ascension to celebrity but also plays as a virtuosic turn, where, in her portrayal of both women, she can demonstrate her dexterity by being the aggrieved and resentful Id to her own placid but condescending Ego. The various subtexts of the piece—that one can't shed one's undesirable connections just because one is famous; that celebrities become unaware of their own tendencies to see everything as an extension of themselves; that guilt only goes so far in forcing one to accommodate unpleasant relatives—are given a further twist by virtue of Blanchett's playing both sides of the equation.

With *The Missing*, the actress took on one of her biggest risks, starring in a genre that has, for the most part, fallen out of favor with audiences and that traditionally does not place women at its center. As a young mother of two who goes on a quest for her abducted older daughter with the help of her own estranged father (Tommy Lee Jones), Blanchett doesn't falter, embracing the physical demands of the role and asserting her right to be at the center of the action while never making her authority anachronistic. The maternal force embodied by Magdelena Gilkeson is a new dimension for the actress, and her fierceness in conveying Maggie's resolve to find her daughter gives the film most of its emotional heft. For much of the film she remains unyielding in her response to the blandishments of Jones, fueled by resentment and bitterness. Yet her face conveys longing for an intimacy that was forfeited during her childhood, which also imbues the possibility of losing her own child with even more resonance. Often echoing *The Searchers*, but with Blanchett at least partially filling John Wayne's boots this time round, *The Missing* provides the actress with one of her most commanding roles. Ron Howard's direction is surprisingly spare, even tough, and Blanchett's grim determination throughout provides the actorly complement to the gnarled and elemental landscapes that serve as backdrop to the film's extended journey.

Having anchored four heavyweight dramas in the course of as many years, with *Charlotte Gray* (2001) and *Heaven* (2002) in addition to *Veronica Guerin* and *The Missing*, Blanchett demonstrated her bona fides as the foremost dramatic actress of the early 2000s, though most audiences would first connect her to the unsettling portrait of Galadriel that she created for the first installment of *Lord of the Rings*, playing the powerful queen of the elves in a register that combined both luminosity and menace.

★★★★★   **The Rewards of Seriousness**

"It has become clearer than ever," wrote David Denby, "that the movie year is divided into two parts, [the second of which is] the Oscar-focused final three months of the year, which are devoted to movies about failure, abjection, death, and the Holocaust, most of them starring Kate Winslet and Cate Blanchett" ("A Better Life," *New Yorker*, 22 December 2008). While it may not have been part of any master plan, especially given that at least half of her films from the latter part of the decade saw their original release dates altered, Kate Winslet became the de facto Queen of the Academy Award Season, Junior Division, matched only by the triumvirate of established grande dames: Meryl Streep, Judi Dench, and Helen Mirren. (These four women accounted for eleven Best Actress Academy Award nominations—and two wins—between 2004 and 2008.) Winslet's films tended to be grouped to permit for release dates in the latter part of the calendar year, so much so that she began to appear onscreen biannually: 2004, 2006, and 2008. (The sole exception was 2007, when the barely released and long-delayed oddity *Romance and Cigarettes* opened in the United States, featuring a feisty Winslet singing, dancing, and sporting a broad North England accent. She was having a grand time, but the material was too off-beat and inconsequential to connect with either critics or audiences.) With the exception of *The Holiday* (2006), which was released at year's end for obvious reasons, all of Winslet's other films from the latter part of the decade were envisioned as award season fodder, and all delivered on their promise to varying degrees, save the disastrous remake of *All the King's Men* (2006). The latter, perhaps not coincidentally, gave Winslet her least demanding role and smallest amount of screen time during this period. But otherwise, she had become the focal point of the films in which she appeared, even when the storylines involved multiple characters, as was the case with *Little Children* (2006). Her instinct for challenging material had become unerring, and certainly no other actress in her peer group had a run of as many roles that seemed designed to invite critics' awards as Winslet did from 2004 to 2008. The phrase "preeminent actress of her generation" became attached to her with increasing regularity as the decade progressed, capped by the bestowal in 2009 of the Oscar that had eluded her in five previous nominations. That Winslet might have won the award for either of the two films in which she appeared in 2008 demonstrated how she had come to capture the market on demanding roles.

The pivotal film in establishing Winslet as perennially "eligible" may have been Marc Forster's *Finding Neverland* (2004). Yet another period piece, and one that offered Winslet a somewhat slighter role than many others, it nonetheless had the patina of quality that award-granting bodies prefer, and appeared in the same year as the radically different *Eternal Sunshine of the Spotless Mind*. Due to the caprices of distributors' release schedules, the two films in combination created the impression that Winslet could be convincing in almost any role: the irrepressible Clementine had given way to the demure and motherly Sylvia Llewelyn Davies, as if through effortless transformation. Doubtless, the timely appearance of *Neverland* helped bolster year-end recognition of Winslet's performance in *Sunshine*, a film that had been released early in the spring, usually a guarantor that it would be ignored at Oscar time. By the time of *Little Children*, Winslet's acting had become even more nuanced and focused, and her Sarah Pierce is a finely wrought creation, the character's intricacies perfectly keyed to the film's overall tone. As A. O. Scott commented in the *New York Times*, "Ms. Winslet, as fine an actress as any working in movies today, registers every flicker of Sarah's pride, self-doubt and desire, inspiring a mixture of recognition, pity and concern that amounts, by the end of the movie, to something like love" (*New York Times*, 29 September 2006, E1).

A square peg in the round hole of established New England suburbia, *Little Children*'s stay-at-home Sarah is perpetually dissatisfied but unable to find adequate outlet for her maternal frustration until the opportunity arises for an affair with an available father from the neighborhood, Brad Adamson (Patrick Wilson). Sarah's palpable displeasure with her life manifests itself in all manner of ways, not the least of which is a distinct lack of interest in parenting. She treats her young daughter like an obligation, and Winslet expresses Sarah's disdain for the limitations the child places on her without reserve. With her furrowed brow and darting eyes, the actress gives full range to Sarah's wariness and weariness, and her hesitant responses and slightly slouched posture reveal the defeat of an intelligent person who has settled for too little in life and hates herself and her world for doing so. Although Sarah is self-aware, she is also self-pitying, and Winslet gives weight to both sides of the character's experience, never asking for sympathy but also never stooping to satirize Sarah's weaknesses. In one of the film's most impressive scenes, Sarah joins a reading group that is taking up, of all books, *Madame Bovary*. There she finds herself having to defend the book as a covert rationalization for her own adultery. Winslet's growing responsiveness to the logic of the argument that she devises defending Emma Bovary as a proto-feminist conveys Sarah's conviction that her own affair is her way of regaining a sense of self; at the same time, Winslet also communicates how Sarah finds energy in conveying her thoughts, which she had long abandoned since choosing the comforts of suburban life. Winslet doesn't flinch from the unlikeable aspects of Sarah's behavior, but also gives full expression to the pleasure, release, and power Sarah finds in uninhibited sex. If Brad is a somewhat vacant underachiever, that only makes the fantasy of illicit irresponsibility that much easier to achieve, and its dissipation that much more inevitable. Winslet allows us to understand that if Sarah's actions may be delusional, they are also recognizable.

April Wheeler, the heroine of Sam Mendes's *Revolutionary Road* (2008), is another denizen of suburbia, but this time during the Eisenhower era. April is a woman who believes she is destined for greater things than a stifling life of manicured lawns and houses with picture windows, but she has attached herself to a man who doesn't have the capacity to help her realize those dreams (Leonardo DiCaprio). As the feeling of entrapment escalates, Winslet's performing rhythms become ever tighter, her shoulders constricted and her brow severe. She lashes out at her hapless husband, because his failure to understand the desperateness of her dilemma only confirms her condemnation to a life that she has grown to loathe. April is a difficult character to essay without the inner thoughts supplied by the omniscient narrational voice of Richard Yates's source novel, but Winslet embraces the highs and lows of April's behavior wholeheartedly: she moves from buoyant optimism as she makes plans for her family to move to Paris to bitter rage when she realizes that a third pregnancy has condemned her to extended domesticity in suburban Connecticut. There is a precision and even a steeliness to April that tempers her most emotional outbursts, confirming her as a mismatch for the more open and amiable Frank. Yet Winslet's very tightness in the role shows us how April is bursting at the seams, a determined dreamer with no outlet for her dreams.

Revolutionary Road (Sam Mendes, DreamWorks SKG, 2008) finds Winslet trapped in suburbia again, two years after *Little Children*. Collection Charlie Keil.

In the film that won Winslet her Oscar, *The Reader* (2008), she undertakes a far less sympathetic role, that of Hanna Schmitz: not only does Hanna engage in a sexual relationship with a minor, fifteen-year-old Michael Berg (David Kross), but she is revealed at the film's midpoint to have been an SS guard who actively participated in Holocaust atrocities. Like the novel upon which it is based, the film invites contemplation of human weakness, complicity, and moral choice. It would be easy enough to dismiss Hanna as purely evil, someone who takes advantage of those less powerful than herself and then dispenses with them when circumstances dictate. And Winslet refuses to soften the edges of Hanna's personality to render the character likeable. She is often harsh with Michael and holds her body tight, refusing responsiveness until the intimacy of sex provides the opportunity of release. Later, when interrogated by a judge about her actions as a guard, Hanna is unrepentant: she sees her job in terms of what was demanded of her, not the moral dilemmas it posed. Largely closed off, Hanna seems to have refused herself the opportunity to reflect on the devastation that she has been responsible for and yet her resolve often slips sufficiently to intimate that she harbors a pain she cannot articulate. Ultimately, there are no easy answers when it comes to a character like Hanna. She is not simply a monster, though she has done monstrous things. She responds to beauty and innocence even as she has been responsible for their destruction. After Hanna is sentenced to life imprisonment, the film presents brief glimpses of her existence behind bars. As Hanna ages in virtual isolation, Winslet resolutely presents us with the same largely inscrutable figure, one whose actions are unforgivable but who still seems somehow worthy of redemption. It is a largely grim and restricted performance, but it could be no other way given the design of the film. What is remarkable is that Hanna emerges nonetheless as a figure that the viewer wishes she could understand better, not simply dismiss. That Winslet could play so many unlikeable characters so compellingly is to her credit, but one hopes for another performance soon where the role and its playing might afford some pleasure, for she is in danger of having us forget that she possesses a fine sense of humor, a trait too seldom engaged. Anyone requiring a reminder need only see her guest turn on the first season of "Extras" (2005), playing herself to fine effect and happily spoofing her own determination to snag an Oscar via high-minded drama, all the while proving most adept at improvising phone sex. One thing is certain: through this riotous performance she has eliminated any chance of ever being able to play a nun onscreen and being taken seriously.

★★★★★ **She's Not There**

If Winslet spent the latter part of the decade demonstrating increased acuity for dispassionately embodying flawed characters, Blanchett continued to meld with her creations, without regard for nationality, prior fame, or even gender. Blanchett's reputation as a chameleon—a term that she despised, as it implied facile mimicry rather than a skilled process of becoming—gathered credence from 2004 onward, as the majority of her characterizations were either portrayals of known figures (Katharine Hepburn in *The Aviator* [2004], Bob Dylan in *I'm Not There* [2007], and Elizabeth I—again—in *Elizabeth: The Golden Age* [2007]) or drew from preexisting sources (Jane Goodall in *The Life Aquatic* and a composite of 1940s-era screen goddesses in *The Good German* [2006]). Arguably, only four of her performances, of the ten she provided from 2004 to 2009, were of figures who existed on their own fictional terms, without recourse to a referent from life and/or media. (For the record, these were her roles in *Little Fish* [2005], *Babel* [2006], *Notes on a Scandal* [2006], and *The Curious Case of Benjamin Button* [2008].) If one were to suggest that a certain degree of artificiality intruded on some of her performances, causing them to seem either mannered (as in *The Life Aquatic, The Aviator,* and *Indiana Jones and the Kingdom of the Crystal Skull* [2008]) or but one step removed from the vitality of her most vibrant and intense work (as was the case with *The Good German* and *Benjamin Button*), one can scarcely blame her entirely, for on each occasion her performance was at the service of a director's vision. And, of course, when that vision met its ideal representation through Blanchett's devotion to it, the results could be transformative, as evidenced by her stunning evocation of mid-sixties Dylan in Todd Haynes's *I'm Not There*.

The tendency toward stylization started amiably enough with the one-two punch of *The Life Aquatic* and *The Aviator*. Both performances are game, and Blanchett's take on the rather self-important and perpetually perturbed Jane Winslett-Richardson in *Aquatic* is as amusing as any of the many off-center portrayals in Wes Anderson's determinedly fey curio. Her portrayal of Hepburn in *The Aviator* garnered much more attention—and an eventual Academy Award for Best Supporting Actress—in part because of the ambition of Scorsese's biopic of Howard Hughes, but also because Blanchett met the challenge of attempting to distill the essence of a cinematic icon. Perhaps recognizing that the Hughes-Hepburn relationship was not based on erotic frisson but rather mutual admiration of each other's iconoclastic nature, Blanchett emphasizes Hepburn's New England individuality, going for verve and gumption over movie-star mystique. For that reason, her Hepburn seems more the gawky social misfit of 1936's *Sylvia Scarlett* (the film that Hepburn is working on when first she meets Hughes) than the elegant woman of accomplishment established once the star was reborn at MGM in 1940. But if Blanchett doesn't capture every facet of Hepburn's persona, that is scarcely her job in *The Aviator*, whose main concern is how the star entered into Hughes's orbit for a brief period. Blanchett aims to create an indelible impression of a distinctive personality, and that she does effectively, employing finely honed technique while tearing into her Hepburn with often giddy abandon.

Her next two films, *Little Fish* and *Babel*, offer the strongest correctives to the general image of Blanchett as the Great Imitator that emerged during this period. The former film in particular provides examples of what may be the actress's most heartfelt work. Playing Tracy Heart, an ex-addict whose life becomes progressively complicated as she tries to secure a business loan, reconcile her feelings for a recently returned ex-boyfriend, and help her desperate stepfather (Hugo Weaving) score drugs when his main supply dries up, Blanchett oozes desperation at the same time that she shows how much effort it requires to succeed at keeping her mundane existence on an even keel. If the film cannot quite attain the level of Blanchett's acting, its loose naturalism provides room for her performance to breathe: her Tracy emerges as fully inhabited, from the moments of tenderness and pity with Weaving to the charged confrontations with her mother (Noni Hazlehurst). *Babel* might have offered her similar possibilities if the plot didn't require her to become disabled by a stray bullet early in the narrative. Her first co-starring effort with Brad Pitt, *Babel* emerges, much like their second film together, *Benjamin Button*, as primarily Pitt's show.

Prior to the release of *The Good German*, the *Los Angeles Times* described Blanchett as "a rare breed of star. She is, to her public, tabula rasa, a blank slate upon which a filmmaker's dreams can be projected and believed" (Irene Lacher, "Unpredictable Pays Off," *Los Angeles Times*, 5 November 2006). Steven Soderbergh's dream entailed having Blanchett incarnate the archetypal untrustworthy screen siren associated with 1940s-era studio filmmaking. Her performance operates in the shadows of such actresses as Ingrid Bergman and Marlene Dietrich and borrows heavily from the example of Alida Valli in *The Third Man* (1949). Unfortunately, Soderbergh conceived of the role as little more than a composite of simulacra, and Blanchett's is less a performance than a series of poses. Only if the actress could fill up the empty shell onscreen with her own persona would this conceit be successful, but that is precisely what a skilled shapeshifter such as Blanchett cannot supply. Blanchett's struggles with the character of Lena Brandt come into sharper relief when one compares her performance to that of co-star George Clooney. Clooney, probably miscast, still makes his role over in his own star image, but Blanchett is left floundering because she has nothing to work with but the bones of femmes fatales long gone. A similar sense of her characterization emerging out of the residue of earlier screen incarnations of foreign villainesses informs her work in *Indiana Jones and the Kingdom of the Crystal Skull*, but the latest installment in this action franchise doesn't ask for anything from its actors save an investment in the spirit of arrested adolescence. Blanchett's performance remains true to its source, and her Russian scientist, in long boots and high-waisted khakis, doesn't lack hauteur, but Spielberg's sexless, grinding vision of adventure high jinks drains the character of any interesting undertones.

Notes on a Scandal has sexuality in place, what with an affair between an underage student and his married art teacher (Blanchett's Sheba Hart) and an older female teacher's obsession with the same adulterous instructor. But despite the various intrigues and recriminations, the film leaves Blanchett adrift as well, again because of the difficulties the conception of her character introduces. The novel on which the film is based presents Sheba Hart only from the perspective of her admirer and eventual adversary, Barbara Covet. When envisioned as someone else's object of fascination, Sheba's actions become easier to accept, precisely because they never require full explanation. Still, *Notes on a Scandal* succeeds as long as Blanchett can show us both sides of Sheba: the airy would-be bohemian and the overextended teacher/mother. Once Barbara (Judi Dench) exposes the affair and convinces

Cate Blanchett reprises the role of Elizabeth I in *Elizabeth: The Golden Age* (Shekhar Kapur, Universal, 2007), which treats the monarchy as a form of performance. Collection Charlie Keil.

Sheba to accept her home as a refuge, the film loses its bearings and becomes a more sexually charged version of *What Ever Happened to Baby Jane?* (1962), a freak show where two unhinged women flail at each other. Blanchett's performance in these final stages may be fearless, but it's also improperly calibrated, tilting to overstatement as the quiet menace of the film's earlier sections becomes lost to overly broad strokes.

Heightened theatricality creeps into moments of Blanchett's reprisal of Elizabeth I in *The Golden Age* as well, but the film's suggestion that the monarchy involves displays of self-conscious performance helps to account for the histrionics. Most critics thought that *The Golden Age* sacrificed historical accuracy to mindless pageantry, and substituted stylistic bombast for close attention to court intrigues. Yet such criticism ignores how *The Golden Age* provides Blanchett the opportunity to portray a woman who has come to learn of the demands that power places on the powerful. Unlike its predecessor, the sequel finds the queen at a stage in her reign when she has become an active decision maker, rather than the pawn of competing factions in the court. Too young by almost fifteen years to play the queen at this historical moment, Blanchett finds many facets to delineate convincingly: flirtatious and bemused with Sir Walter Raleigh (Clive Owen), resigned and rueful with advisor Sir Francis Walsingham (Geoffrey Rush), and wistful when alone. And Blanchett masterfully conveys how always being in the public eye makes one wary of letting one's guard down, lest a moment of personal frailty should imperil the monarchy. In this sense, the portrayal is of a piece with her much-lauded take on Bob Dylan in *I'm Not There*, a near-uncanny incarnation of Dylan immediately after he had gone electric and become increasingly leery of fame and its demands. Blanchett has all the famous Dylanisms down pat and bears a striking resemblance to the 1960s-era singer, but what elevates the performance, ironically, is the indisputable fact, due to her sex, that she could never *be* Dylan, but only an approximation of him. The kaleidoscopic nature of Haynes's biographical fantasia ensures that the viewer remains cognizant of how "Bob Dylan" exists as a composite of different representations at different moments, and Blanchett's gender-bending yet deeply felt portrayal drives the point home most forcefully. At the same time, it stands as the most fitting summation of Blanchett's achievement up to this point: that she could melt so convincingly into a conception of a figure whom we think we know and yet who has not really ever existed.

Cate Blanchett serves as a particularly apt choice to play a version of Dylan because, ultimately, "she" is not there either. Like Kate Winslet, she gives herself over to a role so completely that very little residue of a distinct personality remains. Time and again, media profiles of the two actresses speak of their ability to "vanish" into their roles: "fluidity" is a quality Blanchett is said to both prize and embody, and she and Winslet alike prepare exhaustively. Neither embraces the label of "movie star," with Blanchett going so far as to say that "moviemaking becomes a bit pointless after a time" (qtd. in John Lahr, "Disappearing Act," *New Yorker*, 12 February 2007, 38), while, in comparing herself to Blanchett, Winslet has said that "Cate's a glamorous movie star . . . [while] I'm playing the part" (qtd. in David Colman, "The Winslet Way," *In Style*, February 2009). Ultimately, both exude a sufficient amount of dynamism in their performances that the allure of stardom clings to them even as the complicating issue of personality-driven appeal finds itself dismissed. Mark Harris's astute assessment of Winslet can stand as an apt characterization of how both actresses have succeeded as stars without succumbing to a celebrity version of stardom: "She approaches her characters with curiosity and determination, with an anatomist's keenness to discover what makes them tick rather than a narcissist's desire to refashion them into glibly 'relatable' versions of herself" ("Best Actress: Kate Winslet's Moment," *Time*, 19 February 2009). The alchemy of acting enables both Blanchett and Winslet to place characterization over personality and keep celebrity in check as they pursue a rare breed of stardom, predicated on craft: prestige imports, the two actresses can be heralded as the twin Deborah Kerrs of the new millennium.

Brangelina
Celebrity, Credibility, and the Composite Überstar

LINDA RUTH WILLIAMS

There is a stratum of stardom so elevated that it needs only the simplicity of the given name. There *is* no other Elvis or Arnold or Britney of any real significance. This is paradoxical: the more stratospherically remote a star gets, the more familiar their popular moniker—tabloids and celebrity media deal such names to us as if we were personal friends. Some stars are so confident in their status they dispense with family names altogether (Cher, Madonna, Prince). Brad and Angelina (Pitt and Jolie, of course) certainly fall into the former category, but so identified have they become as a couple since starring together in *Mr. & Mrs. Smith* in 2005 that it is now hard to read them separately, and a hybrid noun was invented by celebrity media for this definitive *überstar* couple of the twenty-first century: "Brangelina." The term does double service as both brand name and relationship shorthand. It is a curiously twenty-first-century mode of nomenclature: Richard Burton and Eliz-

---

Brad Pitt and Angelina Jolie.

abeth Taylor never got past Liz and Dick; Laurence Olivier and Vivien Leigh
were never Laureviv. Other hybridizations have come into currency (Ben-
nifer [Ben Affleck and Jennifer Lopez]; TomKat [Tom Cruise and Katie
Holmes]), suggesting cozy coupledom that effaces personal difference. This is
not true of Brangelina, which is somehow more than the sum of its parts,
with Pitt and Jolie remaining simultaneously singular entities. Before the
coupling, the two were established actors as well as figures of paparazzi fascination in their own right, both featuring in a mixed bag of popular and
esteemed film works as well as starring in their own celebrity soap operas
(Brad's marriage to Jennifer Aniston; Jolie's marriages to Johnny Lee Miller
and Billy Bob Thornton). The couple has juggled film roles of various kinds
with highly publicized humanitarian work while both courting and dodging
the popular media. Brangelina also has satellite players: the expanding family of children, Angelina's father Jon Voight, even Brad's ex, Aniston, Brad's
split from whom was one of the biggest gossip media stories of the decade
(see Claude Brodesser, "Splitsville Is Hitsville for Mags," *Variety*, 17–23 January 2005, 5). The couple inspires unprecedented hysteria (the *Washington Post*
claimed that the birth of their daughter was the most anticipated "since Jesus
Christ") and hyperbole (photos of the couple have commanded some of the
highest fees in the history of publishing [see Nicole LaPorte, "Precious
Images," *Variety*, 12–18 June 2006, 3, 6]).

It is then nearly impossible to read Jolie and Pitt's film work without the
insistent noise of the fame machine screaming through, so I don't propose
even to try. With celebrity wattage this intense, it might be forgotten that
these public figures make films (Neal Gabler suggested that "the reports about
Jennifer Aniston, Brad Pitt, and Angelina Jolie have more voyeuristic entertainment value than most of the movies they'll make" [*Variety*, 17 October
2005, 164]). Yet film choices as much as personal/private tittle-tattle and
sanctioned press releases are integral to the celebrity-making process. As
Peter Bart wrote about the power of agents and management, "A star like
Brad Pitt zealously guards his image and sifts his projects cautiously. The
same for George Clooney, who intercuts 'serious films' between his 'Ocean's
Twelve' frivolities. Both Clooney and Pitt insist on being masters of their own
fate" (*Variety*, 16 October 2006, 82). Jolie has constructed her image on three
pillars—role, personal publicity, and humanitarian activity—but the result is
often contradictory. Into this mix comes the gossip media (tabloid and mid-
range magazine fodder), idealizing and judging without the sanction of the
stars' PR machine (see Wilson). Here Jolie has moved from self-harming,
bisexual, incestuous wild child to maternal saint as the nuclear family has
stabilized her image. This transformative narrative "of motherhood as

recovery" (Negra, "Fertile Valley" 60) amounts to a domestic taming. For Pitt the opposite is true; the closer to house-husband he has gotten, the more savagely critical the media's judgment (unkempt beard, unworked torso, ungroomed appearance). So where are the films in this contradictory and conservative narrative of fame, scandal, and speculation?

Academic film studies, of course, usually start with movies or histories of the industry, and has only lately begun to theorize the phenomenon of celebrity. As a field, star studies have attempted to define ephemeral qualities such as charisma and chemistry, and to separate role from (the illusion of) "real self." Pitt and Jolie have embraced celebrity, partly because (or so it is argued by their PR agents) it enables a more intense light to shine on the good causes they espouse. Of course, the right kind of celebrity also keeps their A-list stock high. In a useful 2006 article in *Cineaste*, screen acting coaches and experts (such as, here, James Naremore) were quizzed about aspects of performance and star quality: "Stars are both actors (sometimes very good ones) and iconic, extracinematic characters; their names circulate through all the media, their mannerisms become as familiar as the people we know intimately" ("Acting in the Cinema" 62). This sense of a familiar figure who is at the same time singularly different—human and simultaneously godlike—was one of the founding ideas of star studies, supplemented more recently by celebrity analysis that has demythologized the machinery of fame. Fan material and hagiographies continue to waver between deification and reassurance of the ordinary: "[Jolie's] unpolished manner suggests that without the money and fame, she could be just like you or me, having the same insecurities and concerns" (McFay 7).

Still, the key terms that differentiate character or supporting actor from movie star remain ill-defined: "Beyond such effects of celebrity and charisma," writes Naremore, "there are no absolute rules for what separates ordinary actors from stars" (*Cineaste*). So—and please forgive what may seem like a dumb question—are Pitt and Jolie able to be esteemed actors (they will never be "ordinary") as well as feted stars? Does the dream of honored performance diminish the brighter a star shines? When a celebrity phenomenon such as Brangelina rides so high in the Hollywood food chain, how to distinguish actorly skill in the maelstrom of celebrity overload? Both have earned industry and critical respect, Jolie with *Gia* and *Girl, Interrupted* in the 1990s, and *A Mighty Heart* (2007) and *Changeling* (2008) since; Pitt with *Interview with the Vampire*, *Se7en*, *Twelve Monkeys* in the 1990s, and *Babel* (2006), *The Assassination of Jesse James by the Coward Robert Ford* (2007), and *The Curious Case of Benjamin Button* (2008) more recently. This is despite their continued branding as body-talent and sex objects (Jolie's *Lara Croft: Tomb Raider*

[2001], *Original Sin* [2001], *Beowulf* [2007], *Wanted* [2008], and *Salt* [2010]; Pitt's *Fight Club* [1999], *Troy* [2004], *Benjamin Button*). One film (*Mr. & Mrs. Smith*) created Brangelina itself, and is an intriguing essay on coupledom.

★★★★★ **Bimbo and Himbo**

Whatever the future of their relationship, from 2005 onward Brangelina wrote the book on what it is to be a universally recognized celebrity couple. It is logical to read them together here, since in a number of ways they are male and female equivalents of each other. In 2010 Jolie was voted the most beautiful woman of the 2000s; in 2009 she was the World's Most Beautiful Woman for *Vanity Fair* (Charlotte Duck, *Glamour*, 6 January 2010). Pitt was *People*'s All-Time Sexiest Man in 1995 and 2000, and has topped numerous polls. The superlatives vie for supremacy: inevitably, they have been voted World's Sexiest Couple. Beauty equivalence is then a baseline, preceding any judgment of performance. If their careers are matched in the mix of respected and mass-market movies they juggle, they are also, in a sense, each other's physical equals. Jolie in particular is physically identified in gossip media through focus on her tattoos, her pregnant body, her extreme thinness (disregarding those pneumatic breasts), rumors about cosmetic surgery, all of which feature regularly alongside the more customary adulation and fetishization of certain features such as her lips, undoubtedly the most discussed feature. Robert Sklar reads *Changeling* as a story of lip-adornment:

> Angelina Jolie's lipgloss . . . reveals—starkly or subtly, as you prefer the structure of a classic three-act Hollywood screenplay. Act One, arcing from modest happiness to tragic loss and bitter conflict, those remarkable lips shine with magnificent radiance. Act Two, the "Snake Pit" sequence, in the "psychopathic ward" gloss of course is forbidden; at best she wears a neutral tint. Act Three, her vindication, retribution, and a glimpse of future contentment, a muted luster is restored. (51)

As with pornography, the body of the performer and the nature of the performance are indistinguishable, further unsettling the sense of separation between star (body) and (embodied) role. Rumors about her psychological instability are underlined by further body-related "facts" that are part of Jolie-lore: the vial of Billy Bob Thornton's blood she carried around her neck when married to him, self-harming and S&M, and the ambiguously sexual comments she has made about her brother (inventing what came to be known as "incest chic"). Sexy, deviant, *and* mad—a combination traded on by gossip stories claiming that Pitt still craves calmer solace in the arms of ex-wife Jen. "Real life" images attempt to counter the mad glamour by featuring Jolie as a saintly figure campaigning as a U.N. goodwill ambassador and Pitt emasculated by the drudgery of trooping the pair's expanding family in and out of international airports.

Some of this emerges through the films of the period, pointing to a struggle to achieve credibility while also not abandoning the core attributes that helped make the pair stars in the first place. Both continue to promote themselves through physical means, whilst also choosing roles that suggest thespian seriousness (Jolie) or actorly versatility and range (Pitt). Those aforementioned "world's most beautiful" plaudits are not just the stuff of celebrity reporting: even respected critics are lost for words. This is Roger Ebert reviewing *Salt*: "How does she look? She looks beautiful by default, and there's a scene in an office where she looks back over her shoulder to talk with Schreiber and you think, oh, my" (*Chicago Sun-Times*, 21 July 2010). "Oh, my"—that's all? The couple have even been praised by Michelle Tauber in *People* for the magnificent aura they cast over their nearest and dearest: "He's a two-time Sexiest Man Alive. She's the world's Most Beautiful woman. . . . Is it any wonder, then, that Brad Pitt and Angelina Jolie—who await the arrival of their first child together any moment now—preside over what might only be deemed the World's Most Beautiful Family?" ("World's Most Beautiful Family," *People*, 8 May 2006).

To start with the films, one must start this story somewhere in the middle, a middle that is also a beginning. The pair had successful film careers prior to 2005, but then, following rumors and cast changes, Jolie was finally confirmed as co-star to Pitt in *Mr. & Mrs. Smith*. The Brangelina behemoth was created in this slick vehicle, which is impossible to read now outside of the frame of real couple as fictional couple. Is it Mr. and Mrs. Smith we are watching, or Brad and Angelina? The story of a couple whose domestic boredom is framed by the clichés of affluent American home life is a witty comment on what these particular megastars would never again experience or become. Indeed, it turns out that they aren't even that in the fiction. Jane meets John Smith during the chaos of a South American revolution; they marry and set up home, going their separate ways to work by day, reunited in relationship torpor by night. We discover that each is really an assassin working for rival hit companies, and each is then sent on the same assignment—to kill each other—at which point they each discover what the other has been doing all this time. After a series of set-piece sequences in which they try to fulfill their mission, they discover they like—and desire— each other more because of the dangerous reality that lurks beneath the mundane suburban veneer. The film is framed by a to-camera consultation

Mrs. Smith's kitchen arsenal in *Mr. & Mrs. Smith* (Doug Liman, Regency, 2005). Digital frame enlargement.

between the couple and a relationship counselor. In the sequence that plays out over the opening credits, the pair are frosty and unfulfilled; over the closing credits they are sexually energized and in love. Problem with your marriage? Try killing each other to spice things up a little.

As a whole, *Mr. & Mrs. Smith* provides a series of visual commentaries on domestic spaces and the confinements of the family: their opulent suburban house hides their weapon collections (Jane keeps hers in a secret compartment below the oven, where John would never look; John keeps his below a trapdoor in the garage where Jane would never look), and when they turn on each other the interior architecture is imaginatively used in the battle. The final showdown takes place in a furniture and lifestyle store, where homely consumption becomes the landscape of semi-comic violence. However, just as it's hard to imagine the stars ever really entering such a place, it is also hard to imagine anyone other than Brad being the Mr. to Angelina's Mrs. Smith, and vice versa, even though the pair weren't a couple when they were cast. At the same time, the film plays with images that are refuted in wider "real-life" publicity. Jane's image is antidomestic, despite the curtains she buys and the dinners she dishes up (it emerges that she never cooked them anyway); her sexy deadly woman recalls other femme fatale roles such as Bonnie Castle in the erotic thriller *Original Sin* (see Williams 119–22), the morally ambivalent protagonist of *Salt*, and the snake-entwined oedipal mother of *Alexander*—a "dragon lady . . . like a combination of Mata Hari and Count Dracula" (Todd McCarthy, *Variety*, 22 November 2004; see also Peter Bradshaw, "Alexander," *Guardian*, 31 December 2004). Since childbirth and charity Jolie has been popularly represented as a cross between Mother Earth and Mother Teresa, adopting babies across the world, making good causes newsworthy, talking about the sexiness of pregnancy. The antidomesticity of

Mrs. Smith is, then, in sharp contrast to the hyper-maternalism of Jolie's public face. At one point Mr. and Mrs. Smith visit a neighbor's party in order to reinforce the veneer of suburban normality. Ushered into a group of mommies and required to hold a baby, an expression of terror fixes on Jane's face unmatched by anything she shows when in mortal danger as an assassin. Contrast this to the "real-life" family photo Diane Negra analyzes ("Brangelina") that promotes Jolie as a kind of *übermother*.

If *Mr. & Mrs. Smith* is impossible to read outside of the subsequent gloss of its stars' real-life relationship, it is also one stop on the developing story of Pitt and Jolie's body careers. After winning her Oscar in 2000 for the wild-child craziness of *Girl, Interrupted*, Jolie embraced the training regime she underwent preparing for *Lara Croft*. For Sklar, the role traded on an image of "a vibrant, unpredictable, sexually daring, slightly dangerous, completely alluring but not quite knowable figure" (52). Although Jolie attended the Lee Strasberg school, complex vistas of the interior self are not needed here: Croft is a cipher from a videogame who kicks ass. Aside from the Tomb Raider sequel in 2003, the seductive Grendel's mother in *Beowulf*—which is all body, but digitally fleshed body—it is principally through *Wanted* that Jolie recently maintained her "embodied" profile, with physical performances animated by stunt-work and action spectacle. *Wanted* is a comic-book wish fulfillment fantasy that has otherwise fine actor James McAvoy as a wimpy accountant who discovers he's genetically an assassin. He is whisked off to join a secret society guided by action-mentor Jolie. Some critics read her as "basically an honorary male" (Peter Bradshaw, "Wanted," *Guardian*, 25 June 2008) or as transcending gender,

> the way a thermonuclear warhead overrides boundaries. In her videogame-avatar roles, with her sharpened cheekbones, telescopic-sight intensity, and a chest-forward walk like the coming of an icebreaker's prow, Jolie's default setting is an omnivorous, dehumanized take-no-prisoners sexuality that begs for military metaphors. . . . She's there mostly as a presexualized adolescent boy's sex object. (Jim Ridley, "Wanted: Irony-Free Escape-Fantasy," *Village Voice*, 24 June 2008))

Wanted played well at cinemas in the summer season of 2008, just months before the release of *Changeling*, a radically different Jolie performance for a rather different audience. The only thing missing from this demonstration of range across diverse markets is a voice role in a kids' movie, and 2008 also saw the release of *Kung Fu Panda*, with Jolie as Tigress.

Pitt is also a renowned physical performer. Reviewing *The Mexican* (2001), Mark Olsen wrote that he is "one of the sharpest, smartest assayers of dumb guys today . . . [his] trademark Tex Avery–like elasticity serves him

well, as he stretches and contorts as if giving physical form to the roiling con-
fusions underneath his surfer-boy exterior" (*Sight & Sound*, May 2001, 54).
The melodrama of victimhood has been played out on his body (the wounds
of *Fight Club* and *Snatch* [2000]; his gestural invitation to assassination in
Jesse James), but he remains more often the heroic outsider, sometimes a
warrior-villain or morally ambivalent maverick figure. *Spy Game* (2001) saw
him as a rookie CIA agent "gone rogue" after putting love before duty.
Rarely has he played true darkness; Jesse James gets close, Tyler Durden—
appetite-fueled alter-ego of *Fight Club*—perhaps closest.

In many ways these stars exemplify contemporary hyperfemininity and-
hypermasculinity. In 2000 Pitt was deemed "a poster boy for manhood in the
new millennium" (qtd. in Robb 216). Yet like the worked-out icons of cinematic masculinity in the 1980s and 1990s, Pitt's body work can often present
as static spectacle as well as action stunt-work. It may seem remarkable that
of the pair the woman is more physically prominent in action and motion
whilst the man's body roles present him more spectacularly in static form, but
Troy, *The Curious Case of Benjamin Button*, and *Snatch* do bear this out. The latter is not a significant performance; Pitt cameos as feral Romany One Punch
Mickey, in demand because of his physical prowess as a bare-knuckle boxer.
When he strips to fight, the film seems to hold its breath, more because of the
star factor than any Mulveyesque "to-be-looked-at-ness." When clothed, the
slightly comic character is little more than stupidly amiable (an A-List star
slumming in a cool film); when unclothed he *is* Brad Pitt. The climactic fight
is a combination of slow-mo, jump cuts, and freezes, perhaps in homage to
Raging Bull (1980) or, of course, *Fight Club*; the suffering body is fetishized.
Benjamin Button might also be seen as a body performance, since the whole
film focuses on the main character's *un*developing body but, like Grendel's
mother, the acting is done through and around digital embodiment and elaborate make-up effects. Nevertheless, at each stage the appearance of Button
is the film's spectacle. The story of a person who lives his life backwards, Button is born baby-sized but very old, "grows up" into adolescence and young
adulthood with his body moving backward from aged to late middle-aged,
then—for a brief moment—is at the peak of adult perfection in body while
also being an adult in mind and experience. As chronologically the years pass
his body gets younger, until he shrinks to baby form. Through this process
Pitt's familiar features come and go, with the move from baby old man to old
man baby a process through which a recognizable star blurs in and out of
focus. Here Pitt is playing with his looks—uglying up, to deploy that mid-
2000s phrase—making us look to see how much we might discern under the
wizened and whiskered latex. It is no accident that the sartorially coolest

era he lives through, the 1950s, coincides with Pitt at the height of movie-star perfection, enabling him to throw off the make-up, don Brando-esque T-shirt, and be his muscled-up self.

He is, of course, also not beyond pumping himself up into prime beef-cake for some chest-exposing roles that have marked him as consummate "himbo." *Troy*, a sand-and-sandals epic based on Homer's *Iliad*, takes the physique we see glimpses of in *Button* and *Snatch* and magnifies it tenfold. Here Pitt plays Achilles, half-divine hero of the ancient Greek war against Troy. Our first view of him is lying naked in bed with two prone women, all glistening post-coital flesh. In the action sequences he is fearless, quick, and acrobatic, but as the individualistic outsider he fights for himself rather than for "any flag." This rebel heroism marks a number of Pitt roles. In one exchange, Agamemnon (Brian Cox) worries that "he can't be controlled—he's as likely to fight us as the Trojans," to which Nestor (John Shrapnel) replies: "We don't need to control him—we need to unleash him." The elab-orately choreographed fight sequences are clearly one demonstration of this, but there is no question that the film's primary spectacle is Pitt's pumped-up chest, unleashed for all of his ample screen time. For *Variety*, "What's really going on . . . is the cinematic fetishizing of an actor on a virtually unequaled level. Appearing almost impossibly buffed, bronzed and chiseled, Pitt is lav-ished with elaborate photographic attention by Petersen and lenser Roger Pratt, in the way Greta Garbo and Marlene Dietrich—but very few men—have been" (Todd McCarthy, 10 May 2004, 51; for more on the politics of masculinity in sand-and-sandals epics, see Courcoux). Certainly this is inter-esting for sexual political readings; Cintra Wilson sees this spectacular ado-ration as a formation of the male pin-up from an earlier age. For her the himbo (she cites Pitt as our prime contemporary example) is exemplary sex-symbol who nevertheless does not threaten heterosexual male viewers, and whose key physical feature is the honed torso:

> A classic leading man . . . is gifted enough to inspire sexual insecurity in the viewer, but a himbo works within the boundaries of a more accessible fantasy range; he's a blunt obelisk with which Hollywood hits America's libido. Chests are key. In the '50s, the male body was a hairless silo projecting straight up from the pelvis. In the '70s, Burt Reynolds and Sean Connery tried to subvert the himboism of the '50s by rolling out their manly breast-carpets.   (*Variety VLife*, September 2005, 32)

Just as the 2000s' interest in reviving historical epics looked back to the genre's 1950s heyday, so Pitt as Achilles apes 1950s rather than 1970s ideal physiques, more Kirk Douglas than Burt Reynolds. Wilson downplays the sexual potency of such an image; the himbo is not "brilliant enough to be

Muscular Himbo Brad Pitt, the male spectacle of *Troy* (Wolfgang Petersen, Warner Bros., 2004). Digital frame enlargement.

intimidating, they are easy-to-chew, bland fantasy snacks for the sexually toothless" (32). The extreme molded cut of pecs and abdominals also owes much to the mainstreaming of body-building made cinematically famous by Arnold Schwarzenegger and Sylvester Stallone in the 1980s and 1990s. These figures played out onscreen the popularization of pumping iron that was taking place in local gyms everywhere. No longer were six-packs the sole preserve of muscle beach fanatics or specialist sportsmen. Of course the red-carpet Pitt does not parade such a heavily worked-out torso. Achilles the war-machine displays a fleshly armor put on for the role. Pitt is then a performer who works up and works down, cutting his physical cloth as well as his acting chops to the measure of varied roles: honed classic beefcake (*Troy*); hyperactive and feeble (*Burn After Reading*, 2008); feral killing machine (*Snatch*); antihero of Americana (*Jesse James*).

★★★★★ "A Real Hero for the People": Seriousness, Versatility, and Good Causes

Given these body roles, how then to be more than a pretty face? How have Pitt and Jolie secured respect for their body of work rather than just their bodies? This is ever more urgent given Peter Bart's worry that "all the silliness involving Brad and Angelina [has] compromised their ability to assume serious roles as serious people" (*Variety*, 20 June 2005, 4). Beauty is historically seen as exclusive of talent. Cintra Wilson allowed Pitt the honor of being the exemplary beefcake on the condition that "we never have to watch him over-pronouncing all his consonants in a costume drama" (32). Of course, that is pretty much what he has wanted to do; Jolie even more so. As the 2000s progressed, a certain seriousness inflected her cinematic and extra-cinematic worlds with *A Mighty Heart* and *Changeling* in particular; she was also featured in Robert De Niro's CIA movie *The Good Shepherd* in 2006, and the FBI movie *Taking Lives* in 2004. Yet there is still a tension between star elements; humanitarian activism does not necessarily reinforce serious thespianism. The public partnership and parading of family life on the global stage suggests both an acceptance of media intrusion and an awareness that espousal of good causes is well served by the global currency of superstardom, and in turn bathes star images with a more beatific glow. The traffic of positive regard is two-way: "When celebs advocate, audiences pay attention," *Variety* noted in 2005 (Kathy A. McDonald, 25 July 2005, A1). In June 2005, Pitt's appearance on an ABC news program "instantly doubled primetime news coverage spent on Africa" (McDonald A4). Yet of course the apparent selflessness of charity endorsement serves to make the star seem even more nobly superhuman, less a frivolous celebrity and more an esteemed statesperson. "Finally there's something to vie with conspicuous consumption in Hollywood: conspicuous giving. . . . Being socially responsible, it seems, is now the rage," wrote Elizabeth Guider in 2006. "The practice may soon become part of every self-respecting celeb's routine, as common as getting Botox injections or berating subordinates. Credit Angelina Jolie, at least in part, for Hollywood's change of heart" ("H'wood's Latest Craze: Generosity," *Variety*, 10 July 2006, 4).

Pitt, too, has benefited from aggrandizement through philanthropy (despite earlier having disparaged celebrities who intervene in world affairs):[1] as Ted Johnson wrote in 2009,

> One Monday afternoon in early March, MSNBC cut to a live shot inside the Capitol, where House Speaker Nancy Pelosi stood before a row of media cameras and introduced "a real hero for the people of New Orleans and a real model for the country." It was Brad Pitt, who was there to pitch, promote and lobby for efforts to rebuild the Lower 9th Ward of the city.
>
> ("Causes and Effects," *Variety*, 15 June 2009, 1)

I am not arguing that these are unworthy causes; simply that the cause of stardom is also served as Brad speaks for the Big Easy or Angelina against landmines. Is not "real hero for the people . . . and a real model for the country" exactly the ideal fleshed out by so many of Pitt's characters? For her part, Jolie has tried to mitigate through charitable works the "just a pretty face" image she claims to dislike. Some critics have found this somewhat self-seeking, making the world see her "less as a man-stealing vixen than as a politically aware and morally engaged celebrity activist. While Jolie gets to address deep questions about world hunger in interviews, all Jennifer Aniston is asked to talk about is . . . Vince Vaughn" (Guider 4). In turning the cameras onto international disasters, have they turned the cameras away from themselves, or simply secured a more flattering angle? Do their movies have any wider role (other than bankrolling charities) in augmenting these hero images?

Three Jolie films veer into the "issuetainment" arena, combining serious performance with discussion of world events. *Beyond Borders* is essentially a romance that commutes between famine-stricken Ethiopia and war-torn Cambodia and Chechnya. Todd McCarthy called it "a tourist's sampler excursion to Third World trouble spots" ("Love in the Third World," *Variety*, 20 October 2003, 40). *A Mighty Heart* is the story of journalist Daniel Pearl's kidnap and murder in Karachi by al-Qaeda. Jolie's most significant performance comes in *Changeling*, which starts as a maternal melodrama but takes on police and governmental corruption in a network of conspiracy (I turn to this in the final section of this chapter). In all these films the personal is the political. Though perhaps the world's highest-profile mother and partner, Jolie has come to specialize in women experiencing the loss of children and partners. *Beyond Borders* has a three-part structure; in each, privileged socialite-turned-aid-worker Sarah loses, then has to find, her lover again in the midst of international conflict situations. *Changeling* begins with the abduction of Christine Collins's real son and the police's attempt to put a substitute child in his place. Though a much sillier film, even *Beyond Borders* features Sarah rescuing a starving baby, notwithstanding that she also leaves her own children when it's time to run to the next troubled hotspot. Roger Ebert found this offensive: "When the suffering of real children is used to enhance the image of movie stars who fall in love against the backdrop of their suffering, a certain decency is lacking. 'Beyond Borders' wants it both ways—glamour up front, and human misery in the background to lend it poignancy" (*Chicago Sun-Times*, 24 October 2003).

Framed by the wider canvas of international tension, the emotional focus of *A Mighty Heart* is pregnant Mariane's loss of her husband, whose death is confirmed shortly before she gives birth to their child. This personal lens might be surprising from a serious auteur director comfortable with the politics of conflict situations—*A Mighty Heart* is often seen as the third in Michael Winterbottom's post-9/11 triptych, following *In This World* and *The Road to Guantanamo*. But the film was produced by Brad Pitt, and Winterbottom was Jolie's directorial choice. Political confidence and gravitas were clearly needed to bring Mariane Pearl's memoir convincingly to a wide audience. When production was announced, *Variety* saw this as "the quintessentially independent and serious-minded Winterbottom [becoming] an incongruous supporting player in the Brangelina circus" (Adam Dawtrey, "Helmer takes

'Heart' at Par," *Variety*, 17 July 2006, 3), but the film was not received as a star-serving circus-trick. Certainly Winterbottom lends Brangelina the requisite seriousness:

> The hoopla that surrounds Pitt and Jolie couldn't be further from the fierce commitment to authenticity that Winterbottom has always displayed. . . . The choice of helmer sends a clear message that Jolie and Pitt's creative ambitions are far more elevated than the tabloid frenzy around their relationship, let alone popcorn fare such as "Mr. and Mrs. Smith," would suggest.
>
> ("Helmer Takes 'Heart' at Par," 3)

From Jolie's point of view, the film might be read as a neo-woman's picture, prefiguring the work she would do a year later on *Changeling*. Once Daniel is kidnapped, *A Mighty Heart* moves between scenes in the manhunt control room at Mariane's house, with a cast of investigative characters; chaotic Karachi street scenes; and private focus on Mariane. Winterbottom was conscious of this personal/political dynamic: "The film is about the relationship between the two: the small group inside the house who are making all these connections and what's going on outside, where all the energy, chaos and confusion is. . . . That's the structure of the story: the quiet and calm inside contrasted with all the noise from outside" (Ali Jaafar, "A World Without Pity," *Sight & Sound*, October 2007, 26). Mariane exemplifies this "quiet and calm," her face registering ephemeral hope and anticipated dread as the five-week investigation continues, her composed dignity followed by explosive grief and punctuated by flashback memories of her husband. Playing a mixed-race Cuban/French woman, Jolie is nearly unrecognizable in dark contact lenses and frizzed hair, and performs Mariane with French accent and clipped, slightly combative delivery. Contemporary reviews lauded Jolie for a characterization devoid of stardust. For Justin Chang in *Variety*, "This isn't the sort of commanding star turn in which the performer vanishes behind a well-known celebrity mask" (28 May 2007, 20). Jolie's involvement with Afghan refugees in Pakistan documented in her straightforward account of activism, *Notes from My Travels*, might also serve as an interesting counterpoint to Mariane's story (Mariane herself contextualizes her husband's death with all the others who died due to terrorism that same week in Pakistan). When the star dared to advocate for Afghan people shortly after 9/11 on "The Tonight Show" she received death threats (Jolie 191).

Aside from the perfunctory roundup of historic hotspots that Pitt visits in *Spy Game* (Vietnam in 1975; Cold War–era Berlin; Beirut in 1985), the nearest a Pitt movie gets to a serious current-affairs film is *Babel*. An ambitious, global-reach movie about the connectedness of things in a paranoid world, Pitt features in only one section of this three-cornered story (though it was marketed as a Brad Pitt film), where he performs grief and impotence, rage and desperation after his wife is shot in the Moroccan desert (an accident misinterpreted as a terrorist attack on U.S. citizens abroad). Unlike *The Mexican*, *Babel* doesn't posit him as center of the story, since, like other overlapping, multi-stranded narratives, it has no center (it is often compared to Paul Haggis's *Crash*, but has a direct lineage back to director Alejandro González Iñárritu's earlier *Amores perros* [2000]). But if a serious performance weren't enough, his presence in such a serious film also serves his star image. This is only one of a range of ensemble cast and supporting roles that Pitt has taken on. Jolie makes fewer movies, but these are more significant events with her as singular star presence. Pitt, by contrast, isn't afraid to provide a bit of starlight in ensemble casts, co-starring, cameoing, or sacrificing prominence for the sake of a smaller or more interesting kind of movie, or to work with a hip director. There are many reasons for taking the small part of an obscure loser like Chad in *Burn After Reading*; playing feckless stupidity in a Coen brothers movie provides a reputation boost outside of it. There may also be the greater chance of award success: "Ensemble pics may not deliver big paydays, but they can polish a resume with shiny kudos," wrote Dave McNary in *Variety* in 2006 ("Band in the Run," 11 December, B1). This is hardly true of the three *Ocean's* films (*Ocean's Eleven* [2001], *Ocean's Twelve* [2004], and *Ocean's Thirteen* [2007]). Neither small nor particularly interesting, the franchise served up some of the biggest box-office successes of the decade, but Pitt is only one of a gang of A-listers and is not in any sense carrying each movie (though the first face we see in *Twelve* is Brad's, hot and handsome, a beautiful woman awaiting him: in the disparate roll-call of ensemble cast introductory sequences, Brad gets the sequence that rolls before the credits). Certainly they keep his stock high, and reinforce some of his singular star traits—the likeable rogue, the action man with a penchant for comedy. There is little that is memorable about these popcorn caper/heists aside from the starry cast list, and the franchise's increasing playfulness and self-reflexivity.

The *Ocean's* films were no ordinary ensemble outing—such movies, particularly common in indie sections of the U.S. movie industry in the 2000s, were usually a gathering of acting talent but with only one or two A-list stars in the mix. Connectedness is a common narrative hallmark: the globalization tract of *Babel*; the circling plot pyrotechnics of the *Ocean's* franchise. *Snatch* and *Inglourious Basterds* (2009) saw Pitt sharing the limelight with a cast of more locally known talent. In the former, Pitt, surrounded by rough-looking unknowns who rarely speak, is paradoxically the most recognizable and the least understandable. This is boyish Brad, showing off his quirky acting chops in a cool Brit Pic. Perkily spouting a near-impenetrable cod-gypsy argot, he is nevertheless the star shining out among anonymous bit-players. *Variety* commended his willingness to subjugate star-individuality to collective requirements, praising him for "melding seamlessly into the large ensemble cast" ("Snatch," *Variety*, 20 September 2000), while Mick LaSalle read *Snatch* as "a mess—but it's a mess with a big star, and that's a plus. Brad Pitt has a supporting role, and the movie wakes up when he's on" (*San Francisco Chronicle*, 19 January 2001, www.sfgate.com). Stardom is then still at the fore even when Pitt steps back from it.

His part in Tarantino's movie is more significant, but he still isn't wholly shouldering the story. Somewhere between multiplex popcorn and auteur film, *Inglourious Basterds* courted wide audiences with a semi-comic treatment of a serious subject (World War II and the Holocaust). Pitt plays another outlaw character, the snarling leader of a feared band of vengeful Jews who hunt out Nazis in occupied France. The Tarantinoesque comic-brutal violence comes largely from the eponymous group's practice of killing and scalping their victims. Pitt is scarred, wrinkled, sporting a small, graying mustache as well as a rather pantomimic Tennessee accent; this is not the Brandoesque physique of *Benjamin Button*'s 1950s sequence. Nevertheless, it is still unmistakably a blackly comedic Brad who shines out to U.S. audiences as the prime recognizable Hollywood star in the ensemble cast of Europeans. The U.S. poster showed Pitt in close-up, but in other territories co-stars Christoph Walz, Diane Kruger, and Til Schweiger are more prominently featured. The president of Universal, David Kosse, told *Variety*, "We don't want people to think the film is just Brad Pitt kicking ass. . . . We want to show off the whole cast. It's the kind of film where the French people speak French and the German people speak German" (Pamela McClintock, "H'w'd Spins the Globe," *Variety*, 13 July 2009, 33). One interviewer remarked to Tarantino that he "went in expecting Brad Pitt to be the star, but surely it's Christoph Walz, right?, to which Tarantino replied, 'To me it's a three-way star thing. Aldo [Pitt], Shosanna [Mélanie Laurent] and Landa [Walz]'" (Ryan Gilbey, "Days of Gloury," *Sight & Sound*, September 2009). *Burn After Reading* similarly featured Pitt in a supporting role but sharing the limelight with Clooney, Frances McDormand, and John Malkovich. Like many Coen antiheroes, Pitt's character is blinded by greed, seizes his chance, and pays for it. "I didn't think [Chad] would be such a dumbbell," Pitt told *Sight & Sound*, ". . . a gum-chewing, Gatorade-swilling, iPod-addicted bubble-brain" (J. M. Tyree et al., "League of Morons," November 2008, 37). Although muscles are Chad's stock-in-trade (he is a gym instructor), this is a long way from a himbo hero like Achilles.

★★★★★ Reflecting on Stardom

It has recently been argued that stardom changed dramatically in the 2000s. "While movie stars today can help open a picture, they sure as hell can't guarantee success," wrote Peter Bart in 2007. "Has the basic concept of a movie star become something of an anachronism?" (*Variety*, 22 October 2007, 6). Received wisdom is that the field has shrunk. There are fewer stars, who are paid more but perhaps valued less. Matthew Ross concludes that Brangelina will "always have the presale juice point," though there "are very few bankable stars these days" (*Variety*, 11 May 2009, A42). Some of this is attributed to the global media and marketplace. Star power is a necessary but not sufficient condition for the success of a movie, according to David Garrett, president of Summit International. "One big reason, in my opinion, is the Web has allowed word of mouth to travel incredibly quickly around the world. . . . And that's going to affect the success of any film, regardless of who's starring in it" (Ross). Pitt and Jolie have embraced this global exposure and, so far, have played it effectively. As the decade closed, Pitt reached his mid-forties (a less perilous time for a male than a female actor) and Jolie her mid-thirties, with both maintaining secure positions as stars able to greenlight movies (see Anne Thompson, "No Country for Real Men," *Variety*, 1 September 2008, 7, 13).

They also made their two most significant and interesting films. Pitt's *The Assassination of Jesse James by the Coward Robert Ford* is his best performance of the decade, while Jolie's *Changeling* is a career best. Both roles meditate on the nature of fame, Pitt's through the stardom of an outlaw, Jolie's through the unwelcome fame of a justice-seeker. Jesse James is another in Pitt's long list of explorations of perverse and glamorous masculinity; Jolie's *Changeling* explores motherhood and activism, issues as acute for her image outside the movie as for the character within it. In movie form, Pitt had been there before: there is something starry about the half-god, half-man Achilles who, it is rumored, cannot be killed. He is a warrior-celebrity, fighting to achieve posthumous fame ("Think how many songs they'll sing in your honor") rather than because of allegiance to a cause. Jesse James is the dark version of Achilles, acutely aware of the circulation of his mythic image in dime novels, newspaper editorials, and postcards, manipulating the adoration of the stalker/fan who will eventually kill him, perhaps shaped by Jesse's own death wish.

There are many things to say about this work of art. It is cinematographically stunning. It has pitch-perfect performances and a poetic and beautifully structured script. Pitt plays Jesse as a glamorous psychopath, at first calm and controlling, then paranoid and nasty. The "all-time sexiest" face is haunted, prematurely aged, yet still exudes the allure of power. But Jesse is a Garboesque star in hiding, as well as an outlaw on the run: "He went everywhere unrecognized," the opening voiceover tells us. Yet he has a magnetism that could betray him at any time: "Rooms seemed hotter when he was in them. Rains fell straighter. Clocks slowed. Sounds were amplified" (compare this to the comment of producer Patrick Hasburgh who had cast Pitt in 1988: "Brad walking into a room was more exciting than most actors doing a scene" [Halperin 50]). Against Jesse's confident cool, Casey Affleck plays creepy young Bob Ford as callow and gauche, adoring and humiliated. Both kill, but as Ebert put it, one of them kills "with style" (Jesse *defines* style here). Both shoot men in the back, but only one of them is branded a coward. Bob—the "coward"—shoots Jesse in a back that is suicidally proffered to him, using a weapon provided by Jesse himself. The dance of control is fascinating. Of course, the Mark Chapmans of this world notwithstanding, fans don't (usually) murder their heroes; and although the love/death courtship the pair play out is the center of the movie, how the relationship ends isn't the point. What is interesting is how much like the star-fan dynamic this is. Which is not to say that Pitt is playing himself. This is a radically different characterization to the jittery dork Chad or the comic-gypsy One Punch Mickey. But Pitt, celebrity and actor, surely has a significant stake in such a powerful exploration of image control and the magnetism of fame.

The commingling of real self and the performed self, conveyed through the role and presented onscreen, is what acting coach Jeremiah Corney defines as charisma, which "is the combination of the actor's personality and talent. Charismatic actors leave the audience with an overwhelming impression of who they are. Their personalities are more important to the audience than any character that they may play" ("Acting in the Cinema"). Pitt's screen charisma is what makes him so watchable, but it is also why we never forget we're watching Brad Pitt, this consciousness overwhelming the immersive experience of the story. This might mean that charismatic stardom and quality screen acting are mutually exclusive; charisma militates against conviction. Of course, cinema history shows this is not the case, which may be why the role of Jesse James was such a smart choice for Pitt. For Naremore, star images onscreen "usually create a double impression that some films can use to their advantage: it's both Norma Desmond and Gloria Swanson coming down the stairs at the end of *Sunset Boulevard*" (*Cineaste*). In Jesse James, the outlaw star "is" both Jesse James and Brad Pitt. So, in a supremely homoerotic scene when Bob watches his idol bathing, Jesse/Pitt's question to his acolyte—"I can't figure it out, you want to be *like* me, or you want to *be* me?"—resonates with the uneasy relationship between the adoring and their objects, between Pitt and his admirers. Jesse is a more powerful and convincing figure precisely because we never forget he is Pitt. Jesse, too, despises as well as uses the proto-celebrity media. When Bob (who keeps a shoebox of Jesse-related fan material under his bed) lovingly confesses, "Many's the night I've stayed up . . . reading about your escapades in the Wide Awake Library," Jesse responds, "They're all lies, you know." Lies that flatter: he becomes an even more heroic celebrity after death. Bob also grasps whatever he can, despite his coward fame, performing a tableau of the murder on music hall stages and garnering some ignoble celebrity until he too is "assassinated."

The question of whether celebrity gets in the way of performance also exercised Nick James reviewing *Changeling*: "Angelina Jolie does about as good a job as is feasible for someone of her extreme fame of subsuming herself in the role of Christine Collins" ("He Who Dares," *Sight & Sound*, July 2008, 21). Of course this is not the only real person whom Jolie has performed: Mariane Pearl, like Jesse James, is also real (interestingly, *Changeling* is confidently subtitled "A True Story," whereas *A Mighty Heart* is only given to be "Based on real events," despite Mariane's recent memoir being its source). It may be that Pitt can slip more easily into a historical character whose reality is now entirely mediated by heroic stories of the Wild West. Jolie has to perform ordinary, unlooked-for heroism. Christine Collins is no longer famous, but she starts the movie as an unwilling celebrity. *Changeling*'s conspiracy thread, its serial-killer story, its madwoman-in-a-nuthouse sequences, all veer close to exploitation fare, but Jolie—as directed by Clint Eastwood, a convincing helmer of the contemporary woman's picture—holds these lurid strands in credible focus.

To argue that some of Jolie's roles are body performances and some are mind performances would strip *Changeling* of its understated physicality. With such raw and ambivalent emotions at play, the body still signifies; it's just not particularly acrobatic or sexualized. In the pursuit of a credible performance Jolie also made herself look drawn, lined, gaunt. The body that launched a thousand magazine covers is clothed in concealing 1920s fashions, and the palette is muted. Certainly she looks as classically handsome as ever, but the film does not promote her sexually: men look at Christine Collins with admiration rather than lust. The lower half of her face (pulled-down cloche hats enshroud the upper half) is the canvas upon which a range of wild emotions play—desperation, anger, frenzied grief, impotence, self-doubt. Jolie's famous lips are then not fetishized objects here, but are

Angelina Jolie in *Changeling* (Clint Eastwood, Imagine Entertainment/Malpaso, 2008): Maternal Melodrama for the 2000s. Digital frame enlargement.

part of the performance. As she watches the boy whom her son saved from death recounting his harrowing story, we are given Jolie's face hesitating in the threshold between restraint and release. Since her eyes are shadowed by those hats, her iconic mouth is allowed to speak through expression as well as dialogue. Yet Jolie does not overplay this; the dignity of the character rests in buttoned-up stillness. Here, as we watch her flat profile for a sign—finally some news of her son!—tears make tracks down her cheeks, and once or twice the bottom lip trembles complex emotional response, but all else is held closed. In a fictional dialogue with Jack Warner, Peter Bart has the old studio head exclaiming, "I don't want to see Angelina Jolie looking for lost children. She should be doing Bette Davis pictures" ("Recession '08: Angst for the Memories," *Variety*, 24 November 2008, 46). It's hard to disagree with this phantom voice from Hollywood's past. For all its chilling horror/conspiracy threads, from score to script to performance, *Changeling* is an old school melo, with Jolie stepping into the shoes of Joan Crawford or Barbara Stanwyck, if not the feisty Davis.

With these recent films, Jolie has attempted to subsume the "Brangelina circus" in screen performance. By contrast, Pitt has used star quality to augment a role investigating stardom. Pitt excels in roles where he can capitalize on aspects of his stardom, Jolie in roles where she buries it. Securely established as accomplished performers in auteur works (by Fincher, Tarantino, the Coens, Winterbottom, Eastwood), the pair is nevertheless still capable of slumming it with high-paying formulaic performances in mass-market multiplex entertainment fodder. Brangelina is then a contradictory public entity. As Julia Wilson argues, Jolie has variously been "model humanitarian, neglectful mother, generous celebrity, happy homemaker, manipulative self-promoter, suffering daughter, jealous girlfriend"

(28). Although he is still something of a contradictory figure, Pitt is less vulnerable to the judgments of gossip media consumers. Perhaps this is
because he is a man and more of an American national treasure. Cinematically Brangelina remains fairly consistent, with working profiles that,
though diverse, seem equally to be struggling for respect while simultaneously cherishing popcorn-friendliness.

NOTE

1. Writes Jolie biographer Rhona Mercer, "It's somehow ironic that Pitt should have
been so impressed with Angelina's charity work and political views, given that years previously he had laughed at the idea that he should have a valid view on any such matters.
'Reporters ask me what I feel China should do about Tibet,' said Pitt. 'Who cares what I feel
China should do about Tibet? I'm a fucking actor! They hand me a script. I act. Basically,
when you whittle everything away, I'm a grown man who puts on make-up'" (238).

12 ★★★★★★★★★★★★
George Clooney
The Issues Guy

DAVID STERRITT

George Clooney has the looks of a classic Hollywood star, somewhere between Gary Cooper and Cary Grant, and his most memorable roles—the eponymous Michael Clayton and Danny Ocean, for instance—take full advantage of the fact. Yet his most significant contribution to American cinema comes less from his appearances in crowd-pleasing entertainments like *The Perfect Storm* (2000) and *Ocean's Eleven* (2001) than from his participation in films that take considerable aesthetic risks (e.g., *Solaris* in 2002 and *The Good German* in 2006) and those that share his strong political sensibility, such as the geopolitical thriller *Syriana* (2005) and the brilliant legal drama *Michael Clayton* (2007). Of particular note are two of the films Clooney himself has directed: *Confessions of a Dangerous Mind* (2002) and *Good Night, and Good Luck* (2005), both of which deal with intersections between popular culture, represented by the television industry, and political machinations, treated satirically in the earlier production and soberly in the later one. Broadly speaking, Clooney's career since 2000 reflects an

George Clooney.

expanding interest in public affairs that has placed him in the front ranks of Hollywood progressivism. This essay looks at the connections among his activities as actor, activist, and celebrity, with attention to his skills and abilities, the regular-guy reputation that sticks to him despite his iconic status, and the question of how his political views feed into movies he decides to make, engaging with some of Clooney's critics along the way.

★★★★★ The Side of Justice

Clooney's activism on and off the screen, including his antiwar activities and advocacy for humanitarian causes, has made him one of the few contemporary movie stars to place his celebrity at the service of both cinematic innovation and sociopolitical progress. Political activism is central to his image as a movie star and a pop-culture icon, as reportage and comment on his career demonstrate. "Unseating old-time liberal 'actor-activists' such as Warren Beatty, Tim Robbins and director Rob Reiner," a British journalist wrote in 2005, "Clooney has now emerged as the leading political voice in Hollywood, winning plaudits from liberals and stinging attacks from conservatives" (Paul Harris, "Hollywood Politics—How a Heart-Throb Became the Voice of Liberal America," *Observer*, 27 November 2005, 18). Clooney is "an outspoken Darfur activist who sees his fame as a means to draw attention to a conflict often ignored by the world," said an NBC reporter in 2009 (Ann Curry, "In Darfur, Clooney Is an Activist First, Then Actor," *Dateline NBC*, 16 March 2009). The actor "manages to balance Hollywood stardom and serious activism," CNN stated in 2010 (Jay Kernis, "Intriguing People for January 18, 2010," 18 January 2010).

Clooney has often encouraged the perception that strong political views and forays into political activism are among his most important concerns. "I'm a liberal," he said to television interviewer Larry King in 2006, adding that "the liberal movement morally, you know, has stood on the right side of an awful lot of issues. We thought that blacks should be allowed to sit at the front of the bus and women should be able to vote, McCarthy was wrong [and] Vietnam was a mistake" (interview with George Clooney, "Larry King Live," CNN, 16 February 2006). Making a similar point more recently to a German magazine, he said he finds it "quite amazing that 'liberal' nowadays has become a swear word [since] in the history of our country it always meant to be on the side of justice. It started with the witchhunt in Salem; the conservatives' point of view was: 'Burn them at the stake,' and the liberals' point of view was: 'There are no witches.' And that's how it continued with the civil rights movement and women's suffrage" ("My World—George

Clooney," *Brigitte*, qtd. in Deborah White, "The Politics of George Clooney, Actor and Liberal Activist," www.about.com). Clooney's many efforts to foster a resolution of the civil war and humanitarian crisis in Sudan are widely known, as are the activities of Not on Our Watch, an organization "committed to stopping mass atrocities and giving voice to their victims," which Clooney founded with five other influential figures in 2005 ("Who We Are," notonourwatchproject.org/who_we_are).[1] All of this notwith-standing, Clooney has soft-pedaled his politics at times, seeing downsides as well as advantages to the activist image he has acquired. (This accords with the great liberal tradition of finding more than one reasonable response to every question.) "After *Syriana* and *Good Night, and Good Luck*," he remarked in 2008, "I was offered the Richard Clarke book and every issues movie. I didn't want to be the issues guy because if the issues change, you're done. . . . If you're a young heartthrob—which I never caught on as—those fans not only abandon you, but they're embarrassed to have liked you. It's the same thing with issues movies. I want to just be a director" (Joel Stein, "George Clooney: The Last Movie Star," *Time*, 20 February 2008).[2]

Facts bear out this assertion. Clooney strongly supported Barack Obama in the 2008 presidential election, for instance—"I love that guy, I love him," he told a reporter—but apart from introducing the candidate at one event in Cincinnati, he turned down requests to campaign for Obama because he feared his efforts would be distorted by "Hollywood versus the Heartland" media spin and wind up doing more harm than good (Ian Parker, "Some-body Has to Be in Control," *New Yorker*, 14 April 2008).[3] Along similar lines, he reduces his hydrocarbon footprint by driving an electric car and a Lexus hybrid, but chooses not to advocate for environmental causes because he persists in using a private jet plane (Stein).

In sum, Clooney's career rests on a cluster of dialectical relationships: between celebrity status as a profession and as a source of influence, between work in front of the camera and behind it, between taking direc-tion and giving it, between managing a public persona and safeguarding a private self, between performing in fiction films and performing in real-life arenas, between acting as entertainment and acting as intervention—between acting and *acting*, one might say. He has juggled these intercon-nected spheres so artfully that for most observers, from movie fans to media pundits, it doesn't seem like juggling at all. "His strategy for being a movie star is pretty simple, if counterintuitive: he makes fun of himself," opined Joel Stein in the 20 February 2008 issue of *Time*, which featured Clooney on the cover. "It's the by-product of every successful person's strategy," Stein added, "which is to figure out what the other person is thinking" (Stein).

Exhibit A for Stein's observation could be his own *Time* article, which spends an inordinate amount of space expressing self-absorbed astonishment that Clooney came to his house for dinner—a canny maneuver on Clooney's part, suggesting that he knew what the journalist was thinking and then addressed his hopes in a way that got results in the form of a highly flattering profile. "Clooney was the only star who could have said yes," Stein coos, "because no other star wears his celebrity so easily" (Stein). Yet the question remains as to whether Clooney's alternating modes of political outspokenness ("I'm a liberal") and reticence ("I want to just be a director") bespeak true uncertainty about how best to exercise his influence on public affairs, or, alternatively, a wish to stave off the appearance of being merely a pampered millionaire by engaging in good works when he isn't busy on the set. While he declines to be an issues guy, his movie work between 2000 and 2010 indicates that he is willing and able to invest large amounts of movie-star capital in film projects charged with evident sociopolitical content.

☆☆☆☆☆ From Supernumerary to Superstar

A brief recap of George Clooney's biography casts light on important aspects of his career in the first decade of the 2000s. He was born in 1961 in Lexington, Kentucky, to a former beauty-contest winner and a television news anchorman who later became known as an American Movie Classics presenter. (An aunt was Rosemary Clooney, the great pop singer.) After attending both Roman Catholic and public schools, he majored in history and political science at Northern Kentucky University and the University of Cincinnati, without earning a degree. He entered television in the late 1970s as an extra, appeared with Elliott Gould and Mary McDonnell on CBS's one-season hospital sitcom "E/R" (1984–85), made little impression as a heartthrob on NBC's boarding-school sitcom "The Facts of Life" in the 1985–86 season, earned considerable fame in the debut season of ABC's blue-collar sitcom "Roseanne" (1988–89), and eventually became a star on NBC's medical drama "ER" (1994–2009) during its first five seasons. (CBS's "E/R" and NBC's "ER" have no connection other than their hospital settings and Clooney's presence.) His first notable movie was the Robert Rodriguez vampire film *From Dusk Till Dawn* (1996) and his first politically inflected role was the army intelligence officer in *The Peacemaker* (1997), directed by Mimi Leder from a screenplay (about purloined nuclear weapons) based on an article by Leslie Redlich Cockburn and Andrew Cockburn, two politically engaged journalists. His last film of the twentieth century was David O. Russell's dramatic comedy *Three Kings* (1999), about rogue American soldiers whose plan to steal a stash of gold after the first Persian Gulf War is sidetracked by Iraqis who need rescuing from Saddam Hussein's army. His first project of the twenty-first century was *Fail Safe*, a television movie about the crisis that ensues when an American aircraft is inadvertently sent to drop a nuclear warhead on Moscow; directed by Stephen Frears and featuring executive producer Clooney in a small role, it was the first full-length narrative broadcast live on CBS-TV in thirty-nine years, underscoring Clooney's longtime interest in television and anticipating his TV-themed films *Confessions of a Dangerous Mind* and *Good Night, and Good Luck*. Aired on 9 April 2000, the show used the screenplay that Walter Bernstein wrote (based on an eponymous 1962 novel by Eugene Burdick and Harvey Wheeler) for the 1964 movie *Fail-Safe*, directed by Sidney Lumet. (A very similar novel published in 1958, *Red Alert* by Peter George, was the basis for Stanley Kubrick's Cold War comedy *Dr. Strangelove or: How I Learned to Stop Worrying and Love the Bomb* [1964].)

Reviewing these facts, one observes that Clooney's background has been marked by both public affairs and show business, the former via his politically involved father and (abbreviated) college career, the latter via his beauty-queen mother and celebrated aunt. One also notes that his professional beginnings were fairly humble, with considerable time as a TV extra followed by modest achievements in mid-1980s sitcoms; only with his appearances on "Rosanne" and "ER" did he truly begin to rise "from failed TV actor into A-List Hollywood actor," in the words of *New York* magazine, and his movie breakthrough in *From Dusk Till Dawn* came a full dozen years after his "E/R" debut (Mark Graham, "Vulture: George Clooney Turns On the Charm One Last Time on *ER*," *New York*, 13 March 2009). His gradual ascent from supernumerary to superstar bespeaks a willingness to work and bide his time as well as patience, seriousness about his career, and a realistic awareness that one can't (usually) succeed in entertainment without really trying. And whether or not he is an issues guy, there has been substantial overlap at times between his private and political life, on one hand, and his professional decisions, on the other. After he spoke out in 2003 against the American invasion of Iraq, he was attacked by right-wingers and included in a pack of "weasel" playing cards along with Barbra Streisand, Jane Fonda, and other left-wing personalities. Surprised and outraged, Clooney channeled his feelings into *Good Night, and Good Luck.* "I was really angry when I made it," he told Ian Parker of the *New Yorker*. "I was out of my mind, I was so furious. Being called a traitor to your country?" He pressed his counterattack further in interviews promoting the film. This throws intriguing light on Clooney's motivations. Viewed positively, the episode casts him as an

George Clooney said right-wing attacks on his patriotism made him "really angry" when he directed and acted in *Good Night, and Good Luck* (George Clooney, Warner Independent Pictures, 2005), his drama about the McCarthy era. Digital frame enlargement.

unfairly insulted citizen who uses his professional status and abilities as tools for publicly challenging his adversaries. Viewed negatively, it suggests that he may at times "read politics through the prism of his own expertise in handling public perception," in Parker's words.

Since greeting the turn of the twenty-first century with *Three Kings* and *Fail Safe*, Clooney has made both entertainment vehicles and the "issues movies" of which he professes to be wary. His roles in the former category include a convict on the lam in the Coen brothers' boisterous farce *O Brother, Where Art Thou?* (2000); a fishing-boat captain in Wolfgang Petersen's action drama *The Perfect Storm* (2000); the leader of a super-spy outfit in Rodriguez's fantasies *Spy Kids* (2001) and *Spy Kids 3-D: Game Over* (2003); a safe-cracker in the crime comedy *Welcome to Collinwood* (2002); a philandering lawyer in the romantic comedy *Intolerable Cruelty* (2003); high-rolling thief Danny Ocean in Steven Soderbergh's trilogy *Ocean's Eleven* (2001), *Ocean's Twelve* (2004), and *Ocean's Thirteen* (2007); and a football hero in his own sports comedy *Leatherheads* (2008). In films that count one way or another as "issues movies" he has played an agent and recruiter for the Central Intelligence Agency in the dark comedy *Confessions of a Dangerous Mind*; legendary TV producer Fred Friendly in the historical drama *Good Night, and Good Luck*; the burned-out CIA agent Bob Barnes in Steven Gaghan's *Syriana*; the eponymous "fixer" for a corporate law firm in the legal thriller *Michael Clayton*; a womanizing State Department official in the crime comedy *Burn After Reading* (2008); a corporate personnel terminator in Jason Reitman's *Up in the Air* (2009); and a member of a paranormal unit in the U.S. Army in the military comedy-drama *The Men Who Stare at Goats* (2009). He has also lent his voice to Wes Anderson's offbeat animated feature *Fantastic Mr. Fox* (2009) and acted in two Soderbergh movies that are difficult to categorize apart from broad genre labels: the science-fiction drama *Solaris* (2002, from the novel by Stanislaw Lem and the 1972 film by Andrei Tarkovsky), wherein he plays Chris Kelvin, a psychologist on a space station, and Soderbergh's *The Good German* (2006), in which he plays Jake Geismer, a journalist in war-ravaged Berlin.

And all the while Clooney continued to polish his moviestar credentials. He won his first Academy Award in 2006, for Best Supporting Actor in *Syriana*, and received Best Actor nominations for *Michael Clayton* and *Up in the Air*. He also received Best Actor nominations from the Screen Actors Guild for the latter two films, and the cast of *Good Night, and Good Luck* was nominated by that organization for Best Ensemble. The New York Film Critics Circle named Clooney Best Actor of 2009 for the one-two punch of *Up in the Air* and *Fantastic Mr. Fox*. Lower on the prestige scale, he won his first Golden Globe for *O Brother, Where Art Thou?* and others for *Syriana*, *Michael Clayton*, and *Up in the Air*. Lower still on the scale, in 2006, at age forty-five, he became the second person to be named the "Sexiest Man Alive" by *People* magazine not once but twice (having won the first time in 1997; his friend Brad Pitt [1995, 2000] is the other two-time honoree). Clooney's other acting honors since 2000 include a nomination for *Solaris*, Academy of Science Fiction, Fantasy & Horror Films; American Cinematheque Gala Tribute, 2006; a nomination for *O Brother, Where Art Thou?*, American Comedy Awards; nominations for *Michael Clayton*, *Up in the Air*, *Syriana*, and *Good Night, and Good Luck*, British Academy of Film and Television Arts; a nomination for *The Perfect Storm* (2000), Blockbuster Entertainment Awards; nominations for *Syriana*, *Michael Clayton*, and *Up in the Air*, Broadcast Film Critics Association; nominations for *Michael Clayton* and *Up in the Air*, Chicago Film Critics Association; a nomination for *Michael Clayton*, Irish Film and Television Awards; nominations for *Michael Clayton* and *Up in the Air*, London Critics Circle; wins for *Michael Clayton* and *Up in the Air*, National Board of Review; nominations for *Michael Clayton* and *Up in the Air*, Online Film Critics Society; a nomination for People's Choice Awards, 2005; and a win for *Michael Clayton*, San Francisco Film Critics Circle.

★★★★★ Head Bobbing

Sexy, busy, and honored he may be, but is Clooney a first-rate actor? This question has circled him so steadily, even at the height of his success in the first decade of the 2000s, that the very uncertainty about his expertise has contributed to his mystique, keeping his name in constant circulation between projects and suggesting that even detractors regard his performances as substantial cultural artifacts calling for analysis and debate. Comments by his admirers generally run along these lines:

> MovieActors.com: Charm. If George Clooney had a British accent he could have been James Bond. . . . His look is almost old-fashioned in its all-American, classic, matter-of-fact handsomeness, with a perfect resonant voice to match. . . . His smile is literally a multi-million dollar charmer. . . . And the brains you see onscreen are based in reality.
>
> (Nate Lee, "The George Clooney Review," www.movieactors.com)

> Men'sFlair.com: An amalgam of Cary Grant, JFK, and Orson Welles, Clooney has created a distinct persona that is unique in today's celebrity culture: a socially conscious, intellectual sex symbol. He is also one of the few actors who can truly be called classic. It's very easy to imagine him working with someone like Gary Cooper or Humphrey Bogart. . . . The son of a reporter, George Clooney is articulate, inquisitive and intelligent. . . . Clooney's own fashion sense is an integral part of his timeless look. . . . Clooney also has an approachability that is very un-celebrity.
>
> (Chris Hogan, "Icons of Timeless Style— Part 1: JFK, George Clooney," www.mensflair.com)

As is typical for remarks by fans, these say little about Clooney's acting techniques or his success in using them. His charm, stylishness, and other star qualities are to be celebrated, not analyzed, and the compatibility between his private life and celebrity persona are to be assumed, not argued for.

Some commentators have been even more unstinting in their praise, and no less reputable a source than *The Observer* has portrayed Clooney as something of a martyr, not just in an ideological sense—risking low box-office returns by parading his Hollywood-liberal views—but physically as well. "Clooney has . . . suffered for his art," wrote Paul Harris. "He gained 35 pounds to play the pudgy middle-aged spy in *Syriana* and hid his good lucks [sic] behind a bushy beard. He also damaged his spine during filming, which saw him in such agony that he ended up drinking heavily to dull the pain" (Harris). Others set forth more nuanced views supported by salient facts. In a wry observation on Clooney's earnings in 2009, for example, a writer for *Movieline* reported that the star took in a total of $22 million dollars for acting in three features—*Up in the Air*, *The Men Who Stare at Goats*, and *The American* (Anton Corbijn, 2010)—and another $5 million for appearing in foreign commercials; lest we think this is big money, however, the journalist then noted that the teenaged Rupert Grint and Emma Watson each received almost 50 percent more ($30 million apiece) for acting in *Harry Potter and the Deathly Hallows*, the two-part finale of the J. K. Rowling franchise (S. T. Vanairsdale, "Shock and Awe: Rupert Grint and Emma Watson Out-Earned George Clooney by Almost 50 Percent," *Movieline*, 4 February 2010).

Reports geared to business and political concerns have little to say about Clooney's artistic strengths and weaknesses, however—traits that are central to his star persona among average moviegoers, if not among the uncritical fans he sought to please during the heartthrob period that he later disavowed. Thoughtful comments on his professional abilities are more likely to come from sources with balanced, even skeptical approaches to the matter, and, strange to say, head wobbling frequently plays a part in the discourse. This last has interested Clooney critics at least since his mis-calculated appearance in Joel Schumacher's miscalculated movie *Batman & Robin* (1997), which prompted a blogger to describe the star's "look down, up, and shake method of acting" (*Celebrity Outhouse*, "Batman & Robin," www.celebrityouthouse.com). Similarly, a *New York* writer marked Clooney's fleeting return to "ER" in 2009 by admitting he was "slightly disappointed that Clooney didn't reinstitute the head-bobbing acting style he patented in the early days of his career," a wily phrase that waxes hot and cold on Clooney at once (Graham, "Vulture").

The opinionated critic David Thomson offered a more substantial eval-uation in the 2002 edition of *The New Biographical Dictionary of Film*, describ-ing Clooney as

> a little reminiscent of William Holden in the early fifties—he seems able to sustain anything. . . . But there's something flippant or facetious in his atti-tude—a touch of Mel Gibson—that stops him short of the anguish, or com-mitment, that Holden commanded. . . . He's likable and versatile, to be sure, but not for one minute in *The Perfect Storm* . . . did he make me think of a Massachusetts fisherman. . . . It was *Out of Sight* and then *Three Kings* . . . that suggested a real following . . . and his flair for humor brought a lot to *O Brother, Where Art Thou?*. . . [He did] nothing to save *Ocean's 11* . . . by exud-ing a bland self-satisfaction that made one all the more mournful for [Frank] Sinatra's self-hating grandeur.   (164)

Thomson's back-and-forth appraisal suggests great ambivalence about Clooney, although he recognizes that the actor has a solid fan base. I'll return to Thomson's views later, but first I note an interesting take on Clooney's acting that appeared in 2009 in *Variety*, where show-business observer Andrew Barker wrote that even "well-known marquee thesps like George Clooney" may be seen by their peers—including those who vote on Academy Awards and other industry honors—as charismatic stars rather than authentic actors when they play characters who seem to resemble their own offscreen selves. "In this year's *Up in the Air*," Barker continued, "Clooney plays a suave, lifelong bachelor who jet-sets across the country lounging in chic hotels. As the actor himself exhibits all these qualities [*sic*] in real life, viewers can't help but wonder how much he is simply playing himself." Yet the critic then speculated that "in Clooney's case, as a major star, that similarity may well have its advantages," since his portrayal of "the loneliness and alienation inherent in a lifestyle similar to his own" could be taken as an act of candid self-exploration, allowing his followers—and Oscar voters—a privileged look at the dark side of his famous lifestyle (Andrew Barker, "Are They Really Acting?," www. variety. com, 29 December 2009). In a commentary on this commentary, Kae Davis found support for Barker's argument in an *Entertainment Weekly* interview with Dave Karger where Clooney said of the script for *Up in the Air*,

> There were some things that sounded like they were taken from a Barbara Walters special that I had done. I'm not completely unaware of people's perceptions of me. I sort of felt like, if you were ever going to deal with it, this is probably the best way to do it and the best person [director and co-writer Reitman] to do it with. If you can't point at what people think are your shortcomings, then you're boxing yourself in.
>
> (Dave Karger, "The Oscar Dance," www.ew.com, 1 January 2010, qtd. in Kae Davis, "George Clooney Acting Ability Called into Question before Oscar Awards," www.examiner.com, 31 December 2009)

When a movie star says, "I'm not completely unaware of people's perceptions of me," one can take the statement as either disarmingly unguarded or evasively oblique. But however one chooses to interpret the words, they merit attention for their implicit acknowledgment that standing guard over his image is never far from Clooney's mind, and that a role conveying impressions of candor and vulnerability can place useful notions about his forthrightness and approachability into the minds of professional peers and popular audiences alike. Clooney was nominated for Best Actor in the 2009 Academy Awards race, but lost to Jeff Bridges in Scott Cooper's *Crazy Heart*. None of the film's other nominees won their races either: Reitman for Best Director, Vera Farmiga and Anna Kendrick for Best Supporting Actress, Reitman and Sheldon Turner for Best Adapted Screenplay, and the movie itself for Best Picture.

★★★★★ Playboy-Politico Perfection

All of which bears out the idea that Clooney's stardom rests to a large extent on the snug connection between his private and public

George Clooney's face would be perfect on a Roman coin, and he often looks like a statue of himself, as in this image from *Michael Clayton* (Tony Gilroy, Warner Bros., 2007) with Tom Wilkinson. Digital frame enlargement.

personae—not as they are in fact, necessarily, but as they operate in and on the moviegoing imagination. His leading-man looks are as precisely configured as those of Cary Grant and Robert Redford, to mention two of the Hollywood celebrities he most resembles; his countenance would be perfect on an ancient Roman coin (with or without the Caesar haircut he has somehow managed to popularize), and in almost every setting and circumstance he has a remarkable tendency to look like a statue of himself.[4] Also like heroes and emperors of old, Clooney is an expert at having a terrific time, forever pictured in the press as a freewheeling playboy who spends countless leisure hours sipping champagne on his yacht, tooling around on his private plane, going on dates with supermodels, and hanging out with his playboy and glamour-girl friends. In sum, he embodies every man's fantasy (and many women's fantasies, mutatis mutandis) of being a carefree Hollywood star.

What makes Clooney's situation more complex, slippery, and interesting than this stereotype is the double-edged nature of such chiseled moviestar perfection. One potential liability is that people who are initially seduced by his celebrity aura may feel resentful when they realize how entirely serious he is about the liberal ideology that he openly espouses and assertively promotes. More broadly and importantly, Clooney's playboy-politico image is so vividly established that it discourages people from sensing deeper, more exotic elements in his personality. Every top star must be an instantly appealing surface on which the public can inscribe the shapes of its desires; yet offering oneself as a tabula rasa is a dangerous game in the twenty-first century's highly charged media environment, inviting the celebrity-world equivalents of graffiti artists—unsympathetic critics, journalists, and buffs—to make their mischievous, irreverent, or malicious marks thereon in front of everyone who cares to watch. With his coin-worthy features and statuesque demeanor, Clooney runs the risk of looking like he's all veneer, all outward show. If the character he's most associated with is Danny Ocean, it's not only because Danny's adventures stretch across three successful pictures; the other, more revealing reason is that Danny's glibness dovetails with Clooney's star persona more seamlessly than do the interiority of a Michael Clayton, the melancholia of a Chris Kelvin, or the world-weariness of a Bob Barnes.

☆☆☆☆☆ Racing Away

Above I quoted David Thomson's assessment of Clooney's career in 2002. Four years later, when Clooney was rolling toward middle age, Thomson speculated that if the forty-five-year-old star sometimes seemed older than he was, this was partly because he was still racing away from his pretty-boy phase, "when he was a big attraction on *ER* and not much else." After leaving "ER" he passed through a "very routine" period, Thomson continued, "smirking his way through bad pictures, and flopping in anything more adventurous," before arriving at 2005, when he came into his own with *Good Night, and Good Luck* and *Syriana*. Three lessons should be drawn from this, Thomson concludes. The first: "Every young star in this year has reason to look at George Clooney with great respect." The second: "You have to make a few *Ocean's 11* pictures to be able to do *Good Night, and Good Luck*," so "you might as well take full responsibility for what you make." The third: "The longer you stay around the more the public thinks you're good company" ("The Crop of Young Male Actors Taking Over Our Screens," *Independent*, 15 January 2006).

Although the third and final point sounds like a truism, it marks the spot where (as often in Thomson's writing) accuracy loses out to spin. Whether or not the public had discovered Clooney was good company, few movie-goers had a shred of interest in seeing *Good Night, and Good Luck*, which scored a humble ninety-two on the list of worldwide grosses for 2005 despite six Academy Award nominations, or *Syriana*, which garnered two Oscar nominations—and, as noted, a win for Clooney—yet barely recouped its $50 million budget in domestic earnings.[5] The lesson actually to be drawn is that while moviegoers may value Clooney's political and humanitarian serious-ness even if they don't share his progressive views, they haven't been impressed in sufficient numbers to make box-office hits of serious films like *Good Night, and Good Luck* or semi-serious ones like *Confessions of a Dangerous Mind*, much less odd items like *Solaris* or *The Good German*.

Thomson is on solider ground in a 2008 update of *The Biographical Dictionary of Film*, where he takes a more realistic look at the "philosophy" whereby Clooney makes "this [picture] for the business, and the next one for himself." In actuality, Thomson says, "one for the system and the business can lead to the next being for you (and the system and the business)." It is most often the case, Thomson continues,

> that your films begin as something dangerous, but end up pleasing the system. After that, you are left with little else than seeing the resemblance between the gangs in the *Ocean's* films and Clooney's sentimentality for male groups having a good time, making a packet and doing cool work. There's nothing that determines artistic personality so much as stark failure with a project you really care about. And I doubt Clooney has run that risk yet.
>
> ("Biographical Dictionary of Film No 34:
> George Clooney," *Guardian*, 4 April 2008)

Thomson isn't a particularly prescient observer. Awaiting the release of *Leatherheads*, for instance, he correctly foresaw that it would be "a rowdy gang/team film that fulfills Clooney's dreams of a male huddle," and that it would be "a step down in ambition from the first two films he directed." Thomson also says it is "likely to be a considerable hit," however, whereas the neo-screwball comedy proved to be a considerable fiasco, costing $58 million to produce and earning a woeful $41.3 million in lifetime grosses (boxofficemojo.com). In a judgment more wrong-headed still, Thomson goes on to declare that *Good Night, and Good Luck* initially "seemed daring— low-budget, black and white, all about paranoia—but in hindsight . . . is full of craft and empty of risk" (Thompson "No. 34"). His sole, simplistic reason for making this statement is that the film's portrait of McCarthyism takes place not today but during, well, the McCarthy era. Far from being safe and crafty, as Thomson claims, *Good Night, and Good Luck* bravely takes a double risk, holding up McCarthyism as a mirror for the increasingly ugly, bellicose tone of the 2000s while honoring the sense of history that postmodern culture seems bent on warping, minimizing, and subverting.

Turning to *Syriana* near the end of this essay, Thomson calls it the work of "a serious-minded actor anxious to prove his respectability, talking to everyone in Washington DC and making a movie about American foreign policy now." But serious-mindedness isn't enough for Thomson, who then asks and answers two questions: "Was it risky or dangerous? Or was it simply complicated and unclear? I fear it showed a fatal irresolution, an unwillingness to attack, a horror of not still being the urbane, worldly, unflappable George Clooney." The lesson Thomson now draws is a moralistic one: "If you want to make real movies about the world today, you need a dangerous mind prepared to give up being The Sexiest Man in the US and all those glossy titles. Clooney has not faced that one yet, and I can see a way in which he never will" (Thompson "No. 34"). The only hope Thomson sees is that Clooney's relatively young age and the rottenness of the world might possibly conspire against his material interests, propelling him beyond the understandable desire to be rich, glamorous, and loved. The critic offers no clue as to what forms Clooney's artistry would then take, however; nor does he explain why Clooney should have to choose *between* glossy titles and "serious-minded" projects instead of continuing to work on both sides of the art-entertainment divide, which is an arbitrary and artificial division to begin with.

I've engaged with Thomson's opinions at some length because they indicate a trap into which Clooney's critics fall when they envision him as an idealized archetype of the socially conscious celebrity, and then punish him for not living up to standards he has never claimed to have. Publicists, compliant journalists, and other confederates start the trouble by presenting Clooney as the world's most likable *and* serious star, living the high Hollywood life both on and off the screen, yet regularly risking his industry cred by speaking his mind politically and taking on projects that are unconventional (*Fail Safe*, for example) or original (*Good Night, and Good Luck*) or political (*Syriana*) or all three (*Michael Clayton*). The trap is sprung when moviegoers (including critics) buy into this image and then buy out of it again, imagining first that Clooney is a one-of-a-kind Hollywood figure—a hero who transmutes the clout bestowed by Danny Ocean into Important Films about political and corporate corruption—and then deciding that he's an ordinary player after all, compromising with the system whenever it suits his purposes. This is the pattern that Thomson follows, saying in his earlier commentary that every young star should regard Clooney with "great respect" because he takes "full responsibility" for what he makes, but backpedaling fast when *Syriana* turns out to be more intricate and challenging than he'd prefer. It seems to me that the "fatal irresolution" of which Thomson speaks lies in his own sensibility, not that of the star he's observing.

All of this said, I think there actually are present-day models for the kind of filmmaking—at once commercial, responsible, and adventurous—that Thomson appears to want but fails to define or describe. I'll mention two of them, although several others would serve equally well. One is the body of work created by Richard Linklater since 1991, when *Slacker* made him an indie to reckon with. Linklater's films are often strikingly original in subject and style, ranging from the romanticism of *Before Sunrise* (1995) to the minimalism of *Tape* (2001), from the deliria of *Waking Life* (2001) to the dystopia of *A Scanner Darkly* (2006), and—underscoring his similarity with

Clooney—from the political preoccupations of *Fast Food Nation* (2006) to the candidly commercial agendas of *School of Rock* (2003) and *Bad News Bears* (2005). Linklater's formula appears to be "one for the system, several for himself," and it has served him well for decades. The other model I have in mind is close to Clooney's own career: the filmography of Steven Soderbergh, who has moved effortlessly (if not always successfully) from the personal expressions of *Schizopolis* (1996) and *Full Frontal* (2002) to the political concerns of *Traffic* (2000) and the two-part *Che* (2008), from the art-house aesthetics of *Solaris* and *The Girlfriend Experience* (2009) to the commercial *and* responsible dynamics of *Erin Brockovich* (2000) and *The Informant!* (2009)—and of course the *Ocean's* trilogy, frankly commercial from start to finish, entertaining a large and diverse audience while bestowing clout, cred, and dollars on a director and star who then invested their takings in a variety of bolder, riskier ventures.

☆☆☆☆★ The Eccentric Actor

I've pointed out the comparisons frequently drawn between Clooney and bygone stars, such as Cary Grant, Gary Cooper, and (something of a stretch) Humphrey Bogart; in my eyes he most resembles Grant, at least when he's performing at his best. In the most perceptive analysis of Grant's style to date, film scholar James Naremore describes him as an actor who operates more in the tradition of Lev Kuleshov, the great Soviet director and montage theoretician, than by the principles of Constantin Stanislavski, the Russian theorist whose ideas became the basis of so-called Method acting. "More concerned with mechanics than with feeling," Naremore writes, Grant was "especially effective in comedy or in the [Alfred] Hitchcock films, where everything depended on timing, athletic skill, and a mastery of small, isolated reactions. He seldom seemed preoccupied or thoughtful and rarely displayed intense emotionalism. . . . Nevertheless, he is an expert at crisp expressiveness and movement, a player whose understanding of classical film rhetoric is equal to anyone's" (224). I would modify this in a couple of ways. Clooney can be a capable comedian, as in *Welcome to Collinwood*, *Burn After Reading*, and *Leatherheads*, but he can also be the overeager *farceur* of *O Brother, Where Art Thou?* and the unpersuasive comic lead of *Intolerable Cruelty*. Although introspection and introversion are not among his specialties, he shows an instinctive talent for thoughtfulness in *Good Night, and Good Luck*, for preoccupation in *Syriana*, and for off-kilter intensity in *Michael Clayton*. (On the other side of the ledger, Grant, too, could be an overemphatic comic, as in Frank Capra's *Arsenic and*

Old Lace [1944], and his range was not impressively wide—it's hard to imag- ine him doing first-rate work in films like *Syriana* or *Michael Clayton*.)

Clooney is certainly a Kuleshovian rather than a Stanislavskian, how- ever, more attuned to the techniques and *trucs* of acting than to psycholog- ical detail and the simulation of deep feeling. He also recalls Grant in that he resembles, in Naremore's words, "what the early Soviet directors liked to call an 'eccentric' actor—a highly stylized creation made up of peculiar movements and an interesting combination of expressive codes" (Naremore 235). This returns us to the overlapping qualities of Clooney's three per- sonae—the celebrity self, the actor self, and the activist self—and to the challenges set up for him, as for Grant and such fellow eccentrics as James Stewart and Burt Lancaster, by the modern media environment, which strives "to make obvious theatrical eccentricity seem invisible," as Nare- more puts it. A star's image, he continues, "is a valuable commodity, affect- ing her or his every public appearance, so that popular actors seem to become the very figures they play, shading their fictional behavior into their celebrity appearances" (235).

And vice versa, I will add. Like earlier Hollywood stars as different as Charles Chaplin and Katharine Hepburn, or Joan Crawford and John Wayne, Clooney has put his most inspired work into the creation of himself, or rather of himselves, an ever-shifting dialogic matrix of public-private, outer-inner, artificial-authentic traits, skills, qualities, and tics. If it's still uncertain whether he will be an actor for the ages or a star for the firma- ment—and the jury is still out on these questions—it's because today's mass-media milieu is vastly more difficult to navigate than in the studio days of old, flattening all but the most prodigiously gifted actors (my per- sonal American pantheon includes Robert De Niro, Gena Rowlands, Meryl Streep, Forest Whitaker, Philip Seymour Hoffman, Denzel Washington, and quite a few character actors) into two-dimensional products of the celebrity marketing industry. Clooney's movie-star looks and footloose reputation have been both his blessing and his curse, propelling him to archetype sta- tus at the expense of the spirited eccentricity that shines through his most fully realized performances but merely glimmers in the rest.

The most affecting and enduring art invariably comes from individuals who have the creative derring-do to burrow deep within themselves, tap the mysterious wellsprings of their most inward natures, and then share what they've discovered in emotionally intelligible forms—and the more peculiar, particularized, and idiosyncratic their findings are, the more swiftly they will reach and the more profoundly they will move the audiences who see and hear them. Clooney has too readily given up the particularities that might

George Clooney has done much of his best acting when embedded in an ensemble cast, as in *Good Night, and Good Luck* (George Clooney, Warner Independent Pictures, 2005), which was nominated for the Screen Actors Guild's Best Ensemble award. Digital frame enlargement.

have made him a great actor as well as great star; he runs with packs of friends, embraces mainstream Democratic politics, and often makes the best impression when he's embedded in an ensemble cast, as in *Good Night, and Good Luck* and all the *Ocean's* movies. This is fine for an archetype—a star— but it works against the singularity that lifts an actor's achievements to the highest levels. Clooney might become a true and luminous artist if he learns to contradict the crowd and cultivate the most instinctive, unruly, and unpredictable resources he can find in his creative personality. If he keeps running with the pack, he may succeed as a celebrity, an activist, and an issues guy, but his full aesthetic potential will remain undeveloped, unheeded, and unknown.

NOTES

1. The group's other founders are actors Don Cheadle, Matt Damon, and Brad Pitt, producer Jerry Weintraub, and human-rights lawyer David Pressman, who at this writing is Director for War Crimes and Atrocities for the National Security Council in the Obama administration. *Not on Our Watch* is also the title of a best-selling book about the need for humanitarian activities in Darfur, eastern Congo, northern Uganda, and other gravely troubled places, written by Cheadle and John Prendergast, a human-rights activist. Don Cheadle and John Prendergast, *Not on Our Watch: The Mission to End Genocide in Darfur and Beyond* (New York: Hyperion, 2007).

2. The article doesn't clarify Clooney's reference to "the Richard Clarke book," but since *Good Night, and Good Luck* and *Syriana* were released in 2005 and Stein's profile appeared in 2008, the likely candidates are Richard A. Clarke's novels *Breakpoint* (2007), about terrorists seeking to destroy the world's computer and communications resources, and *The Scorpion's*

Gate (2005), about global turbulence sparked by revolution in Saudi Arabia. Before writing these books Clarke held various government positions relating to U. S. counterterrorism policy.

3. Clooney's father, a well-known television personality in the Cincinnati area, once ran unsuccessfully for Congress, and Clooney believed the campaign had been undermined by opposition rhetoric pitting Hollywood against America at large.

4. Thanks to Murray Pomerance for this witty formulation.

5. *Good Night, and Good Luck* cost $7 million to make and took in combined domestic and international grosses of $31. 6 million, ranking number seventy-six among pictures that never reached the top five, while *Syriana* had a production budget of $50 million as against lifetime domestic earnings of $50. 8 million and foreign earnings of $43.2 million (boxofficemojo.com).

In the Wings

MURRAY POMERANCE

In the last days of 1919, the star of "Fatty" Arbuckle was most spectacularly on the ascendant, and his legion fans were hardly in a position to suspect that before another two years were out his fame would collapse almost overnight in the harsh glare of the Rappé scandal. A somewhat similar fate befell Errol Flynn in the 1950s, the early (and as yet unreconstructed) career of Rob Lowe late in the 1980s, the burgeoning career of Winona Ryder in 2001 (thanks to a brief shoplifting spree at Saks Wilshire Blvd.), and dozens of other stars whose light went off with great—and utterly unpredictable—abruptness. The case of stars dying young—Carole Lombard, Bobby Driscoll, Tommy Rettig, Brandon De Wilde, River Phoenix, Heath Ledger—also gives pause to any who would try to predict how movie careers will soar, hit their apogee, and gracefully decline into a culturally approved sunset. Thus, as at the end of the 2000s one tries to look forward to what is beyond, only speculation, bald and flagrant as it is, will do.

There seems no reason for believing that the most well-established box office draws will not, for at least the next decade—since they are none of them yet in late middle age—continue unobstructed to seduce audiences around the world. Johnny Depp, whose publicity agents have made something of a fetish the listing in advance of his future plans, was slated after the release of Michael Mann's *Public Enemies* (2009), his last film of the decade, for considerably more than a dozen projects at one point—although at this writing, late in 2010, and with his twerpy Mad Hatter (for Tim Burton) and beleaguered American tourist (in the film of that name, with Angelina Jolie) in release, there are only five films in his foreseeable future. One of these, of course, is the fourth *Pirates of the Caribbean* venture, which will pay him enough money to retire on and at the same time titillate the hunger of Depp fans everywhere. George Clooney will open a film in 2011 and is writing and directing a project with Evan Rachel Wood and Ryan Gosling set for 2012. Not yet fifty when the decade came to a close, and still considered by hordes either the most beautiful male figure on Earth or in close contention for the status with Depp, he has begun buying into his films and gives off all the signs of the actor sliding behind the camera. Meryl Streep, a little older, is rumored to be lined up for various roles, but she has a monumental career behind her and little need to satisfy external expectations with continued performance—yet part of her star quality has been an apparent hunger for bizarre and challenging roles, a hunger that if perhaps not yet sated may soon be after she incarnates Margaret Thatcher. The aging, but still monarchical, Jack Nicholson has a James L. Brooks comedy ready for release, and is working on another project with the equally mercurial Philip Seymour Hoffman. Nicole Kidman has numerous projects on the way, all in the popular vein (by contrast with her stunningly offbeat 2000s work in such films as *Birth* [2004], *The Interpreter* [2005], or *Fur* [2006]). The indomitable Nicolas Cage is filming a sequel to *Ghost Rider* (2007) and has completed filming *Drive Angry 3D* (the tagline for which, "All Hell Breaks Loose," may set a record for banality). Tom Cruise will return in, among other things, another *Mission Impossible* adventure, this one written by J. J. Abrams, who will bring along a young and addictable fandom. There can be little doubt, too, that we will see other stardoms grow onscreen: Zac Efron, Dakota Fanning, Michael Cera, Jesse Eisenberg, Carey Mulligan, and Andrew Garfield, among a long list of distinct possibilities.

All of the above films will most likely net between twenty and sixty million dollars on their opening weekends, and proceed to earn back their investments in DVD and Internet releases later (but not much later) on. As film budgets have soared, and the number of films released per week has risen, there is a very tiny window for active marketing in which any title has some chance to make a dent in the (increasingly) astronomical production budget that subtended it. Diversification of distribution platforms has thus been the most important single change in Hollywood cinema since 2000. A film that is suitably advertised may do well for one or perhaps two weekends; and in order for the revenue to be substantial these opening onslaughts must be organized in several countries simultaneously. But the movie theater is no longer the principal venue for film watching, or even more importantly for their own success, for watching stars. Their appearances on television—for example, Anne Hathaway's as co-host of the 2011 Academy Awards—solicit new fans and consolidate already existing fan bases.

If that appearance doesn't do the trick, perhaps her frequent semi-nude moments in *Love and Other Drugs* (2010) will already have done so anyway, Hathaway, along with her co-star Jake Gyllenhaal, here cresting what may well be a new wave in mainstream stardom, skin shots. While plenty of screen performers have done nude or semi-nude scenes, it has not typically been the case that the distanced and elevated star has shown considerable flesh, but as we learn from IMDb's "Parents Guide" for the film, Hathaway exposes her left breast for a doctor; shows her panties in a kitchen scene; removes a topcoat to reveal bare breasts; shows her butt in bed with Gyllenhaal, and shows her breasts in a lovemaking scene, while for his part, Gyllenhaal stands completely naked covering his genitals in front of a male doctor, and so on. Might the decade of the 2010s not open this door wider, with nubile young big shots all over Hollywood baring it all in scenes artfully (or not) contrived for the purpose, thus going where no one has gone before? Thanks to exploding DVD and BluRay sales, all this heartfelt nature can be brought home, into the sanctity of what had many years ago been for most film viewers a rather chaste hearth.

DVD sales—which make possible the presentation of multiple versions of scenes or entire films, backstage commentary, and even scholarly interpretation—constitute a very significant portion of any film's overall "box office." But more than merely allowing viewers to take the movie theater home, indeed to reconstitute their homes as movie theaters (and thus to cover the overhead costs initially borne by theater ownership), DVDs and palm device downloads allow for interactive viewing—stop and start, freeze frame, replay, not to mention the dubious thrill of watching a motion picture while listening to the director as he whispers what he actually intended to do, in our ears. Being born, then, is a new "microstardom," that of performers whom we watch through devices reduced in size and immensely flexible in usage. Two aspects of microstardom are worth noting especially.

First, no matter how plump the bank account of the home user, the home or palm screen is comparatively small, and thus the performance of the actor and the stardom of the star are shrunk to fit. In most cases, indeed, the screen is that of a computer or standard-size television, and the movie star is converted, willy-nilly and in an invisible puff, to the magnitude of all those luminaries who since the earliest days of the 1950s beguiled us on TV. Take the case of William Shatner. He starts out in the 1950s, unknown to the world, playing Shakespeare at Stratford, Ontario. In the mid-1960s he is cast in "Star Trek," and becomes an icon across North America, so beloved of his fans that they lobby to bring him back when the series is cancelled (all this, part of the apocrypha of the Star Trek universe). In the "Star Trek" universe as we see it, Shatner is about six inches tall (as King Kong was, too). In 1979, Robert Wise opens the *Star Trek* film saga, and Shatner, still rather fit looking but clearly also corseted, explodes into mega-human size, an Olympian figure of the screen (along with Spock, McCoy, Uhura, and the rest of the motley crew). But if the *Star Trek* movies continue for twenty years, Shatner becomes progressively slower-moving and bored. Early in the 2000s he is cast as the spectacular Denny Crane in "Boston Legal." Now he is back on the small screen, but he has become bigger than ever, literally bursting out of his two-thousand-dollar suits (decorated with lavender neckties) and touting a characterological ego so huge that he spends most of his time waltzing around a law office pronouncing his name. Is he big, or is he small? The role has expanded, and so—ironically—has the body, yet the image is shrunk again. As in the 2000s the image download terminated with increasing frequency not in a desktop device but in a hand-held or laptop unit (an iPhone, iPad, or BlackBerry, for examples) the figure of the star—Judi Dench in *Casino Royale* (2006), Tom Cruise in *Valkyrie* (2008)—became literally no more than a manikin. In 1940, Michael Powell predicted in *The Thief of Bagdad* exactly such tiny, lifelike, charming figurines caught in a proscenium that was only a toy.

Movie stars after 2010 will have to "work" for us when their images are quite tiny, just as well as they do when the images are huge, since there will no longer be any way to predict which kind of venue fans will use for seeing them. The increasing popularity (and circulation) of *Vanity Fair*, for example, which lards itself monthly with glossy pictures of Hollywood celebrities, makes sense when we see that the pages of this magazine are only freezes of a typical downloaded movie projection. The star consists of, inheres in, and is fully embodied by the miniaturization through which we accept her.

Beyond size changes, it is also true that DVD, Internet, and all forms of broadband downloading require the digital image, and so all of these simulacra we have been getting used to are also pixilated (thus, as images, editable). While a certain telltale softness in lighting and a certain range of color representation are both precluded in digitization, many exciting effects are made possible; but most importantly, the screen image appears noticeably sharp and thus seems to replicate unaided vision: digitized star performance brings a new and vastly marketable thrill (witness the closure, by Technicolor, of its San Fernando Valley processing plant in late 2010). But more: if digital editing has been around since the late 1980s, filmmakers have now begun to shoot digitally as well, so the film star is no longer "originally" on film. The image shot digitally requires less light; indeed can be made in virtually any lighting conditions. A related thrill is provided by what David Bordwell has called "intensified continuity," in which shots last for a shorter time, shot juxtapositions are typically organized around the principle of discontinuity, camera positions wildly shift. In this artistic territory, the kind of work required of stars has changed. In many cases, they need only model costumes and take poses, since the film will be constructed out of action modules put together digitally, not out of "scenes" played through with the rise and fall of characterization that stage actors and early screen actors accomplished. More and more, Hollywood would be looking for bright young faces that can look pretty in a close-up, youthful bodies good for holding a pose and draping a garment or for racing through a sewage plant before the world blows up. Vocal modulation, social charm—these are no longer particularly necessary since the voice will be shaped on a digital system and charm belongs to a day gone by, a day before the advent of continuous, ubiquitous hustling, telegraphic communication (as in texting), and tourism (that is, racing through a scene rather than inhabiting it).

Thus, the stars of the new age are all cell phone and digital device compatible, all best seen as they move past us. Matt Damon, wounded and driving toward a Russian tunnel in *The Bourne Supremacy* (2004); Jennifer Garner, looking for bombs in *The Kingdom* (2007); Ellen Page, one-lining her way through high school in *Juno* (2007); Jesse Eisenberg, one-lining his way through *The Social Network* (2010) or *The Squid and the Whale* (2005); Daniel Radcliffe, if he can go beyond stripping onstage in *Equus* and actually find some film roles that eclipse Harry Potter. Andrew Garfield had an auspicious introduction as Robert Redford's sassy favorite student in *Lions for Lambs* (2007), and then took over the screen with his eloquent classical performance as Anton in *The Imaginarium of Dr. Parnassus* (2009), before going very big as the chum/nemesis Eduardo Saverin in *The Social Network*. His star turn in *Never Let Me Go* (2010) and the planned Spider-Man "reboot" (2012), in which he will play the cult hero, suggest the beginning of an active star career. Anne Hathaway seems also poised to replace both Julia Roberts and Emma Thompson. Most young actors will not need breadth of ability and serious training, however. To work at any size, in a wisp of a moment, they will need instantly recognizable physical characteristics—Zack Gallifianakis, Adam Sandler, Jack Black, Jennifer Garner, Gwyneth Paltrow, Angelina Jolie, Michael Cera—and the twinkly charm that makes us want to hold them in the palm of our hands. So it may come to be that the great Kong with Fay Wray or Jessica Lange, or Luke Skywalker with his holographic Leia, were harbingers of an unseen and untold future where the greatest objects of collective fascination would become, as they had been in childhood, our dolls.

WORKS CITED

★★★★★★★★★★

Fan magazines and other primary materials are cited in the text of individual essays.

"Acting in the Cinema: Commentary by Authors and Critics." *Cineaste* (Fall 2006): 60–63.

Amaya, Hector. "*Amores Perros* and Racialized Masculinities in Contemporary Mexico." *New Cinemas: Journal of Contemporary Film* 5.3 (2007): 201–16.

Anderson, Christopher. *Hollywood TV: The Studio System in the Fifties*. Austin: U of Texas P, 1994.

Barthes, Roland. *Camera Lucida*. New York: Hill & Wang, 1981.

Becker, Christine. *It's The Pictures That Got Small: Hollywood Film Stars on 1950s Television*. Middletown, Conn.: Wesleyan UP, 2008.

Beltrán, Mary. *Latina/o Stars in U.S. Eyes: The Making and Meanings of Film and TV Stardom*. Urbana: U of Illinois P, 2009.

Bennett, James. "The Television Personality System: Televisual Stardom Revisited after Film Theory." *Screen* 49.1 (Spring 2008): 32-50.

Berg, Charles Ramírez. *Latin Images in Film: Stereotypes, Subversion, and Resistance*. Austin: U of Texas P, 2002.

Bingham, Dennis. *Acting Male: Masculinities in the Films of James Stewart, Jack Nicholson, and Clint Eastwood*. New Brunswick, N.J.: Rutgers UP, 1994.

———. *Whose Lives Are They Anyway?: The Biopic as Contemporary Film Genre*. New Brunswick, N.J.: Rutgers UP, 2010.

Butler, Judith. *Gender Trouble: Feminism and the Subversion of Identity*. New York: Routledge, 1990.

———. *Precarious Life: The Powers of Mourning and Violence*. New York: Verso, 2004.

Caldwell, John T. *Televisuality: Style, Crisis, and Authority in American Television*. New Brunswick, N.J.: Rutgers UP, 1995.

———. "Welcome to the Viral Future of Cinema [Television]." *Cinema Journal* (Autumn 2005): 92.

Cornell, Drucilla. *Clint Eastwood and Issues of American Masculinity*. New York: Fordham UP, 2009.

Courcoux, Charles-Antoine. "From Here to Antiquity: Mythical Settings and Modern Sufferings in Contemporary Hollywood's Historical Epics." *Film & History* (Fall 2009): 29–38.

Davis, Therese. *The Face on the Screen: Death, Recognition, and Spectatorship*. Bristol: Intellect, 2004.

DeCordova, Richard. "The Emergence of the Star System in America." *Stardom: Industry of Desire*. Ed. Christine Gledhill. New York: Routledge, 1991. 17–29.

Desjardins, Mary. "Lucy and Desi: Sexuality, Ethnicity, and TV's First Family." *Television, History, and American Culture: Feminist Critical Essays*. Ed. Mary Beth Haralovich and Lauren Rabinovitz. Durham, N.C.: Duke UP, 1999. 56–74.

Doane, Mary Ann. "Film and the Masquerade: Theorising the Female Spectator." *Screen* 23.3–4 (1982): 74–88.

Dyer, Richard. *Heavenly Bodies: Film Stars and Society*. New York: St. Martin's, 1986.

243

————. *Stars*. London: British Film Institute, 1998.

Eberwein, Robert. *The Hollywood War Film*. Malden, Mass.: Wiley-Blackwell, 2009.

Ellis, John. *Visible Fictions: Cinema, Television, Video*. Rev. ed. New York: Routledge, 1992.

Faludi, Susan. *The Terror Dream: Fear and Fantasy in Post-9/11 Media*. New York: Metropolitan Books, 2007.

Gabbard, Krin. *Black Magic: White Hollywood and Black American Culture*. New Brunswick, N.J.: Rutgers UP, 2004.

Genz, Stéphanie, and Benjamin A. Brabon. *Postfeminism: Cultural Texts and Theories*. Edinburgh: Edinburgh UP, 2009.

Gill, Rosalind. "Postfeminist Media Culture: Elements of a Sensibility." *European Journal of Cultural Studies* 10.2 (2007): 147–66.

Halperin, Ian. *Brangelina: The Untold Story of Brad Pitt and Angelina Jolie*. New York: Transit, 2009.

Henderson, Brian. "*The Searchers*: An American Dilemma." *Film Quarterly* (Winter 1980–81): 9–23.

Hilmes, Michele. *Hollywood and Broadcasting: From Radio to Cable*. Urbana: U of Illinois P, 1990.

Holmes, Su, and Sean Redmond. "Introduction: Understanding Celebrity Culture." *Framing Celebrity: New Directions in Celebrity Culture*. Ed. Su Holmes and Sean Redmond. New York: Routledge, 2006. 1–25.

Hughey, Matthew. "Cinethetic Racism: White Redemption and Black Stereotypes in 'Magical Negro' Films." *Social Practice* (Autumn 2009): 544.

Hunter, Stephen. *Now Playing at the Valencia: Pulitzer Prize–Winning Essays on Movies*. New York: Simon & Schuster, 2005.

Jermyn, Deborah. "'Bringing Out the Star in You': SJP, Carrie Bradshaw and the Evolution of Television Stardom." *Framing Celebrity: New Directions in Celebrity Culture*. Ed. Su Holmes and Sean Redmond. New York: Routledge, 2006. 67–85.

Jolie, Angelina. *Notes from My Travels: Visits with Refugees in Africa, Cambodia, Pakistan, and Ecuador*. New York: Simon & Schuster, 2003.

Kelly, Richard T. *Sean Penn: His Life and Times*. London: Faber and Faber, 2004.

King, Barry. "The Star and the Commodity: Notes Towards a Performance Theory of Stardom." *Cultural Studies* 1.2 (1987): 145–61.

————. "Stardom, Celebrity, and the Money Form." *Velvet Light Trap* 65 (Spring 2010): 7–19.

King, Samantha. *Pink Ribbons, Inc.: Breast Cancer and the Politics of Philanthropy*. Minneapolis: U of Minnesota P, 2006.

Kord, Susanne, and Elisabeth Krimmer. *Hollywood Divas, Indie Queens, and TV Heroines: Contemporary Screen Images of Women*. Lanham, Md.: Rowman & Littlefield, 2005.

Landy, Marcia. *Cinematic Uses of the Past*. Minneapolis: U of Minnesota P, 1996.

Leys, Ruth. *Trauma: A Genealogy*. Chicago: U of Chicago P, 2000.

Maddux, Kristy. "Winning the Right to Vote in 2004." *Feminist Media Studies* 9.1 (2009): 73–94.

Maltby, Richard. *Hollywood Cinema*. Oxford: Blackwell, 1995.

Mann, Denise. "The Spectacularization of Everyday Life: Recycling Hollywood Stars and Fans in Early Television Variety Shows." *Private Screenings: Television and the Female Consumer*. Ed. Lynn Spigel and Denise Mann. Minneapolis: U of Minnesota P, 1992. 40–69.

Marshall, Sarah. *Jennifer Aniston: The Biography of Hollywood's Sweetheart*. London: John Blake, 2007.

Martin, Adrian. "The Misleading Man: Dennis Hopper." Ed. Angela Ndalianis and Charlotte Henry. Westport, Conn.: Praeger, 2002. 3–21.

Martin, Nina. "*Down with Love* and Up with Sex: Sex and the Post-feminist Single Girl." *Jump Cut: A Review of Contemporary Media* 49 (Spring 2007). Online at www.ejumpcut.org/archive/jc49.2007/ninamartin/index.html. Accessed 28 June 2010.

McConnell, Frank D. *The Spoken Seen: Film and the Romantic Imagination*. Baltimore: Johns Hopkins UP, 1975.

McDonald, Paul. "Star Studies." *Approaches to Popular Film*. Ed. Joanne Hollows and Mark Jancovich. Manchester: Manchester UP, 1995. 79–97.

McFay, Edgar. *Angelina Jolie: Angel in Disguise*. Edmonton: Icon Press, 2005.

McGilligan, Patrick. *Clint: The Life and Legend*. New York: St. Martins, 2002.

McLean, Adrienne L. *Being Rita Hayworth: Labor, Identity, and Hollywood Stardom*. New Brunswick, N.J.: Rutgers UP, 2004.

McRobbie, Angela. "Postfeminism and Popular Culture: Bridget Jones and the New Gender Regime." *Interrogating Postfeminism*. Ed. Yvonne Tasker and Diane Negra. Durham, N.C.: Duke UP, 2007. 27–39.

Mellencamp, Patricia. "Situation Comedy, Feminism, and Freud: Discourses of Gracie and Lucy." *Star Texts: Image and Performance in Film and Television*.Ed. Jeremy G. Butler. Detroit: Wayne State UP, 1991. 316–32.

Mercer, Rhona. *Angelina Jolie: Portrait of a Superstar*. London: Blake, 2009.

Metz, Walter. "The Old Man and the C: Masculinity and Age in the Films of Clint Eastwood." *Clint Eastwood, Actor, Director: New Perspectives*. Ed. Leonard Engel. Salt Lake City: U of Utah P, 2007. 204–17.

Morin, Edgar. *The Stars*. Trans. Richard Howard. Minneapolis: U of Minnesota P, 2005.

Morrison, James. "Clint Eastwood and Bruce Willis: Enforcers Left and Right." *Acting for America: Movie Stars of the 1980s*. Ed. Robert Eberwein. New Brunswick, N.J.: Rutgers UP, 2010. 223–42.

Mulvey, Laura. *Death 24x a Second*. London: Reaktion, 2006.

Murray, Susan. *Hitch Your Antenna to the Stars: Early Television and Broadcast Stardom*. New York: Routledge, 2005.

Naremore, James. *Acting in the Cinema*. Berkeley: U of California P, 1988.

Negra, Diane. "Brangelina: The Fertile Valley of Celebrity." *Velvet Light Trap* 65 (Spring 2010): 60–61.

———. "Failing Women: Hollywood and Its Chick Flick Audience." *Velvet Light Trap* 64 (Fall 2009):91–92.

———. "'Queen of the Indies': Parker Posey's Niche Stardom and the Taste Cultures of Independent Film." *Contemporary American Independent Film: From the Margins to the Mainstream*. Ed. Chris Holmlund and Justin Wyatt. New York: Routledge, 2005. 71–88.

———. "Structural Integrity, Historical Revision, and the Post-9/11 Chick Flick." *Feminist Media Studies* 8.1 (2008):51–68.

Ouellette, Laurie, and James Hay. *Better Living Through Reality TV*. Malden, Mass.: Blackwell Publishing, 2008.

Pomerance, Murray. *Johnny Depp Starts Here*. New Brunswick, N.J.: Rutgers UP, 2005.

Powell, Anna. *Deleuze, Altered States and Film*. Edinburgh: Edinburgh UP, 2007.

Projansky, Sarah. *Watching Rape: Film and Television in Postfeminist Culture*. New York: New York UP, 2001.

Rich, B. Ruby. "Brokering *Brokeback*: Jokes, Backlashes, and Other Anxieties." *Film Quarterly* (Spring 2007): 44–48.

Robb, Brian J. *Brad Pitt: The Rise to Stardom*. London: Plexus, 2002.

Rodríguez, Clara E. "Introduction." *Latin Looks: Images of Latinas and Latinos in the U.S. Media*. Ed. Clara E. Rodríguez. Boulder, Colo.: Westview, 1997.

Schickel, Richard. *Clint: A Retrospective*. New York: Sterling, 2010.

———. *Clint Eastwood: A Biography*. New York: Alfred A. Knopf, 1996.

Sklar, Robert. "Changeling." *Cineaste* (Winter 2008): 51–52.

Stacey, Jackie. *Star Gazing: Hollywood Cinema and Female Spectatorship*. London: Routledge, 1994.

Stern, Lesley, and George Kouvaros. *Falling for You: Essays on Cinema and Performance*. Sydney: Power Publications, 1999.

Tasker, Yvonne, and Diane Negra. "Introduction: Feminist Politics and Postfeminist Culture." *Interrogating Postfeminism*. Ed. Yvonne Tasker and Diane Negra. Durham, N.C.: Duke UP, 2007. 1–25.

Thomson, David. *The New Biographical Dictionary of Film*. 4th ed. New York: Alfred A. Knopf, 2002.

Tracy, Kathleen. *Morgan Freeman: A Biography*. Fort Lee, N.J.: Barricade Books, 2006.

Valdivia, Angharad. "Is Penélope to J.Lo as Culture Is to Nature? Eurocentric Approaches to 'Latin' Beauties." *From Bananas to Buttocks: The Latina Body in Popular Film and Culture*. Ed. Martha Mendible. Austin: U of Texas P, 2007. 129–48.

Walters, Ben. "The Departed." *Time Out Film Guide*. Ed. John Pym. 16th ed. London: Time Out, 2008. 263.

Weiss, Margot. "Mainstreaming Kink: The Politics of BDSM Representation in U.S. Popular Media." *Journal of Homosexuality* 50.2–3 (2006): 103–32.

Westman, Karin E. "Beauty and the Geek: Changing Gender Stereotypes on 'The Gilmore Girls.'" *Geek Chic: Smart Women in Popular Culture*. Ed. Sherrie A. Inness. New York: Palgrave Macmillan, 2007. 11–30.

Williams, Linda Ruth. *The Erotic Thriller in Contemporary Cinema*. Edinburgh: Edinburgh UP, 2005.

Wilson, Julie A. "Star Testing: The Emerging Politics of Celebrity Gossip." *Velvet Light Trap* 65 (Spring 2010): 25–38.

Yalom, Irvin. *Staring at the Sun: Overcoming the Terror of Death*. San Francisco: Jossey-Bass, 2008.

CONTRIBUTORS
★★★★★★★★★★★★

MARY C. BELTRÁN is an associate professor of communication arts and Chicana/o-Latina/o studies at the University of Wisconsin–Madison. Her research is focused on the production and narration of notions of race, gender, and class in U.S. entertainment media and celebrity culture and the ways in which media texts and media producers articulate group and national identities. She is the author of *Latina/o Stars in U.S. Eyes: The Making and Meanings of Film and TV Stardom* and co-editor (with Camilla Fojas) of the anthology *Mixed Race Hollywood*.

CORINN COLUMPAR is an associate professor of cinema studies and English at the University of Toronto, where she teaches courses on film theory, the body in visual culture, and the filmmaking practices and textual politics of various counter-cinematic traditions (feminist, Aboriginal, "independent," and queer). In addition to publishing in numerous journals and anthologies, she is the author of *Unsettling Sights: The Fourth World on Film* and a co-editor of *There She Goes: Feminist Filmmaking and Beyond*.

ROBERT EBERWEIN is distinguished professor of English emeritus at Oakland University. He is the author of *Armed Forces: Masculinity and Sexuality in the American War Film, Sex ED: Film, Video, and the Framework of Desire*, and *The Hollywood War Film*; and editor of *The War Film* and *Acting for America: Movie Stars of the 1980s*.

MICHAEL K. HAMMOND is senior lecturer in film history in the Department of English at the University of Southampton. He is the co-editor and contributor to *Contemporary American Cinema* with Linda Ruth Williams and is author of *The Big Show: British Cinema Culture in the Great War 1914–1918*. He is presently working on a British Academy–funded project on the impact of the First World War on Hollywood aesthetics in the 1920s and 1930s.

VICTORIA E. JOHNSON is chair of the Department of Film and Media Studies at the University of California, Irvine, where she is also an associate professor in the Ph.D. Program in Visual Studies and affiliated faculty in African American Studies. Her *Heartland TV: Prime Time Television and the Struggle for U.S. Identity* won the Society for Cinema and Media Studies' Katherine Singer Kovacs book award for 2009. Her other publications include chapters and articles in collections and journals such as *The Television Studies Reader, Cinema Journal,* and *Film Quarterly*.

CHARLIE KEIL is the director of the Cinema Studies Institute and an associate professor in the Department of History at the University of Toronto. He has published extensively on the topic of early cinema, especially the pivotal "transitional era" of the early 1910s, in such publications as *Early American Cinema in Transition*; *American Cinema's Transitional Era* (co-edited with Shelley Stamp); and *American Cinema of the 1910s* (co-edited with Ben Singer). He has also published on documentary, contemporary cinema, and stardom, including an essay on Katharine Hepburn and Cary Grant in the Star Decades volume devoted to the 1940s.

DOMINIC LENNARD is a lecturer in film and literature at the University of Tasmania, Australia. His research interests include genre film (especially horror films and westerns), versions of masculinity in popular culture, and the representation of children in film and literature. He has also published on Michael Jackson.

JERRY MOSHER is an associate professor in the Department of Film and Electronic Arts at California State University, Long Beach. His research focuses on American cinema and its representation of the body. He has published essays on film and culture in numerous anthologies.

CLAIRE PERKINS is an assistant lecturer in Film and Television Studies at Monash University, Melbourne. She is the author of *American Smart Cinema* (forthcoming) and co-editor of *Film Trilogies: New Critical Approaches* (forthcoming).

MURRAY POMERANCE is professor of sociology at Ryerson University and the author of *Michelangelo Red Antonioni Blue: Eight Reflections on Cinema*, *The Horse Who Drank the Sky: Film Experience Beyond Narrative and Theory*, *Johnny Depp Starts Here*, and *An Eye for Hitchcock*, as well as editor or co-editor of numerous volumes including *A Little Solitaire: John Frankenheimer and American Film*, *Cinema and Modernity*, *Enfant Terrible! Jerry Lewis in American Film*, *A Family Affair: Cinema Calls Home*, and the forthcoming *Stars of David: The Jewish Experience in American Cinema*. He edits the Horizons of Cinema series at SUNY Press and the Techniques of the Moving Image series at Rutgers, and, with Lester D. Friedman and Adrienne L. McLean, respectively, co-edits the Screen Decades and Star Decades series at Rutgers. In 2009 he appeared on Broadway in conjunction with *The 39 Steps*.

DAVID STERRITT is chair of the National Society of Film Critics, adjunct professor of film studies at Columbia University and the Maryland Institute College of Art, film critic of *Tikkun*, and chief book critic of *Film Quarterly*. He reviewed many of George Clooney's movies during his long run as film critic of the *Christian Science Monitor*. His books include *Mad to Be Saved: The Beats, the '50s, and Film*, *The Films of Jean-Luc Godard: Seeing the Invisible*, *Guiltless Pleasures: A David Sterritt Film Reader*, *The B List*, and *The Honeymooners*.

BRENDA R. WEBER is an associate professor in gender studies at Indiana University. Her books include *Makeover TV: Selfhood, Citizenship, and Celebrity* and *Women and Literary Celebrity in the Nineteenth Century: The Transatlantic Production of Fame and Gender*. Her current projects include *Reality Gendervision: Decoding Gender on Transatlantic Reality TV* and *Mediating Masculinity: Conceptualizing "American" Masculinity in a Post-Millennial Mediascape*.

LINDA RUTH WILLIAMS is a professor of film in the Department of English at the University of Southampton. She is the author and editor of books including *The Erotic Thriller in Contemporary Cinema* and *Contemporary American Cinema* (co-edited with Michael Hammond), as well as numerous articles on feminism, sexuality, censorship, and contemporary culture.

I N D E X

★☆☆★★★★★★★★★

Pages in italic contain photographs.